IMPROVISING THEORY

IMPROVISING THEORY

Process and Temporality in Ethnographic Fieldwork

ALLAINE CERWONKA

AND

LIISA H. MALKKI

The University of Chicago Press

Chicago and London

ALLAINE CERWONKA is associate professor in and chair of the Department of Gender Studies at Central European University, Budapest. She has written articles for various professional journals and is the author of a previous book, *Native to the Nation: Disciplining Landscapes and Bodies in Australia*.

LIISA H. MALKKI is associate professor of cultural authropology at Stanford University. The author of numerous published articles, she is also author of *Purity and Exile: Violence, Memory, and National Cosmology among Hutu Refugees in Tanzania*, published by the University of Chicago Press.

The University of Chicago Press, Chicago 60637
The University of Chicago Press, Ltd., London
© 2007 by The University of Chicago
All rights reserved. Published 2007
Printed in the United States of America

16   15   14   13   12   11   10   09   08   07   1   2   3   4   5

ISBN-13: 978-0-226-10030-2   (cloth)
ISBN-13: 978-0-226-10031-9   (paper)
ISBN-10: 0-226-10030-8   (cloth)
ISBN-10: 0-226-10031-6   (paper)

Library of Congress Cataloging-in-Publication Data

Cerwonka, Allaine.
   Improvising theory : process and temporality in ethnographic fieldwork / Allaine Cerwonka and Liisa H. Malkki.
      p.   cm.
   Includes bibliographical references and index.
   ISBN-13: 978-0-226-10030-2 (hardcover : alk. paper)
   ISBN-13: 978-0-226-10031-9 (pbk. : alk. paper)
   ISBN-10: 0-226-10030-8 (hardcover : alk. paper)
   ISBN-10: 0-226-10031-6 (pbk. : alk. paper)
      1. Ethnology—Australia—Melbourne (Vic.)—Field work.   2. Cerwonka, Allaine— Correspondence.   3. Malkki, Liisa H.—Correspondence.   4. Ethnologists— Australia—Melbourne (Vic.)—Correspondence.   5. Ethnologists—California—Irvine— Correspondence.   6. Electronic mail messages—Australia—Melbourne (Vic.) 7. Electronic mail messages—California—Irvine.   I. Malkki, Liisa H. (Liisa Helena) II. Title.
GN346.C45   2007
305.800945′1—dc22   2006036523

∞ The paper used in this publication meets the minimum requirements of the American National Standard for Information Sciences—Permanence of Paper for Printed Library Materials, ANSI z39.48-1992.

To Mimi and Lucie

CONTENTS

Acknowledgments *ix*

Nervous Conditions:
The Stakes in Interdisciplinary Research *1*
ALLAINE CERWONKA

The Fulbright Proposal *41*

Fieldwork Correspondence *44*
ALLAINE CERWONKA, LIISA MALKKI

Tradition and Improvisation
in Ethnographic Field Research *162*
LIISA MALKKI

References *189*
Index *199*

ACKNOWLEDGMENTS

The authors together would like to thank the following friends and colleagues for their generous help with this book: Erica Bornstein, David Brent, Jim Ferguson, Michael Herzfeld, Emily Noonan, and Christina Schwenkel.

Liisa Malkki

It goes without saying that without Allaine Cerwonka, this book would not exist. Her intellectual courage and imaginative nomadism drive this project. I am honored to have accompanied her on a small part of her journey. The decisive part of the research and writing for my part of this manuscript was done during a wonderful year as a Fellow at the Center for Advanced Study in the Behavioral Sciences in Stanford, California. I remain deeply grateful for that time. Thinking, research, and writing occur in complex webs of interrelationship. To untangle these for the sake of giving thanks is a daunting task. At the University of California at Irvine, I taught for several years a Practicum on Fieldwork Techniques in which I used our correspondence as a pedagogical device, sometimes together with Allaine. I thank all the students there who so generously engaged with our text. Likewise, many students at the Department of Cultural and Social Anthropology at Stanford University have been wonderful critics and colleagues. I am privileged to be able to work with them. At the risk of forgetting someone, I would especially like to thank the following colleagues, students, and friends:

Olli Alho	Erica Bornstein
Talal Asad	Donald Brenneis
Elif Babül	David Brent
Susan Ma Diego Beach	Teresa Caldeira
Alissa Bernstein	Jean Comaroff

John Comaroff
Paulla Ebron
Harri Englund
Johannes Fabian
Jim Ferguson
Ute Frevert
Ulf Hannerz
Laurie Kain Hart
Michael Herzfeld
Miyako Inoue
Jean Lave
Georgia Lawrence
Staffan Löfving
Purnima Mankekar
Emily Martin
Bill Maurer
Ray McDermott
Ramah McKay
Lynn Meskell
Amanda Moore
Sally Falk Moore

Chrisy Moutsatsos
Nick Murray
Zhanara Nauruzbayeva
David Nirenberg
Francis Nyamnjoh
Kevin O'Neill
Richard Perry
Mary Louise Pratt
Anna Rastas
Angel Roque
Renato Rosaldo
Selim Shahine
Uli Schreiterer
Christina Schwenkel
Rania al-Sweis
Stanley J. Tambiah
Ulla Vuorela
Thet Shein Win
Sylvia Yanagisako
Mei Zhan

Allaine Cerwonka

I would like to thank the numerous people who provided help with this book, as well as people who helped me in various ways to conceptualize the project that it documents. This group includes people who showed me in one way or another what high-quality interdisciplinary research might look like. I am grateful to the Fulbright Foundation for the funding to conduct ethnographic fieldwork in Australia, to the members of the Fitzroy Police for their generous help from December 2004 to October 2005, and to the members of the East Melbourne Garden Club during that same period. I also thank the Politics Department at Melbourne University for hosting me during my research time in Australia. I received various forms of financial and intellectual support from the Department of Political Science and the University of California at Irvine, and the University of California Humanities Research Institute, for which I am grateful. My colleagues and friends in the Department of Gender Studies and in the Department of Sociology and Social Anthropology at the Central European University have helped me as well by providing a much-appreciated intellectual community.

I also thank my Cerwonka and Weberman family members for their enthusiasm, and my mother for her unfailing help with my writing projects. I am especially grateful for my husband David's many forms of help with this project, for his moral support, and for making me laugh despite myself. Thank you to Lucie who, at one-and-a-half years old, is a model of critical inquiry. I also extend a particular thank you to Mark Petracca for his faith in me, and my appreciation to both him and John Cash for helping me think through some important aspects of my ethnographic project. And, of course, it is very clear from the correspondence in this book what an insightful and generous mentor Liisa Malkki has been to me at crucial points in my development as a scholar. It has been very enriching to work together on this book and to see our relationship evolve into one of colleagues and friends since our UC Irvine days.

In addition to those mentioned already, I also wish to thank Elizabeth Beck, the members of the Burgess family, Eva Crow, Jim Devlin, Yehuda Elkana, Emanuela Guano, Eric Kaldor, Mathilde Lochert, Kristen Maher, Thu-Huong Nguyen-Vo, Mark Poster, Gaby Schwab, Susan Talburt, Robyn Wiegman, David Easton, and Jim Ferguson (for his particularly useful comments on my foreword to this volume). The collective help of those mentioned here, and of others less directly involved in this project, have helped make my scholarly work better than it would otherwise be.

Nervous Conditions

The Stakes in Interdisciplinary Research

ALLAINE CERWONKA

To: Liisa Malkki lhmalkki@orion.oac.uci.edu
From: Allaine Cerwonka allaine_cerwonka@politics.muwaye.unimelb.edu.au
Date: Thursday, March 16, 1995 12:28
Subject: those brave boys in blue

Hi Liisa,

. . . I'm in an opaque space at the moment. Nothing is clear but there is the hint of lots of interesting things. I feel frustrated at my inability to think these issues through in a clear and fresh way. I need some help at this point. And I'm not exactly sure what I need from you. Direction, confidence, optimism. Whatever you have handy in your bag of tricks at the moment. This all seems very complicated on my end, but it would be great it if strikes you as child's play. Let me hear from you.

"Dazed and confused,"

Allaine

Introduction

The e-mail correspondence at the heart of this book took place between Liisa Malkki, the anthropologist on my interdisciplinary dissertation committee, and me as I conducted ethnographic fieldwork in Melbourne, Australia, in 1994 and 1995. Our extended e-mail exchange chronicles my experience of navigating an interdisciplinary project through ethnographic research. In our exchange, Liisa and I discuss the process of doing a multisited, urban ethnography. This discussion of fieldwork includes threads of dialogue about research ethics, the emotional experience of fieldwork, and aspects of our personal lives that shaped our intellectual pursuits. Among other things, the correspondence highlights the closeness between emotions and ethics, and illustrates moments in fieldwork that are not only tense social situations, inevitable in social research, but also ethical quandaries that are signaled in the body.

The e-mails begin in November 1994, when I first wrote to Liisa from Melbourne, and end shortly before my return from fieldwork in August 1995. They are presented in their original chronological order and run through the entire year of my fieldwork. Liisa corresponded mainly from California, except for a brief period in Montreal, Canada. The correspondence thus began more than a decade ago. At the time, I was a graduate student in political science, and Liisa Malkki was an assistant professor of anthropology at the University of California, Irvine. We wrote to each other as part of a research process, with no thought of publication. Only after teaching with this correspondence in an ethnographic methods course did we think to publish it because of the way it captures the process of ethnographic research as it unfolds in real time and as it is embedded and embodied in the concrete details of the researcher's everyday life. In this regard, our correspondence is valuable and unusual for the way it illustrates an interpretive approach to knowledge production and disrupts many still-normative ideas about empirical research.

The "interpretive approach" has received a considerable amount of attention within anthropology, especially in the 1970s when Rabinow and Sullivan edited a collection of essays entitled *Interpretive Social Science* (1979). That interdisciplinary collection reflected a lively dialogue in anthropology, philosophy, literary studies, and elsewhere about interpretive modes of knowledge production as an alternative to positivism. Rabinow and Sullivan's collection complemented the writings of others in anthropology, such as Sally Falk Moore, Pierre Bourdieu, Clifford Geertz, and many others interested in the unique hermeneutics of ethnography. However, while questions of hermeneutics and epistemology have remained important since the 1970s for philosophy and literary studies, in anthropology these issues came to be eclipsed in the early 1980s by questions about representation and power as scholars turned their attention to what it means to "write culture" (Clifford and Marcus 1986). This book returns to the issue of ethnographic fieldwork as an especially rich form of interpretive knowledge production. It critically addresses ethnography as a research practice rather than as a genre of writing. The correspondence between Liisa and me illustrates several of the principles of the interpretive approach that I address in this foreword. In this discussion of some of the key ideas and theorists in the interpretive tradition, I do not intend to offer a new analysis of hermeneutics; rather, I mean to examine the hermeneutic process involved in an interdisciplinary ethnographic research project. How does an interdisciplinary project involve a unique process in its improvisation and its use of ethnographic details to produce theoretical insights? And how might an interdisciplinary interpretive approach illustrate for us a more generalized process of knowledge production that reflects a more productive, ethical, and realistic approach to understanding than the positivist paradigm? The e-mail correspondence itself chronicles how knowledge is produced hermeneutically and shows how ethnographic interpretation works in real time and in relation to various pragmatic, social, and ethical issues.

The correspondence contains some passages in which Liisa explains aspects of fieldwork strategy that usually go without saying in anthropology. While doctoral programs in anthropology include methods courses, novices in the field are often left to figure out many aspects of fieldwork by listening to stories of others' fieldwork and through the informal socialization that occurs within the discipline. As the excerpt below illustrates, the correspondence demonstrates the pragmatic challenges and choices characteristic of fieldwork as they quite typically intersect with ethical issues (e.g., "Am I somehow misleading my informants?") and with the emotional experience of the researcher. The passage below is one of many moments in the fieldwork correspondence where what often "goes without saying" is made explicit through our exchange. In this particular e-mail, Liisa is addressing my discomfort about having my rights and status undefined in the Fitzroy Police Station, one of my two field sites:

Re: the lack of definition of your location and status at the station. Not to worry too much, though I think worry is inevitable. The more information and insights you are given, the hungrier and more desperate you get. You don't want to be cut off and closed out before you're done. So yes, important to tread with care in what you're doing. But sometimes, given the way institutions think, the people at the station *don't want* to have to make a formal, official decision about where you fit in; it's easier for them and productive and enabling for you to keep you in limbo, and keep your role ill defined. Am I being clear? That way they don't have to acknowledge [formally] that there's this weird, out-of-category person hanging about.

As for your length of stay: it'll dawn on them, and perhaps by that time they won't care, and you'll be more familiar to them. Anyway, people don't track time so carefully in many instances, [especially] if it doesn't concern them and their time directly. (Correspondence, April 5, 1995)

Such moments in the correspondence are not only potentially useful for interdisciplinary scholars, but are also valuable for anthropologists with an interest in the assumptions about the ethics, epistemology, and strategies that inform their own discipline.

Indeed, ethics forms one of the key frames of the project and is, we believe, a very timely topic, as numerous scholars in various disciplines have recently begun to critically rethink it. More important, good social research clearly demands a highly developed, ceaseless, daily engagement with ethics as a process—an engagement that far exceeds the requirements of currently existing "ethics committees" and "human-subjects protocols" on university campuses. It is increasingly clear that the conventional understanding of ethics as a code—rather than as a process, as we see it here—needs to be critically examined.

Additionally, the correspondence documents an interdisciplinary research process that blurs several key boundaries, including the persistent gap within academia between theory and empirical research. The fieldwork process captured in the correspondence suggests how one always reads empirical details in the field through theory, whether self-consciously or not. As philosopher A. C. Grayling explains, our ideas of even the simplest objects, like a chair or table, are shaped by social categories such as those that divide the world into things on which we place bodies and things on which we place other objects (1995, 535). These categories represent a theoretical and conceptual organization of the world that is inherent in even the most taken-for-granted assumptions about the things around us. Thus, the interpretation of empirical details in fieldwork is always a way of reading and dwelling in the world through theory. This correspondence between student and mentor illustrates how theory is challenged and also reshaped by the complexity and richness of everyday social practices and processes. Ethnographic research requires a movement similar to what Ricoeur has called "the dialectic of guessing and validation." The correspondence captures this interpretive process of tacking between theory and empirical detail to show how this hermeneutic process yields claims to knowledge.

One of the central points of the project is that methodology and pedagogy are theoretically consequential subjects that demand further, innovative rethinking—as well as new forms of research practice. This is a work of theory as much as it is a critical examination of ethnographic methods. And just as research methods need to be taught, so too does theory.

This book as a whole also attempts to go beyond the hermeneutic analysis in philosophy and anthropology offered by Gadamer, Geertz, and others by showing how the hermeneutic circle unfolds in real time, within the complexities of an ethnographic project. Because the correspondence illustrates fieldwork in real time as the research process unfolds, we see that the tempo of ethnographic research (like most knowledge production) is not the steady, linear accumulation of more and more insight. Rather, it is characterized by rushes of and lulls in activity and understanding, and it requires constant revision of insights gained earlier. We see the anxiety and euphoria that accompany the uneven tempo of analytical understanding and systematic research. Thus, the correspondence examines the hermeneutic process as it relates to affective experiences such as doubt, elation, hope, fear, confidence, stress, exhaustion, energy, and projection, further complicating the common idea of a neat boundary between objective and subjective, abstract and concrete knowledge.

My e-mail exchange with Liisa amply illustrates the range of emotions involved in the practice of "understanding," as Gadamer called it. The earlier e-mails communicate the anxiety-producing challenge of identifying exactly what one wants to know (as Liisa says in her essay, one's "will to knowledge") and which particular fieldwork strategies will form that knowledge. In an e-mail on March 16, 1995, I described myself as "dazed and confused," and at other points in the correspondence, I melodramatically suggested that I would not be sleeping well again until I figured out whether or not to choose the police station as a second field site (March 7, 1995). The correspondence also reveals moments of anger toward the police when the fieldwork presented me with physical, social, and ethical challenges that stretched me further than I wanted to be stretched (see June 1, 1995, and July 13, 1995). Of course, there were many euphoric moments when the fieldwork was exhilarating, as shown in the e-mail recounting my experience patrolling in the police car. In one e-mail I wrote, "Liisa, it is such a blast! There's so much blood!" (March 31, 1995). And joy and satisfaction came with understanding and hard work, as when I wrote to Liisa, "Well, I am going to spin off this screen. That's it! No more caffeine for a while! Two nights ago, I woke up and realized that as I had been sleeping, the word 'Landscape' was just floating across a scene of a rural landscape in my head. I hate it (and love it, of course) when I can't shut my head off" (May 24, 1995).

The moments of confusion, euphoria, and intellectual *disorder* depicted in my fieldwork represent a realistic model of what all social knowledge production entails. In this regard, the e-mail correspondence offers an important counterpoint to the mythical figure of the ethnographer, sardonically dubbed "The Lone Anthropologist" by Renato Rosaldo (1989) and "The Great White Man" by Trinh T. Minh-ha (1989).[1] This more "realistic" model of fieldwork should not be reduced to or misunderstood as my saying, "No one's fieldwork is perfect." Rather, my point is that the opportunity to examine one particular fieldwork experience as it unfolds in real time is that it can provide valuable insight into the circular nature of interpretation. Presenting the fieldwork process in real time also distinguishes the correspondence stylistically from a novel or memoir. The seeming aimlessness, doubt, and generally circular nature of understanding does not "entertain" as a novel should, for example. But this depiction achieves something rarer in providing a window onto the process of understanding and ethnographic improvisation.

We also witness in the correspondence how ethnographic knowledge production involves strategic and ethical choices that are entwined with the mundane details of the researcher's daily existence "in the field." Gupta and Ferguson (1997a) have analyzed how the traditional understanding of the field in anthropology implies a separation in time and space from the "normal life" of the researcher. Johannes Fabian makes a related critique concerning how anthropological representations position their objects of study in a different temporality from their own, arguing that this tendency functions to primitivize the Other (1983b). To the extent that the correspondence disrupts the image of fieldwork as a mythical, exotic, and purely intellectual experience that is separate from the mundane details of "normal" or "real" life, our book also works against the exoticization of the practices and people whom anthropologists study. Malinowski's *Diary in the Strict Sense of the Term* (1967) undid many of the romantic stereotypes of the anthropologist in the field (e.g., as tolerant, sympathetic, and open-minded). The *Diary* nevertheless preserved the romantic idea of the ethnographer sitting in his bungalow or tent, isolated from normal life and protected by his classic literature. In contrast, the correspondence here depicts fieldwork in a city where the ethnographer is connected to other intellectual producers and social communities, and where the fieldwork is interwoven with mundane details of "normal life" such as babies, unreasonable landlords, and computer glitches. Such a depiction disrupts traditional ideas about fieldwork as a mythical rite of passage, even as it reconfirms ethnographic research as a potentially profound intellectual, physical, and emotional experience. Work and life come to be entangled in the embodied, situational, relational practice that constitutes long-term ethnographic fieldwork. Fieldwork is always already a critical theoretical practice; a deeply and inescapably empirical practice; and a necessarily improvisational practice. Further, as anthropological and interdisciplinary researchers increasingly experiment with newer forms of fieldwork such as multisited ethnography (Marcus 1998)[2] or ethnographies of virtual communities, for instance, ethnographers are increasingly forced to reenvision what their research practices actually look like. And of course, as part of this process, we must consider how the character of fieldwork (city versus remote village, institution versus whole village, the study of Western cultural practices, etc.) relates to what we can claim to know as a result of our field-work practices.

We hope that the correspondence stimulates people to consider how the traditional anthropological ideal of "immersion" in a field site has evolved in an era of globalization. Even in "out of the way places" (see Tsing 1993), more widely available Internet access and affordable international phone rates mean that ethnographers never completely "unplug" from their home communities. Liisa comments in the correspondence that even classical anthropologists like Malinowski were not as isolated as the mythology invites us to believe. The correspondence includes allusions to three experiences of fieldwork that suggest how the anthropological "field" too is one of the many spaces globalization has reconfigured since the 1980s (see also Gupta and Ferguson 1997a). In our e-mail exchange, Liisa and I refer (in varying degrees) to Liisa's fieldwork in western Tanzania (1985–86) and Montreal (1995), as well as mine in Australia. The dialogue thus provides several models of immersion: participant observation in a refugee camp with a Jeep and access to an international community of aid workers; research in a Western city with access to English-language research libraries; as well as fieldwork accompanied by one's family and Internet access in one's apartment. All of these examples deviate from the mythical ideal of immersion and reflect the complex forms of community and isolation one increasingly experiences in contemporary fieldwork.

Additionally, the everydayness of the correspondence between Liisa and me challenges the normative association of knowledge with the abstract and the masculine. The correspondence envisions a different social reality of knowledge production. In many ways the intellectual intensity Liisa and I exhibit here is suggestive of the romantic, masculine ideal of the scholar in high pursuit of Knowledge and Truth. But that aspect sits snugly alongside other elements such as passing comments about childbirth, novels, and the numerous pleasures and frustrations in our lives at given moments in time. Because of the association of the "personal" and the body with the feminine, the correspondence will no doubt strike a number of readers as a "feminine" mode of communication or research. While not necessarily rejecting such an ascription, I see that one productive challenge of the correspondence is that it makes such dichotomies (masculine/abstract versus feminine/personal) harder to sustain (Herzfeld 2004). Instead of abandoning objectivity and abstraction completely for romanticism's formula of truth through subjectivism, the correspondence encourages us to envision knowledge production in richer and more complex ways than these dichotomies that persist in haunting the academy permit. To this end, we are interested in how ethnography

as an interpretive mode of knowledge production involves the empirical, affect, and prejudgment, and ultimately leads to a reconception of objectivity.
Later in this essay I return to the question of how such an approach informs
all knowledge production, all "understanding," rather than being a particular characteristic of "women's ways of knowing" or of the so-called "soft
sciences" like anthropology.

    The remainder of this foreword takes up some of the central ideas of the
interpretive approach in order to explicate the epistemology and hermeneutics of ethnographic knowledge production as a tool for interdisciplinary
research. Drawing from the e-mail correspondence, I also link these philosophical issues to the question of ethics and the improvisational process in
ethnographic fieldwork more generally, which Liisa develops further in her
concluding essay.

Interdisciplinary Research: Liminality in the Academy

The e-mail correspondence chronicles the process of knowledge production,
on my side, of a scholar trained in a single discipline, political science, who is
undertaking a thoroughly interdisciplinary research project. I was engaging
in ethnographic research, an unorthodox approach in political science, in
order to contribute to social and political theories about the spatial processes
of national identity construction, in the specific, urban context of Melbourne,
Australia.

    While many champion interdisciplinary research, there is relatively little
sustained discussion of what such research actually looks like. Disciplines
have their own methodological orthodoxies. Scholars who engage in research that relies upon hybrid approaches therefore often find themselves
having to defend their research efforts more vigorously than do their more
orthodox colleagues. Not surprisingly, it is hard for the interdisciplinary scholar
to avoid feeling like a dilettante, rather than a "real" scholar who has con-
fined herself to the scholarly literature and methodology of a single discipline
(and, thereby, gone "deeper"). Instead, an interdisciplinary scholar's orientation and knowledge base may encompass aspects of three or four fields, as
mine did.

    Many publishers and funding agencies have encouraged interdisciplin-
ary work in the last twenty years. However, my mentors in graduate school
rightly understood that the structure of academic institutions and culture of
individual departments still present obstacles to employment for scholars
whose specialties do not fit neatly into preexisting, discipline-specific categories of expertise. In trying to drive this point home to me early in my graduate

career, my political science advisor, Mark Petracca, used the Kroger Supermarket analogy. Over coffee one sunny Southern Californian afternoon, he patiently explained that the subfields within our discipline were organized like a supermarket. With characteristic irony, he cautioned that for the sake of my employability in political science, I needed to decide on which aisle my research expertise would be located. In other words, without fitting into the discipline's system of subfields, my work would have less credibility, and I would have less marketability as a professional looking for a position in political science. (I have since decided that my work perhaps most appropriately belongs on the "impulse" rack by the cash register alongside the eclectic mix of candy, tabloid magazines and batteries.) And Liisa has remarked with affection on more than one occasion that my interdisciplinarity renders me a "creature with no appropriate cage."

Mary Douglas's famous study of purity and contamination (written in 1966) examines how cultural categories function to organize and regulate social life. She observes that people and things that contradict existing cultural categories or in other ways are "matter out of place," may often be deemed dangerous or impure. Below, she describes how such categorization maintains a social order and creates "unity of experience." She writes,

> The whole universe is harnessed to men's attempts to force one another into good citizenship. Thus we find that certain moral values are upheld and certain social rules defined by belief in dangerous contagion, as when the glance or touch of an adulterer is held to bring illness to his neighbors or children.
>
> It is not difficult to see how pollution beliefs can be used in a dialogue of claims and counter-claims to status. But as we examine pollution beliefs we find that the kind of contacts which are thought dangerous also carry a symbolic load. This is a more interesting level at which pollution ideas relate to social life. (1995, 3)

The borders of disciplines are historically constituted and, while there is a logic to the academy's categorization system, disciplinary borders are nonetheless fundamentally arbitrary. Interdisciplinary work, in addition to devising new epistemologies and research forms, is renegotiating a historical and politically charged categorical system that orders regimes of knowledge, status, and authority.

While admittedly not branded as dirty or profane, the promiscuousness of interdisciplinary scholars is indeed perceived to be unwise and, for some, dangerous to the academy because their work challenges the established divisions of authority and expertise that disciplinary borders conventionally reflect. If political scientists do ethnography and study cultural phenomena, how can anthropologists claim special expertise and authority? If literary scholars talk about the "political," what can we designate as the particular intellectual "jurisdiction" of political scientists? Additionally, scholars often define themselves in opposition to another group within the academy with whom they perceive themselves as having incommensurable differences (e.g., humanists contra social scientists, or positivists contra literary theorists).

Thus, on a more subtle level, interdisciplinary research threatens these quasi-moral communities by blurring what are believed to be fixed epistemological and methodological demarcations of difference. Douglas explains that the purpose of categorization systems is to make an untidy world orderly and more predictable. She writes, "For I believe that ideas about separating, purifying, demarcating and punishing transgressions have as their main function to impose system on an inherently untidy experience" (Douglas 1995, 4). The increase in cross-disciplinary borrowing in the academy potentially threatens every discipline because it undermines the larger system of authority and the dominant ordering of knowledge (along with the system of funding that regulates it) in the academy today.

These disciplinary categories, grounded in disparate cultural and intellectual traditions, became very real for me as my scholarly pursuits took me across the disciplinary border between political science and anthropology, and across the sturdy border between the social sciences and humanities. In the context of my work at the time, the disciplines with which my research engaged included cultural studies, literary studies, architecture history, art history, cultural anthropology, gender studies, and cultural geography. Certainly the positivists in my own discipline were skeptical of my compromising ("polluting") the rigor of social scientific empiricism with "less exact" interpretative methods from the humanities and from anthropology. On more than one occasion political science faculty members told me that I was asking interesting questions in my research but that my papers were (. . . pregnant pause) "somehow literary or something." Many of the questions about epistemology, ethics, and strategy that I raised in the correspondence in this book grew out of my need to justify my process of knowledge production to myself and to the larger political science community, which, on the whole, does not consider ethnography to be a useful method for understanding the political. While political science is a discipline that includes many research methods, since the behaviorist revolution in the 1950s it has come to be increasingly dominated by quantitative empirical approaches, such as statistical methods and rational-choice models. The e-mail correspondence illustrates one scholar's process of resolving important differences between the expectations of empirical political science and the interpretive approach of ethnography. My experience shows that questions about rigor and generalizability, for instance, are not dead letters; they often need to be resolved in legitimating an interdisciplinary approach to positivists (and others).

Although political science takes as its main object of inquiry a social system (i.e., the political), the majority of empirical research in the discipline takes the individual as its basic unit of analysis. Rational-choice theory, survey methods, and various statistically based methods make up the bulk of the empirical work done in political science since the behavioral revolution in the 1950s. To the extent to which political scientists have been concerned to explain the influence of culture, it has been to gauge the likelihood of a polity to support democratic institutions and other structures associated with modernization. Or it has been concerned to explain seemingly irrational political behavior such as ethnic hatred or terrorism. Given this general orientation among empiricist researchers within the discipline, my discipline gave me few models for examining the process of identity production and the complex relationship between the agency of individuals and the social structures that shaped and were shaped by them.

In an *American Political Science Review* article, Lisa Wedeen (2002) offers a careful analysis of how political scientists have employed the concept of culture. Her own study, *Ambiguities of Domination* (1999), is one of very few examples of political science research grounded in an ethnographic study of the subtleties of political domination. Wedeen's article highlights the untenable nature of many political scientists' empirical claims about culture and makes a strong argument for defining culture as a meaning-making process, in keeping with critical anthropology's definition.

Wedeen explains that under the influence of the behavioral revolution in the 1950s and 1960s and of modernization theory, "political culture" scholars have taken culture to be "all politically relevant orientations of all members of a political system" (Verba 1965, 518; see also Almond and Verba 1963). In short, political scientists have conducted large-scale survey research of attitudes and psychological orientations in order to assess how the culture hinders or supports democracy, and to record other markers of "progress." Members of other branches of political science have departed from this approach, most notably "materialists" and rational-choice theorists, who set out to determine how individuals pursue their self-interest in cost-benefit calculations. Culture enters the equation in order to explain why a nation-state fails to democratize or in order to explain political outcomes that deviate in some other way from expected, self-interest-maximizing behavior. What the various approaches share is a tendency to use essentialized "cultural differences" to help explain political phenomena like ethnic violence or religious fundamentalism.

Although they keep a healthy distance from ethnographic *methods,* political scientists have turned to Clifford Geertz's (1973) formulation of culture as a basis for their own research into political culture. However, Wedeen argues that their use of Geertz has actually led the discipline to generate a weaker and incoherent conceptualization of (political) culture. She writes, "Political scientists thereby adopted many of the problems of the Geertzian concept of culture: that the system was reified and fixed, that it was identifiably bounded, and that meanings were always already set in a given 'text'" (2002, 716). In taking culture as a coherent political system and as a set of beliefs and values, political scientists in the main have failed to attend to culture as a process shaped by historical contingency as well as by a dynamic interplay between individual agency and social structure.

Furthermore, while Geertz emphasized the structure of culture, political scientists tended to look at the individual (through surveys), seeing their choices and attitudes as reflections of a reified, essentialized political culture in order to explain or predict various political situations. As Wedeen explains with care and at length in her analysis, political science theories of culture "tended to render historical analyses of practice and process impossible or irrelevant, explaining political outcomes as the result of empirically untenable, untestable assertions of uniformity and fixity. Most political scientists continue to think of culture as connoting fixed group traits" (2002, 716). In her call for more interdisciplinary borrowing between anthropology and political science, Wedeen identifies several disciplinary differences that make political scientists less inclined to borrow from cultural anthropology. These include the continuing emphasis in political science on the individual as the privileged unit of analysis, the greater support among political scientists for the principles of positivism and for modernization theory, as well as a preference in political science for conceptual parsimony over the often lengthy, albeit richly detailed, descriptions in anthropological monographs. Finally, most empirical political science research contrasts notably with interpretive approaches in its less critical reading of the role of power in knowledge production and of the principles of positivism more generally (see Wedeen 2002, 719).

Thus, my interest in interpretive knowledge production and my commitment to interdisciplinarity stand in sharp contrast to the principles that inform King, Keohane, and Verba's influential book *Designing Social Inquiry* (1994) and to those of the many other prominent political scientists who seek an overarching methodology for political science comparable to that of the natural sciences (see, for example, Monroe 1997; Almond 1990; and King 1989).

Alongside the specific concerns of quantitative political scientists about using ethnographic methods, I also encountered skepticism from political philosophers and theorists in the humanities about my use of empirical field research at all to rethink theory. Given that humanists and political theorists have watched universities and outside funding sources increasingly privilege empirical research for its closer approximation of the natural sciences, perhaps my interest in theorizing via empirical research appeared to them to be a kind of sell-out. Since the rise of behavioralism in the 1950s especially, political theory has been removed from empirical research in its focus on philosophical questions. Some political theorists have focused on historical texts and figures, grounding their analyses in political texts of various kinds; and others have turned to the discipline of philosophy as a model for their analyses. Although in some cases they have splintered into rival groups, the various factions within political theory have shared the common vision that political theory can offer an alternative to the hegemonic behavioralism (and a critique of it in many cases) that defines the discipline in the second half of the twentieth century (see Gunnell 1993).[3] Consequently, I found very few models in political science or in humanities-based critical and social theory for interdisciplinary work that drew both on the humanities and the social sciences and tacked between theory and empirical findings.[4]

Thus, one of my motivations for collaborating with Liisa on this book was my sense that as more and more scholars undertake interdisciplinary work, they face epistemological and methodological roadblocks like the ones I confronted in my field research. And I believe that such research is very worthwhile, despite and perhaps even because of its heterodoxy. Liisa notes in her essay in this volume that anthropology is defined less by a strict set of topics, theories, or methodological steps than by a "sensibility." I think that this idea is highly applicable to interdisciplinary work as well. In my own research experience, it did not make sense to me to limit my research to the political science literature and methods, given that scholars in numerous other disciplines have written on topics central to my research—topics like nationalism, empire, and the picturesque. Thus, a central contribution of the e-mail correspondence is that it provides insight into what interdisciplinary research might look like as a "sensibility" or "disposition," to borrow from Bourdieu. Because I approached ethnographic methodology as an "outsider" (as someone who is not an anthropologist or sociologist), my communication with Liisa prompted her to explain many things that typically "go without saying" among anthropologists. The correspondence helps explicate, then, how interdisciplinary scholars might use ethnography in a way that diverges from the way that anthropologists work, but that nevertheless produces defensible and worthwhile scholarship. In fact, the utilization of ethnographic methods by non-anthropologists can enrich what ethnography might be, even allowing for new forms of research. It is beyond the scope of this essay to say what the sensibility of interdisciplinary scholarship might be, and I am not sure that this question has any single answer. But I hope to shift the discussion of interdisciplinarity decisively away from the assumption that it amounts merely to a "failure" to achieve the standards of any particular discipline. We ought to think about interdisciplinarity as a knowledge-production process that flexibly adopts approaches and tools as a consequence of the questions being asked, not as a consequence of the methodological constraints dictated by the history or current hegemony within a given discipline.

Tacking between Whole and Part

Ethnography has traditionally been concerned with how social structures, relationships, and processes produce cultural forms that in turn shape individual consciousness and practices. Ethnographers have pursued such insights by examining social practices and discourses, as well as institutional structures. The empirical nature of ethnography is particularly promising for developing and revising theories concerning social structures, social transformations, cultural negotiation, and "friction" (Tsing 2005). It is particularly useful research practice for interdisciplinary and political science scholars who are dissatisfied with approaches that privilege the individual as the primary unit of analysis. Interpretive ethnography provides a process of data collection and an epistemology that allows one to better understand human agency in the context of social and institutional discourses and that can attend to the influence of history.

Like many scholars of my generation, I was persuaded by post-structuralist and feminist critiques of the limitations of totalizing theories. I appreciated the importance of understanding larger processes such as globalization, modernity, and nationalism by studying their local forms. As many have already pointed out, local differences can help illustrate that these phenomena are not monolithic but are shaped by local realities and the agency of particular groups. For my doctoral dissertation (1997), I turned to ethnography as a means of producing nontotalizing theoretical insights about interconnected contemporary, local practices and global processes. As Michael Herzfeld observes, "It is by dint of the comparatively microscopic focus, I suggest, that anthropology—with its intimate knowledge of alternative conceptual universes and local worlds—offers one of the few remaining critical vantage points from which to challenge the generalizing claims of the global hierarchy of value" (2004, 4). Thus, ethnographic methods have been a means for me of developing theoretical insights that take into account the complexities of local specificities and allow a critical vantage point for understanding the dominant political logic of nationalism and globalization. I was interested in the theoretical insights I could achieve from a continual tacking between ethnographic details and theoretical concepts such as post-coloniality or modernity.

Various scholars in the hermeneutic and anthropological traditions have underscored the dialectical process of moving between the whole and the part in a way that relates to my discussion here. Philosophers (see, for instance, Schleiermacher [1994],[5] Dilthey [1972] and Gadamer [1999]) write about the need to move between the whole of a phenomenon or text and its parts to understand fully the meaning of a phenomenon or text. In her essay in this volume, Liisa traces the idea that ethnographic research involves constant movement between the theoretical and empirical back to Malinowski, who explains how one must investigate the significance of land tenure. Malinowski writes, "And since this idea has gradually to emerge from evidence before him, he must constantly switch over from observation and accumulated evidence to theoretical moulding, and back to collecting again" (Malinowski 1935, 321; see also Malkki's essay in this volume). Similarly, Geertz (1973), in his famous discussion of ethnography as thick description, invokes the metaphor of "tacking" as the movement between part and whole that ethnographers do when interpreting culture. I think it is possible to work with Geertz's conceptualization of the process of interpreting without necessarily reproducing his representation of cultures as closed and coherent systems, in which the part (Balinese theatre for instance; see Geertz 1973) reflects in overly neat ways the dominant meaning in the whole of a culture. The tacking that ethnographers undertake is not so much between the *part of culture* (particular set of symbols) and the *whole of a culture*. The tacking in ethnographic analysis is more a matter of moving in our interpretive analysis between theory and empirical social facts in a dialectic that often reshapes our theoretical ideas as well as our view of the empirical data.

The passage below depicts the movement between theory and empirical detail that I was compelled to make in order to understand the significance of the spatial practices I was observing. In this e-mail message to Liisa during my fieldwork in 1995, I describe the kinds of spatial mapping that police do in "keeping order."

All of these details give the police an amazing spatial overview of the people of the community and of course enables them to better control the spaces in which people move. (So, for instance, when an Aborigine turns up in North Fitzroy at 2:00 a.m., they can jump to the conclusion that he or she is there to burgle a place or other wrong-doing because they are out of their so-called appropriate place.) And, indeed, space is transformed in relation to time. The police's reading of normal Aboriginal space at 2:00 a.m. has to do with a certain constellation of pubs that are open in the district at that time and who they know hangs out at which ones, and where they are in relation to the known Aboriginal hostels. Similar maps are constructed for various groups that the police want to track, of course. It's also interesting how members of the force are regularly walking into the station, frustrated that there is no such address of the place that the "crook" gave as their home address. I guess you could say that a whole series of fictional geographies are improvised as a way of resisting power's control of space (de Certeau's "tactical raids of the weak"). (Correspondence, June 6, 1995)

My observations were shaped by theoretical concepts I had studied before doing fieldwork. For instance, the very conceptualization of given practices as "spatial" comes from certain theoretical discussions in contemporary scholarship (see, for example, Soja 1989; de Certeau 1984; and Massey 1994). The hermeneutics of ethnography, however, involves a reading of social practices through theoretical concepts without simply reducing the practices to a mere "illustration" of the theory. In the case of my own study, these spatial practices were part of a larger process of ongoing state control and practices aimed at rendering Aboriginal geographies transparent to the state. De Certeau has provided some particularly useful language for understanding the resistant nature of what struck the police at this station as merely "irresponsible" or "irrational" (non-Western) behavior. However, the social practices in this field site extend de Certeau's ideas about the power relations operating at the level of spatial practice to postcolonial and national political processes (see Cerwonka 2004, 151–96). Such analytic insights necessarily grow out of a hermeneutic process that continually and self-consciously moves between theory and empirical, ethnographic detail. As the correspondence details, however, disciplinary differences prompted political scientists to see such tacking as problematic for the way "fieldwork is leading the theory" (see, for example, the e-mail dated May 18, 1995). Consequently, the interdisciplinary discussion about theory and methods that took place during the course of my project highlights subtle yet profound disciplinary differences concerning the relationship of theory to empirical research. It also suggests some of the ways in which conceptual and institutional boundaries between social science disciplines that have overlapping objects of study (e.g., politics, culture, society) are reproduced.

Anthropologists have long seen their ethnographic work as part of a process of making theoretical arguments. However, as Rabinow and Sullivan (1979) note, an interpretive approach offers an alternative to the reductionism found in many theoretical models. The various forms of structuralism in the 1960s in anthropology defined themselves as a corrective to prior theoretical schools. Nevertheless, structuralism, as Rabinow and Sullivan characterize it, continued the thesis of "the priority and independence of logical structures and rules of inference from the contexts of ordinary understanding" (1979, 10). Such structural approaches tended to offer totalizing ethnographic accounts of social and symbolic processes and to prioritize order in social life, rather than the discontinuity and disorder that inevitably characterize that life (Moore 1987, 729–30). While there has been a move away from structural ("totalizing") accounts, as Paul Willis notes, the use of theory in the form of a ready-made, interpretive framework continues to impede both creative ethnographic work and the development of new theoretical categories. Willis observes,

> Too many ethnographies are shackled rather than liberated by theoretical obeisance. If there aren't illuminating categories around, don't shy away from developing or adapting your own categories in relation to the world, which is *undoubtedly* developing ahead of us and developing forms, binaries, sensuousness, emergences, cultural forms which *aren't* going to fit easily into prior categories. The over-reification of theories and theorists is a big problem. (Willis, quoted in Mills and Gibb 2001, 411–12)[6]

Thus, as post-structuralism affirms the cultural constructedness of categories, identities, and even bodies, ethnography serves as a particularly useful research practice. Ethnographic research has traditionally examined cultural categories and structures, not primarily through historical analysis, as Foucault did, but by examining them cross-culturally. Consequently, far from illustrating the relationship of theory to ethnographic material for anthropologists alone, this book highlights what a hermeneutical process might look like for scholars of any discipline who seek to develop nontotalizing theory and to understand how larger social processes function in specific local settings.

The correspondence as a whole reflects the process of moving among various levels of interpretation, providing insight into how field research happens in real time. It illustrates how the process is characterized by partial understanding, as well as floods of insight, in a process that is more spiral in nature than linear and cumulative. I started the project with a background in postmodern geography and an orientation in the literature on the senses as constitutive of social categories. But many of the issues and social practices I observed in Australia posed interesting questions about how transnational processes helped to produce the nation in spatial terms. As I encountered people who transplanted the aesthetic of Great Britain to the arid bush landscape of Australia or reproduced Australia as a Western (rather than Asian) nation through police management of bodies and urban space, the established scholarly theories were productively complicated; I was compelled to think about how transnational geographies like the British empire, and geopolitical borders like East and West, are constructed not simply through maps and free-trade agreements, but in struggles over everyday, local landscapes.

Conversely, the local common sense that deemed it natural to divide the Vietnamese neighborhood of Richmond from the Anglo-Celtic neighborhood of East Melbourne meant little without a theory that could help denaturalize it and to draw out its significance for larger structures of power and identity. But the theoretical apparatuses offered by Soja (1989), Lewis and Wigen (1997), Howes (1996 and 2003), and Seremetakis (1994), for instance, required revision in light of the sensual, local spatiality I encountered and inhabited in Melbourne neighborhoods. The following e-mail gives an example of the temporally and socially uneven nature of understanding and the continual movement between part and whole, fieldwork and theory.

To: Liisa Malkki
From: Allaine Cerwonka
Date: Wed, May 24, 1995
Subject: Another Thought

Me again.

I have been thinking, as always, about the structure of all of this madness, dissertation stuff. I think I'm in a bit of a manic phase again, I must warn you. But hopefully it's just too much caffeine.

Could it be that social geography is the key concept around which this all comes together? . . . For instance, when I was talking to Judith, the garden club secretary, about delivering leaflets to the next suburb over, she explained how a road that has been expanded in the last five years, Hoddle Street, acts as a divide between the two communities and keeps people from coming into East Melbourne (although they still deliver the leaflets). And as you walk in the area, the noise is so loud that it repels you and causes you to go in one direction or the other (Richmond or East Melbourne). I would also think that the predominance of one language versus another in a given area might shape the area (like the dominance of Vietnamese on Victoria Street) . . .

I don't want to get bogged down in details, but hope that these few give you a sense of what I mean. Perhaps you have seen how the senses fit into postmodern geography before, but the light just went on over my head. . . . I think the presence of languages and smells might be one way in which the supra-local exists within/shapes the local; I have my eyes open for others . . .

One more thing I am not sure in all of this [. . .] is how [. . .] discourses about the land and indigenous products [. . .] and the supra-national environmental movement link to [. . .] Melbourne spatial politics. Oh, I read a while back the article by Ulf Hannerz [regarding . . .] how modernism has shaped Swedish national identity; that was useful for my thinking about the environmental movement and Australia. . . . As you can see, I haven't given up reading entirely. I can't. I think I started a little behind the eight ball in terms of reading in all these areas when I started my fieldwork anyway, but I also find that it helps me continually fine-tune what I am looking at and how I should approach it all. Otherwise, I find that I get lost in the details of the interviews and can't find the big picture as easily. (Correspondence, May 24, 1995)

The above passage from my fieldwork captures what Rabinow, following Ricoeur, calls the "dialectic of guessing and validation" (1979, 11). Rather than the scientific model, according to which one begins with a theoretical hypothesis, tests it, and then finds it true or false, the interpretive process involves a continuous movement between explanations (theories) about the object or process at issue and the parts that force adjustment or reaffirm the researcher's initial "guessing." Thus, one of its important strengths is that the correspondence offers a window onto a hermeneutic ethnographic process that builds theory—in fits and starts—from the "tacking" between the theoretical (whole) and the ethnographic detail (part). It demonstrates how one might use theory and ethnographic material to think one through the other, and thus avoid imposing prefabricated, theoretical models on the rich complexity of everyday life. In this regard, the correspondence illustrates a process that most methodology books can only describe abstractly and that one must try to infer from finished ethnographic monographs. As anthropologist Sally Falk Moore notes, rejecting neat, totalizing theories in favor of more tentative claims attentive to the non-order and gaps of meaning in social structures is not a compromise in scientific or theoretical rigor.[7] She terms this approach "fieldwork in a post-structural period," inviting more analytic attention to "uncertainty and disorder" within the ethnographic scene (1987, 730).

By giving this process a name in this essay or by illustrating it with the e-mail correspondence, I do not claim to be putting forward a new method of research. To the contrary, the value of the correspondence in this book lies in its illustration of an interpretive process of knowledge production that has always operated in the social sciences and humanities. In other words, it is an illustration of what already exists, not what *could or should be.*

Improvisation in Fieldwork

On many levels, the correspondence illustrates how ethnography is not "a methodology" at all in the traditional understanding of the term. It cannot be reduced to a set of standardized techniques that any practitioner can implement. As Liisa argues in detail in her essay, ethnography relies on improvisation. In the *Interpretation of Cultures* (1973), Clifford Geertz stresses ethnography as a process rather than as a methodological doctrine:

> In anthropology, or anyway social anthropology, what the practitioners do is ethnography. And it is in understanding what ethnography is, or more exactly *what doing ethnography is,* that a start can be made toward grasping what anthropological analysis amounts to as a form of knowledge. This, it must immediately be said, is not a matter of methods. From one point of view, that of the textbook, doing ethnography is establishing rapport, selecting informants, transcribing texts, taking genealogies, mapping fields, keeping a diary, and so on. But it is not these things, techniques and received procedures, that define the enterprise. (1973, 5–6)[8]

Although Liisa also discusses this passage, I would like to underscore two important points that Geertz makes in it. First, "doing ethnography" is more than the sum total of the various tasks one does during fieldwork (interviewing, mapping fields, and such). And second, there is an important connection between understanding the *process* of ethnographic research and understanding ethnographic evidence as a kind of knowledge. Geertz's assertions are an important point of departure for us. As I have already noted and will consider further, this book addresses the connection between the ethnographic process and the more general question of how we make knowledge claims. Additionally, we stress that ethnography demands a certain sensibility, as well as improvised strategies and ethical judgments made within a shifting landscape in which the ethnographer has limited control. Ethnography is not, then, simply the sum total of standard, stable, ethnographic tasks, as the genre of "how-to" books (textbook and methods manuals) on ethnography might imply to the novice ethnographer.

The following passage from one of my e-mails to Liisa provides an illustration of improvisation in fieldwork. It suggests how ethnography entails constantly adjusting one's tactics and making judgments based on particular contexts that one can never fully anticipate. The following passage is taken from a longer e-mail message I wrote to Liisa during my fieldwork.

A [...] breakthrough with the cops yesterday. Finally, I went out and had beers with a few (about ten) of them after the shift. The suggestion has been made a few times, but it's never been in a way where I could seriously take it up. So at last I went out yesterday afternoon when the shift ended. I was pleased that the constable who asked me was the person I had interviewed that afternoon as well. That made me feel it had been a positive experience for him, and it sent out that signal to others as well, which hopefully will make it more of something people want to do rather than are told to [do] by the sergeant...

Some of my most interesting moments of conducting fieldwork have come when police members seem to want to tell me things about these incidents [internal investigations into police misconduct]. The expectation/paranoia (as I read it) is that I will ask and then publicly denounce the police (in combination with their professional culture which rigidly defines an inside and an outside in terms of professional loyalties) about these abuses of power. So I am careful never to ask. That makes it even more interesting when they want to tell me. Yesterday, while I was observing at the station, this sergeant brought up the subject twice that he couldn't do an interview with me that day because he had an internal investigation interview about an incident at the station last week. When he brought it up the second time, I figured he wanted to tell me about it so I asked a bit of a general question and got told quite a bit. It's almost funny that they almost can't conceive that really I want to write about national identity and not about police abuses. (Correspondence, June 1, 1995)

This passage testifies to the ways in which my fieldwork practices (what to ask, under what circumstances, and how) depended on the dynamics of my particular field site and how my informants responded to me as a person. Police-station culture and the particular constellation of personalities among my informants there necessarily shaped my strategies about when to ask questions and when to be silent. Only the fieldwork context could guide me in determining when to pose especially direct questions about internal police investigations of the improper use of force by individual police officers. And it was only by continually assessing my research practices in relation to the shifting circumstances in the field site that I could make good ethical judgments. Similarly, within the East Melbourne garden club, my other fieldwork site, I found that the intimacy I developed with certain people grew out of unpredictable and subtle social and affective negotiations that arose from encounters as diverse as hospital visits, funerals, and seemingly unimportant walks in the garden. Each ethnographer confronts his or her own particular situational dilemmas and must improvise strategies and tactics in light of what he or she is trying to know through the fieldwork. While many have embraced Geertz's idea (see also Rosaldo 1989) of ethnographic methods as something that exceeds a finite and easily agreed upon set of tasks, the informed improvisation so central to its critical practice has hitherto been underexamined.

The improvisational nature of ethnographic fieldwork stands in contrast to the formulaic quality usually associated with the concept of methods. In fact, this quality makes it a useful illustration of philosopher Hans-Georg Gadamer's point in *Truth and Method* (1999) concerning the impossibility of reducing the process of understanding to a set of standardized steps. Gadamer describes "understanding" as a *process*. He argues that method, as canonized in the sciences, is not adequate to capture how our acquisition of knowledge really occurs; the scientific method as a model is not properly transferable to the humanities or social disciplines and research questions, as many positivists in the social sciences have held. Gadamer actually identifies the hermeneutic process as universal. (Geertz too contradicts the popular wisdom that the humanities and social sciences represent entirely different modes of knowledge production. He asserts that rather than being a practice of scientific observation, the work of the ethnographer is "much more like that of the literary critic" [1973, 9].) In the following passage, Gadamer describes the process of understanding in the human sciences as characterized by something different than the inductive logic of the scientific method:

> The hermeneutic phenomenon is basically not a problem of method at all. It is not concerned with a method of understanding by means of which texts are subjected to scientific investigation like all other objects of experience. It is not concerned with amassing verified knowledge, such as would satisfy the methodological ideal of science—yet it too is concerned with knowledge and with truth. . . . The human sciences have no method of their own. Yet one might ask, with Helmholtz, to what extent method is significant in this case and whether the other logical presuppositions of the human sciences are not perhaps far more important than inductive logic. Helmholtz had indicated this correctly when, in order to do justice to the human sciences, he emphasized memory and authority, and spoke of the psychological tact that here replaced the conscious drawing of inferences. What is the basis of this tact? How is it acquired? Does not what is scientific about the human sciences lie rather here than in their methodology? (1999, xxi, 7–8)

Gadamer challenges the hegemony of objectivism while acknowledging that we can identify a number of elements common to the process of understanding (which he discusses at length in *Truth and Method*). With the notion of psychological "tact" (taken from Helmholtz), Gadamer characterizes an orientation to research that is more nuanced. He emphasizes understanding as a nonscripted process wherein the researcher responds to the particularities of what he or she is examining. The researcher expects that understanding will be influenced by his or her own historical and cultural situatedness. In this way, Gadamer seems to be identifying something akin to what Liisa and I call a research "sensibility."

Additionally for Gadamer, because the subjectivity of the researcher (her positionality and prejudgments) can never be erased from the knowledge-production process, as positivists have tried to do, the act of interpreting will always involve a "fusion of horizons" (1999). This fusion is a co-influencing of the historical specificity of the researcher, on the one hand, and of the history and character of the object of research, on the other. In other words, one cannot reduce understanding to a method, because the researcher and object of inquiry are always historically situated and historically related. Gadamer's historical-hermeneutic approach challenges the positivist's sharp division between subject and object, emphasizing instead the dialogue between the two. Lorraine Code observes that "here, the subject/object dichotomy that functions as a basis of positivist-empiricist presupposition yields to a conception of objects of knowledge as neither autonomous in, nor abstractable from, processes in which knower, known, and knowing are bound together" (2003, 8). The fusion at the center of understanding means that we must see knowledge production as a flexible, creative, historically influenced *process*.

In her essay in this book, Liisa lends support to Geertz's early characterization of ethnography (as a nonmethod) when she explores the parallels between improvisation in jazz and the ethnographic process in anthropology. She argues that improvisation has always been a feature of ethnographic practice. And while positivists have shunned ethnography's improvisational features as "imprecise" and "soft," improvisation in ethnographic research grows out of extensive training and lends such research heuristic flexibility and, as a result, a high degree of empirical precision. The improvisational aspects of ethnographic fieldwork are understandably difficult to teach in a methodology seminar. The experiences of the ethnographers reflected in this e-mail correspondence help us to see improvisation as a valuable tactic in ethnographic research and to see it in relation to the larger process of knowledge production.

Interestingly, Claude Lévi-Strauss gives us a suggestive portrait of an alternative approach to understanding in his description of the *bricoleur*'s construction of mythical knowledge. I want briefly to note some of the parallels between the approach of the *bricoleur* and the improvisation of the ethnographer with the aim of further elucidating the latter. In "The Science of the Concrete," Lévi-Strauss sketches an alternative process of understanding.[9] Although he is describing a general approach to knowledge production (in this case mythical knowledge) that can exist alongside modern science, he gives us a useful way of imagining what the ethnographic process might look like when understood as something other than a form of scientific investigation. In fact, Lévi-Strauss' formulation is remarkably convergent with Gadamer's rejection of methods as static (cf. Gadamer 1999, xxii). He describes a "science of the concrete" wherein the *bricoleur* produces knowledge flexibly by "making do with whatever is at hand" (1962, 17).[10] Lévi-Strauss describes the *bricoleur* when he writes,

> His universe of instruments is always closed and the rules of his game are always to make do with "whatever is at hand," that is to say with a set of tools and materials which is always finite and is also heterogeneous because what it contains bears no relation to the current project, or indeed to any particular project, but is the contingent result of all the occasions there have been to renew or enrich the stock or to maintain it with the remains of previous constructions or destructions. (17)

Lévi-Strauss's account gives us a language for describing how the ethnographer produces theoretical knowledge from an engagement with the physical, social, and affective landscapes over which she has only partial control. In contrast to a traditional scientific experiment, the materials used are more than anything else those at hand, be they the people who are willing to help and participate in the research, the situations to which one is granted access, or the food and activities the researcher's body can tolerate.

Additionally, the *bricoleur*, like the ethnographer, inevitably shapes the social landscape and phenomena that she studies through the choices she makes. Lévi-Strauss explains, "He 'speaks' not only *with* things, as we have already seen, but also through the medium of things: giving an account of his personality and life by the choices he makes between the limited possibilities. The 'bricoleur' may not ever complete his purpose but he always puts something of himself into it" (1962, 21).

The idea of deliberate improvisation is captured in the correspondence in one of Liisa's early e-mails to me. Here she reminds me of the heuristic value of the less-structured elements of ethnographic fieldwork:

Uncertainties about interviews: don't be afraid of having exchanges that look more like rambling, long, multifaceted conversations and chats than formal, structured 'Interviews.' It'd be easy to adopt a very rigid [. . .] interview style with Q & A flowing in neat rows and columns. Anthropological fieldwork doesn't look like that—or not only. Often the best material comes in strange forms—chance bits, like *objets trouvés* [found objects]. Besides, you are also doing the observation-side of the participant-observation process, which means you notice your surroundings and make notes on them. . . . You can and should be continually changing and adapting your tactics and techniques of fieldwork. (Correspondence, March 22, 1995)

The eclectic, creative process of the *bricoleur* is helpful for reconceptualizing research as the calculated improvisation that ethnographic fieldwork is. It complements Gadamer's description of all understanding as a complex fusion of horizons between subject and object, and of movement between part and whole. In the next section, I look more closely at the influence of social personhood in ethnographic interpretation, again drawing on Gadamer's hermeneutics.

Positionality and Knowledge Production

An interpretive approach to knowledge production pushes critical discourse in the social sciences beyond the simple denial of the positivist ideal of objectivity and beyond suggestions for self-reflexive strategies. It articulates an alternative epistemology for research and offers a more accurate account of knowledge production. Gadamer again helps us to conceptualize this alternative epistemology when he writes that "understanding is not merely a reproductive but always a productive activity as well" (1999, 296). Rejecting the idea that research is an exercise in recording an objectively observable reality, Gadamer insists on the constructive nature of understanding and interpretation. His theory of interpretation develops an account of how understanding inevitably involves the concrete, historically situated personhood of the researcher. He claims *more* than that the positivist ideal of objectivity can never be reached;[11] he asserts that *we can only ever understand something from a point of view* (see also Haraway's critique of aspirations to a "view from nowhere," 1991). Gadamer writes,

> [The demand that] in understanding history one must leave one's own concepts aside and think only in the concepts of the epoch one is trying to understand . . . is a naïve illusion. The naïveté of this claim does not consist in the fact that it remains unfulfilled because the interpreter does not sufficiently attain the ideal of leaving himself aside. . . . To want to avoid one's own concepts in interpretation is not only impossible but a manifest contradiction. (1999, 396)

In this passage, Gadamer makes a point that he develops from Heidegger's idea of the fore-structure of understanding in *Being and Time* (Heidegger

1962, 191). Both contend that it is only *through* a point of view, or a given "facticity," in Heideggerian terminology, that one can understand something. Heidegger writes,

> When something is understood but is still veiled, it becomes unveiled by an act of appropriation, and this is always done under the guidance of a point of view, which fixes that with regard to which is understood is to be interpreted. (191)

What Gadamer and Heidegger assert in these two passages is that the potentially endless number of aspects or dimensions of an object or phenomenon *can only* be understood from a particular vantage point. As philosopher Linda Alcoff notes of Gadamer's argument, "He offers us a way to conceptualize the inevitable locatedness of knowers not as detriments but as necessary conditions for knowledge" (Alcoff 2003, 232).[12]

Thus, a grasp of what we seek to understand is always mediated by the positionality of the inquirer, without which the information would be meaningless, uninterpreted, "uncooked." A vantage point means having a sociohistorical location, but it might also be understood as the set of priorities, questions, or even hypotheses that one inevitably brings to bear in trying to understand an object or phenomenon. My ethnographic research, like all sustained practices aimed at understanding, confirms Gadamer's and Heidegger's point insofar as one cannot help but understand Australian national identity from a particular point of view. My fieldwork illustrates this insight on a number of levels. It depicts the way in which my historical, cultural location as a middle-class, American woman with various political and social commitments shaped the understanding I developed about my topic. For instance, I was interested in spatial practices and the territoriality of the Australian nation in part because of my location at a historical moment when globalization was challenging the territorial sovereignty of the nation-state. This historical context influenced my understanding and framed my investigation. Had I undertaken this research fifty years earlier, my historical context would certainly have shaped the investigations in some other way. Not only is it impossible to transcend these particularities, but they are necessary (and desirable) ingredients for organizing, interpreting, and making meaning of a phenomenon or text.

In the first months of my e-mail exchanges with Liisa, I weighed the pros and cons of various ethnographic field sites. Each site seemed to me impossibly particular and thus "failed" to promise an overarching (complete) view of Australian national identity. These early e-mail exchanges illustrate my struggle to clarify to myself how my analytical lens—and the social locations of a police station and a garden club—would allow me to understand the social phenomenon of the spatial construction of the Australian nation. A failure to understand the inevitability of partial knowledge often leads researchers to conclude that *no vantage point or field site* is adequate because any one site (or two or three) would provide one kind of information but leave out other kinds, thus fatally hobbling generalizability. The brief correspondence I had via fax with my political science advisor in California illustrates succinctly how this conceptual hurdle I confronted early in my fieldwork was shaped by my disciplinary orientation as a political scientist. In his supportive response to my fieldwork progress report, my advisor expresses concern about my ability to generalize from a field site comprised of middle-aged and elderly gardeners. My anxious decision to select two field sites meant realizing that my research would inevitably involve a particular and situated viewpoint (cf. Haraway 1991) and that that was the only way in which I could understand formations of Australian identity. I could not simply find it at large, as I initially thought I should do. My experience illustrates that the inevitability of partial knowledge means that one's research choices will allow for a certain range of information and insight. Good research thus entails being clear about what one seeks to understand and, in turn, being conscious and deliberate about choosing fieldwork practices that will facilitate insight on the subject. My early goal of selecting "representative" field sites gave way to identifying what I might learn about the spatial construction of the nation from the viewpoint of the practices and discourses of people in the contexts I chose, be they church-goers, police, or garden club members.

In our exchange, Liisa challenged me to recognize that the only way to make defensible knowledge claims about my topic was to speak out of detailed, rich and, as she phrased it then, "sometimes ridiculously deep" knowledge of a particular social location. At this important juncture in my fieldwork, Liisa writes,

To: Allaine Cerwonka
From: Liisa Malkki
Date: Wed, February 15, 1995
Subject: Re: back again . . .

Hi Allaine,

Sorry to get back to you so late. Got your two wonderful communications about fieldwork. YES YES YES: the cops, the gardeners, parishioners are, I think, excellent contexts to situate yourself in!! Can't state this strongly enough. You've hit on fascinating, sociologically important, revealing sites from which to explore your questions. And this is really what

I was talking about. Informants are everywhere, but there needs to be some coherence, some social/sociological logic to the CONTEXTS or SITES in which you are working. So, two things (in answer to your queries about informants' nature, location): 1. Informants are persons whom you generally have more regular contact with. You get to know them, talk to them pretty often (not daily or anything necessarily), see them living and working in their life circumstances/surroundings, earn their trust, learn things about their lives and thoughts from many different angles. Deep (sometimes ridiculously deep) knowledge, thick description. [It's a] very time-consuming process, this developing of relationships with informants—and energy-consuming. This does not mean that chance conversations and casual acquaintances cannot provide valuable material or insights, as well. Simply keep a record for yourself of whom you spoke with at any given time, where, when, how, why, etc.

2. This second point is the one I was really trying to stress. When you come back and write your study into a dissertation and then a manuscript, you need to be able to say something more focused than that you spoke with "some interesting people" in Australia. You need to be able to identify and explain and justify your arguments on the basis of research in specific social locations—because, after all, you can't talk about Australia in general in a serious way. Your informants can, but you as a scholar can't claim that your arguments hold for the whole country. See? You can simply state that in the contexts of which you have thorough knowledge, this and this holds. And from there, other, more general insights might follow. You need to be pretty hard-nosed about this if you claim to do ethnographic fieldwork. And this is, precisely, what you should claim, what you are entitled to claim, and what I (for one) expect from you. I am absolutely tickled pink when I think into the future about your book. (Correspondence, February 15, 1995)

To say that understanding is always a situated practice is not simply to acknowledge that we always bring personal "bias" (conceptual and personal fore-understandings and prejudgments) to our research. It is to say that we always understand *through* a set of priorities and questions that we bring to the phenomenon/object we are researching. While scholars might not acknowledge the elements that inform their research, the elements are nevertheless there, invisibly so. This point bears on the important question of how one's personhood is also a *condition* for knowledge claims, rather than a deterrent to understanding. This issue appears in the correspondence in an e-mail to me from Liisa where she addresses my anxiety that, as a woman studying police, there were things to which I did not have the same access that a male researcher might:

To: Allaine Cerwonka
From: Liisa Malkki
Date: Saturday, August 12, 1995
Subject: Re: travels

Hi,

Good to hear from you, as always. I hope I didn't worry you about access to women, home lives, etc. I was just asking and did not mean to suggest at all that you should have collected X or Y kind of material. I also think it's worth being self-conscious, as you are, about the kind of material and access your being a woman either blocks or enables. I suspect men-scholars working on cops is more usual than women, and I suspect that they do get lots of good material through going to Australian rules football something-or-other. But they do not necessarily get what you have found. Men, cops, people—they have to interact with lots of different kinds of people in the course of everyday life, and one should not assume *a priori* that the most natural or truest "habitat" of men-cops is the company of other men, or other cops. . . .

Another thought: you felt nervous, I think, about not having done the correct thing, or done enough, when I asked you about the cops' home lives. This is a good preview case that gives you a hint of how a returning fieldworker feels—how fragile and inarticulate—when asked by colleagues at the home institution, "So what did you find? What are your conclusions? What are you arguing? What's your evidence? What's your point in a nutshell?" People readily interrogate you in a manner that suggests they expect that you have accomplished a "total ethnography," that is, an in-the-round full ethnography of the whole social universe that you studied in. Of course, this was always a fiction, even when ethnographers did manage to find isolated rural villages in the middle of nowhere. Upon reflection, no one would [explicitly, intentionally] ask such a thing [a total ethnography] of you; [but the post-fieldwork questions from colleagues sometimes add up to give you that impression]. (Correspondence, August 12, 1995)

In the second paragraph of this e-mail, Liisa offers a direct critique of the many ways that expectations of a totalizing, holistic vision persist in "what goes without saying" in anthropology, despite the agreement among most scholars about its impossibility. In the first paragraph, Liisa addresses a different but related tension in anthropology, one she observed in my work as well. She raises the epistemological question of how the understanding achieved in ethnographic research is configured and limited by aspects of the researcher's identity. The positivist approach, of course, has been to treat any influence on the research of the researcher's person as compromising to her results, or "findings."

The positivist research model encourages one to strive for objectivity by erasing all personal influences on the research. Self-reflexivity is an approach to research that is critical of many of the principles of positivism (including the ambition to achieve objectivity). Further, it aims to attend to the imbalance of power in the research encounter that privileges the researcher. With the aid of self-reflexive strategies, individuals strive to reduce their authority and power in the research context through self-awareness and sensitivity. Yet, too often such attempts in the end reproduce the positivist ambition of containing polluting influences on the research (in this case, power) by adhering to certain methodological principles (self-awareness rather than self-effacement).

As previously mentioned, anthropology has historically had an ambivalent relationship with the ideal of objectivity. Both James Clifford (1986) and Mary Louise Pratt (1986) have written about the literary conventions that anthropologists use to offset the fundamental contradiction between the ethnographer's active participation in the research scene and the demands of objectivism.[13] Clifford has described this as the "discipline's impossible attempt to fuse objective and subjective practices" (quoted in Pratt 1986, 32).[14] In disciplines outside of anthropology, it has often been easier to brush aside the question of the inevitable effect of the researcher on his object of study because the researcher's body and participation were less overtly implicated in the research process. In contrast, it is far more difficult to erase completely the researcher's presence from an ethnographic monograph since the ethnographer's claims rest on having observed and participated in the life of a social context. This central fact has left ethnographers without any semblance of distance as claimed by more positivist, objectivist researchers who employ survey questionnaires, don the white lab coat, or seemingly maintain neutrality on the other side of the one-way glass wall in psychological and other social scientific observations.

And, indeed, social science positivists have accorded ethnographic methods scant authority because the researcher is not sufficiently removed from the "data." But the very thing that renders ethnography's knowledge claims suspicious for some is in fact its strength. The nature of the ethnographic encounter (*participant* observation) has prompted anthropologists in particular to confront the inseparability of the ethnographer's "horizon" (Gadamer) from her object of inquiry. For this reason, ethnographic fieldwork is a rich and demanding activity where questions about the relationships among experience, self, and the alterity of the research object are more readily explored than in other research practices. For example, without setting out to do so, I found that the process of fieldwork forced me to question to a

significant degree how my fear of, affection for, and alienation from the police I worked with shaped my research and insights [see the e-mail of March
31, 1995 and "Afterthought," p. 96]. Thus, far from being a deficiency, the
sustained contact and negotiation between ethnographer and the phenomena she researches is really ethnography's creative center and offers endless
opportunities for social science scholars to develop more suitable and creative models for knowledge production.

The idea of positionality in Gadamer's work (what he calls one's "horizon") and in that of others who advocate an interpretive approach is different
from the idea that our insights are simply *reducible* to our subjective bias.
Rather, our point of view *fuses* with the horizon and alterity of what we research and is therefore not a mere projection of the researcher's subjectivity.
In other words, an interpretive approach is not a rejection of all notions of
objectivity in favor of romanticism or indulgent subjectivism. It reconceptu-
alizes objectivity as a theoretical stance. Thus, what Clifford described in the
earlier quotation as anthropology's "impossible attempt to fuse the objective
and subjective" is only impossible if one is trying to adhere to positivism's
very narrow notion of objectivity.

Further, Gadamer problematizes the idea of "absolute objects" and the
"world in itself." As philosopher David Weberman writes, "The object is un-
derdetermined because it is not self-contained, it is not self-contained because
it is partly constituted by its relational properties, and its relational properties vary according to the temporal (and perhaps cultural) position of the
historically situated knower" (2003, 43). For Gadamer, one's understanding
of an object or phenomenon is necessarily and productively shaped by language, which always mediates meaning. Additionally, understanding is shaped
by the relationships of an object or phenomenon to other things and events.
Among the many things that might configure understanding are the researcher's historical and cultural location vis-à-vis what he is studying; the power
relations that underpin the research; and the motivation for the research.

How "bias" or "prejudice" shapes the research process within positivist
models is an issue for epistemology, but also for the ethics of the social sciences. The positivist model has asserted, as well, that research ethics depend
on a strict division between the researcher's opinions, desires, and social orientation, on the one hand, and the research object, on the other. The following passage from my e-mail correspondence with Liisa captures my
growing realization of the ethical dimensions of fieldwork. I came to see
my prime ethical responsibility not in terms of *repressing* ("removing") my
personhood, but in terms of the need to remain consciously aware of my
investment in and even fusion with the "object" of inquiry. I wrote,

There are so many different layers to fieldwork. Issues multiply and intersect in exciting ways. I am forever in a state of trying to work out what I am doing with my methodology and why; and on top of that, the fieldwork and research is very often about me as well. Fieldwork is about me in that it requires a lot of integrity and self-justification for what I am doing and why, and the issues—like identity and feeling a sense of place—end up being issues in my life as well as in the lives of those in my study. (Correspondence, July 4, 1995)

This passage illustrates the kind of fusion of horizons that Gadamer writes about: prejudices, historical situatedness, and the viewpoint of the researcher are an inescapable and *productive* influence on interpretation and understanding (Gadamer 1999). Further, as a result of their fieldwork experience, ethnographers (and feminist methodologists for that matter) potentially offer a more nuanced understanding of responsibility and ethics to philosophers' work on hermeneutics.

The correspondence provides a window onto the way that ethics is embedded even in what seem to be the most trivial of fieldwork choices and strategies: This is quite different from the manner in which ethical issues are presented in most methodology books and courses. Anthropology's long history of thinking about the delicate relationship between inquirer and that which she seeks to understand makes it a particularly rich intellectual location from which to think about the ethics and politics of contact and fusion (in Gadamer's sense).

Given the futility of efforts at neutralizing oneself in the research process, *especially* in ethnographic fieldwork, we clearly need alternative models for picturing what an ethics of engagement would look like. Joanne Passaro (1997b) touches on this issue when she describes the anxiety that others expressed about her being "too close" to the subject matter in her research. People questioned her ability to get an "unbiased" understanding of homeless men in New York City because she was studying her own society and was admittedly invested in understanding homelessness as an important political problem. Passaro explains,

In both cases, the assumption was that an epistemology of "Otherness" was the best route to "objectivity," that as an outsider I would be without the ideological filters or stakes in the outcome of my study that an insider would have. But at this point at the close of the century, we already know that "objectivity" is not a function of "distance"; that "Otherness" is not a geographical given but a theoretical stance; and that we do indeed have a stake in our work. . . . For most people the essential question was whether by doing fieldwork in the United States

I was "distant enough" to produce adequate ethnographic knowledge. Whether I was "close enough" was never an issue. (Passaro 1997b, 152–53)

Passaro challenges the positivist ideal by pointing to the analytical insights and interpersonal understanding that we forego in research that strives to maintain or produce detachment. Objectivity is therefore not a question of proximity (distance); it is a theoretical, epistemological idea.[15] Equally important, we cannot assume that empathy and identification are always the most ethical or analytically useful stance in knowledge production.

Affect and Embodiment as Heuristic Tools

There are numerous dimensions of the significance of personhood and subjectivity in epistemology that we might examine. However, in this last section, I want to consider the place of affect and the body in ethnographic research. The emotional highs and lows of the ethnographer are particularly central to the correspondence. Emotional distance and the "absence" of the researcher's body have long been assumed to be important to achieving objectivity. Of course, the suspicion of emotions and the disruptive influence of the body unregulated by reason are part of the more general mind/body split in Western thought and epistemology following Descartes (see Grosz 1994 and 1993). Affect and the body have also been historically associated with the feminine, rendering them all the more suspect to social science disciplines striving to be rigorous, "hard" sciences.[16] Rejecting the constraints and sexism of positivism, some feminist and self-reflexive researchers have championed affect, (empathy in particular; e.g., Behar 1996).

Taking a somewhat different tack, I would suggest that we look upon affect and the body as hermeneutic resources. The passage I cite below involves an incident in my research that I quickly came to see as a mistake in judgment on my part. Instead of focusing on the ethical issues related to this incident, as I do in "Afterthoughts" to the following e-mail (chapter 3), here I want to think about how my body contributed to my understanding of the cultural practices of the police station. In an e-mail to Liisa, I described a strip search the police conducted on a woman arrested for stealing food at a local supermarket in the following way:

I had a profound experience earlier on in the week when I went in to observe at the station. A drunken woman was arrested for shop-lifting two packages of cheese and some butter from the supermarket. There was only one woman cop on, and so the sergeant said that she would have to do the search before the other two male cops could question her. Someone jokingly suggested I watch the search because the woman (to be searched) was quite overweight. I asked the sergeant seriously if he would mind. He agreed and instructed Rene to do a *strip* search . . .

I think this incident was a mistake in judgment on my part. I was impressed that during the search the woman said, despite her drunkenness, "This is really degrading, you know," and went on to make jokes [directed toward] the woman cop about having bigger boobs than Rene, etc. (The woman cop was very cold in response; maybe because it was true?) I felt quite bad about having participated in that scene. I do not think it was necessary for me in learning about national identity. What I learned about police-"crook" power relations was certainly no surprise and I don't think justified in the face of how my presence added to this woman's degradation. [I've been thinking] about what made me interested in observing the scene, even once I knew it would be a strip search. I think I got caught up in the excitement of being allowed more and more access to station life. There's this lust for more access and knowledge, almost for its own sake. [And during the night shift there is an air of festivity at] the station when someone is brought in. It breaks up the boredom of sitting around staring at each other; I think I also got caught up in the excitement of a person to "process." The experience taught me that the person is talked about [at the police station] in such a way that it is really easy to forget that they are a person. I was consequently caught up short when I was shut in this little room with a very vulnerable naked body that was stripped down and told to lift her breasts to prove she wasn't concealing anything beneath them, all for two packages of cheese and some butter. (Correspondence, July 21, 1995)

Reflecting on this incident here, I am interested in the kind of understanding we arrive at through the body, through embodiment. Being conscious of my emotional investment and visceral response to this strip search allowed me new insights about fieldwork practices and the cultural landscape of the police station. In this situation, it was largely at the level of my own body that I understood the ethical problems of my observing a strip search. My physical feeling of claustrophobia prompted me to see that I had made a misjudgment in my fieldwork. The woman's complete nudity, in contrast to the uniformed police and my own comfortably clothed state, underscored the unequal power relations between us and a general orientation that I shared with the police, if only momentarily.[17] In other places in the e-mail correspondence with Liisa, I explained that I often experienced stomach cramps while making observations at the police station. The stomach cramps were a way that my body communicated to me something about my surrounding environment and about my emotional experience of fieldwork. These examples invite us to think more about how the researcher's body is a site for analytical insight about various aspects of fieldwork.

In her 1999 ethnography, *A Finger in the Wound,* Diane Nelson provides a compelling example of how analysis may be enriched by attention to bodies. She undertakes an analysis of how the Guatemalan state and Mayan ethnic identity are constituted through metaphors of the body and violence inflicted on it. Her theoretical conclusions derive in part from her empirical analysis of the ways that her own *gringa* (North American, white, female) body was constructed as an object of desire and how the *gringa* body also functioned as a landscape for violent retaliation against American economic imperialism in Guatemala.

Nelson notes that the body is unstable and overdetermined in its signification of ethnic and national meaning in Guatemala. Her central point—that bodies "break apart wetly under the weight of signification they are meant to carry, and they overflow and obliterate the messages inscribed on them, messing up any clean, unified categories"—is useful for thinking about how the body functions as an instance of materiality that needs to read as belonging to one's empirical research (Nelson 1999, 209). There are other ethnographies that attend to how the body plays into intellectual activity and the reproduction of knowledge. For instance, Michael Herzfeld's ethnography of artisans in Greece (see *The Body Impolitic* 2004) analyzes how artisanal knowledge and skills in contemporary Greece are passed on to the apprentice by "schooling the body." The body is a plane of the reproduction of artisan identity and knowledge through its embodiment of a particular form of masculinity, as well as through more surprising postures like studied boredom and indifference. And in his characterization of intellectual labor as artisanal in *Spirit and System* (2005), Dominic Boyer undermines Western individualist ideas about intellectual labor as culturally and materially transcendent. These two ethnographies are particularly useful for the way in which they draw attention to the cultural and physical in *male* practices of knowledge production, an issue that tends to receive less critical attention in feminist critiques of knowledge production.

Theorizing the political hieroglyphics of the body would help avoid what Paul Willis has called "flat discursivism" in research (Mills and Gibb 2001, 410). We would benefit from thinking more about how the body of the researcher is a landscape for analytical insight about various issues as well. What erasures, repressions, and disciplines are required to sustain the model of empirical research as a disembodied intellectual practice in which the researcher's body is never decisively implicated in theoretical insights?

Avoiding personal investment in my research and, for example, avoiding any emotional identification with the police officers' enthusiasm for "processing" people arrested on dull night shifts was for me neither possible nor desirable. This example shows instead how we can use our subjective responses heuristically as well as in the service of a more sophisticated, sustained ethical approach to research. In this case, doing so led me to recognize how some of the conditions of station life (boredom or authority) could prompt callousness toward people who were brought into the station during quiet night shifts. Seeing myself respond as the police offers did on the night they conducted a strip search helped me to understand police culture in more subtle ways, and my sense of claustrophobia during the strip search enabled me to understand fieldwork better. Paying attention to one's emotional investment is of course an extension of "situating" oneself in field research (cf. Haraway's notion of situated knowledge [1991]). But I am referring to something that goes beyond just recognizing one's structural position in relation to research informants (e.g., white, English woman conducting research among black, South African children).[18] I see affect and the body as resources that allow a better understanding of our changing investments in the varied contexts of fieldwork that produces more ethical research, and as a way of tapping into another level of information about the subjects of our research.

Ethnography is a particularly rich arena for exploring such questions since its approach is premised on the presence of the researcher's body and personality in the field site.[19] The body may function as a medium that registers useful information and insights. This is not to privilege the body as a source of pure truth or as possessing a "natural link" to some romantic conception of intuition. Yet, at the same time, we would miss an opportunity if we were to deny that the body is a terrain of experience and understanding in research, especially in ethnographic research. As we move further away from the positivist ideal of erasing the researcher's subjectivity from the research, we have an opportunity to think about the heuristic possibilities of various elements of the researcher's subjectivity and thus to reject the binary division between objectivism and romantic "subjectivism." Subjectivity's many forms—embodiment, affect, and so on—should complement and enrich, rather than replace, critical reason as a mode of analysis.

Conclusion

On its most straightforward level, this book offers the reader a snapshot of the year-long process of ethnographic fieldwork as it unfolds. Since it was written in real time, it chronicles the researcher's intellectual questions, as well as her emotional highs and lows. In this respect, the correspondence communicates the tempo of fieldwork in a way that books on ethnographic methods cannot convey, if they attempt to do so at all. The correspondence is a record of ethnographic fieldwork improvisation as it took place in the context of an interdisciplinary research project.

Others have written retrospectively about their experiences of conducting ethnographic fieldwork. Typically these accounts focus on relationships with informants and the emotional challenges of conducting fieldwork, but they also provide a glimpse into how research goals are woven into everyday field encounters (see, for example, Briggs 1970; Rabinow 1977; Behar 1996; and Moreno 1995). In some respects, Malinowski's *A Diary in the Strict Sense of the Term* (1967), in particular, provides insight into fieldwork as a process of theory-building insofar as Malinowski, writing during the course of his fieldwork, captures the spiral-like, abductive process of ethnography's epistemology. However, in the *Diary* and in *Coral Gardens* (1935), Malinowski's discussion of fieldwork methods is not connected to theory in its contemporary sense. The *Diary,* in particular, is an exceptional example of the emotional tempo of fieldwork. Yet this account does not document the development of the researcher's theoretical ideas in much detail. Thus, we are left with the task of putting the "how" of fieldwork into dialogue with theory, post-Malinowski. Rather than offering a *retrospective* account of feelings and choices made in the field, the correspondence presented here illustrates ethnographic fieldwork as a set of continually adjusted practices in real time, out of which theoretical insights are frequently produced.

Our book complements these earlier memoirs and accounts, but differs insofar as it is written in real time, as the fieldwork unfolds. As such, the correspondence between Liisa and me communicates the tempo of research (lulls, fits and starts, as well as floods of information) and provides a window onto the hermeneutics of ethnographic fieldwork. It presents one fieldworker's experience as it moves between the partial, incomplete, and tentative insights of field events and the more abstract theoretical writing that informs the study.

Furthermore, the correspondence illustrates how ethnographic research is embedded in a complex, emotional landscape that should not be viewed as it traditionally has been in the social sciences—as a hindrance to understanding—but as enabling knowledge production. To extend Gadamer's argument about prejudice, to deny affect and positionality in interpretation is not only impossible but a kind of performative contradiction. Understanding does not often occur in a single, lightning-bolt moment (the proverbial light bulb over the head), nor is it a matter of a deliberate, linear accumulation. It requires analytical movement, not stasis. And it forces the recognition that we only understand from a point of view that reflects our social, cultural, historical, affective location. Recognizing the nature of understanding does not lead logically to a relativistic approach in which all interpretations are equally valid, or to the claim that all affective responses are equally ethical and productive. Rather, this recognition invites us to be more deliberate in our approach and allows for more dialogue about the effects and possibilities of our engagements in knowledge production. In comparison with treating method as a formula and approaching theory and empirical research as separate activities, a processual approach to knowledge production yields more complex, ethical, and life-affirming research.

The next part of this book presents the correspondence between Liisa and myself in chronological order, preceded by my original Fulbright proposal for the research project. We have kept our editing of the correspondence to a bare minimum, treating it as much as possible as a primary document. Had we been working with another type of primary document produced by others, editing would of course have been impossible. This is, however, a "working archive" that is meant to be as clear and useful to the reader as possible. To that end, we have made certain alterations. Typographical errors and punctuation have been corrected. Unclear phrasing and unwieldy sentence structure have been altered only when needed for intelligibility. Passages omitted or added appear in square brackets. Names have been deleted in some cases, and pseudonyms are used in others to ensure confidentiality and anonymity where appropriate.

Each of us has later inserted "Afterthoughts" into the correspondence. These appear in the interstices of the original e-mails in a different type, to mark them as distinct from the original, chronologically arranged correspondence. The Afterthoughts contain ideas arrived at with the benefit of hindsight, discussions of methodological and other issues that we wanted to draw out more explicitly, and connections that we thought should be made visible.

The tone of our conversations was, of course, informal, as this was a private correspondence. We hope that our playful and sometimes irreverent tone will not be construed as disrespect or lack of regard by any of the people who have been involved in this process, or who may recognize themselves in these pages. As tempting as it was to polish the correspondence by removing every quip and irrelevance, these seemed too true to the document to omit. It would have been just as wrong to clean it up by omitting discussions of doubts, lack of direction, avoidance, frustration, and worry—the very things that make doing fieldwork such a fraught activity or "nervous condition." (Of course, nerves also quiver in moments of elation and epiphany when everything is going better than expected.) Perhaps it is enough to say what "goes without saying"—that these rough and nervous moments belong to a document produced in the course of a good-faith effort to understand.

Endnotes

1. See Renato Rosaldo 1989 and Trinh T. Minh-ha 1989 for more sustained critiques of the ideal type of the anthropological ethnographer.

2. It is debatable how new multisited ethnography actually is.

3. While notable differences exist between Straussians and other historically oriented political theorists or between political theorists who engage with canonical texts (e.g., Hobbes, Locke, etc.) and those who engage with contemporary theory (e.g., Foucault, Butler, etc.), what these different groups have in common is their reliance on text (rather than empirical data) for their analysis and challenge to the hegemony of behavioralism.

4. Kristen Renwick Monroe's *Contemporary Empirical Political Theory* explores developments within political science in the search for theory that "can be tested by reference to the empirical world" (1997, 1). Thus, although it atypically contains essays by political theorists and political "scientists," it nonetheless reproduces a more scientific model of the relationship of theory to empirical "fact." In combining theory and empirical ethnographic research, I did not envision the latter as a means of "testing" the former.

5. Schleiermacher (1768–1835) does not use the term *hermeneutic circle*; however, he does discuss the process of reading the part in relation to the whole of language. See especially Schleiermacher 1994, 74, 85.

6. Willis also discusses the relationship between theory and ethnographic fieldwork; see Willis 1997.

7. For further discussion of processual ethnography, see Sally Falk Moore 1993.

8. See Eleonora Montuschi 2003 for further discussion of Geertz's definition of ethnography as an "activity," not a method.

9. I want to thank Liisa Malkki for encouraging me to explore the parallels between Lévi-Strauss's notion of the *bricoleur* and improvisation in fieldwork.

10. Lévi-Strauss is concerned in his essay to reject the conception that mythical thought is best understood as a prototype of modern scientific thought, a stage in society's technical or scientific evolution. Instead, he makes the more ambitious claim that science and myth should be understood as "two parallel modes of acquiring knowledge" whose most important distinction is in the kind of phenomena to which they are applied (1962, 13).

In this discussion, he highlights the long legacy of understanding achieved contextually, pragmatically, and inductively through the "ordering and reordering of events," as he phrases it (1962). He calls the alternative approach he describes a "science of the concrete" whose exploitation of the sensible world in sensible terms represents an adaptation to particular forms of discoveries. One of the main distinctions he draws between the science of the concrete and modern science is that the former generates knowledge claims from observation of and induction from the *event* rather than from "structured sets," which science takes as its traditional object of inquiry. And while the results of a science of the concrete will at times be different from those of modern science, Lévi-Strauss notes that "it [is]no less scientific and its results no less genuine" (1962, 16).

11. See Weberman 2003 for further analysis of the radicalism of Gadamer's claims in this respect.

12. See Weberman 2000 and 2003 for further discussion of the scope of Gadamer's relevance for different types of interpretation across the social sciences and humanities.

13. Historically, women researchers have been in a position not unlike that of ethnographers. Under the common association of women with the body, they have struggled with the perception that their gender and emotional response to research material would

compromise the quality of their research. Some women responded by trying hard to perform objectivity as their male colleagues did. However, unlike many anthropologists, feminist scholars more quickly simply rejected the terms of objectivism adapted from the natural sciences. As a result, feminist methodology has been a particularly rich location for the deconstruction of positivist objectivism. See, for example, di Leonardo 1991; Harding 1987 and 1991; Reinharz 1992; Visweswaran 1994; Naples 2003; and Wolf 1996.

14. Mary Louise Pratt describes this tension when she writes, "I think it is fairly clear that personal narrative persists alongside objectifying description in ethnographic writing because it mediates a contradiction within the discipline between personal and scientific authority, a contradiction that has become especially acute since the advent of fieldwork as a methodological norm. James Clifford speaks of it as 'the discipline's impossible attempt to fuse objective and subjective practices.' Fieldwork produces a kind of authority that is anchored to a large extent in subjective, sensuous experience. One experiences the indigenous environment and lifeways for oneself, sees with one's own eyes, even plays some roles, albeit contrived ones, in the daily lives of the community. But the professional text to result from such an encounter is supposed to conform to the norms of scientific discourse whose authority resides in the absolute effacement of the speaking and experiencing subject" (1986, 32). See also Clifford 1986.

15. See also the collection of essays in Gupta and Ferguson 1997a.

16. See also Freeman 2001 and Lutz 1995 for discussion of how theory and empiricism are gendered.

17. For instance, just as the accused woman shoplifter did not have the right to refuse to be strip-searched by the police, neither could she refuse to have me witness all of these activities involving her for the purposes of my research.

18. See also Daphne Patai's (1991) critique of uncritically marking one's "difference" in feminist research as a way of avoiding power and privilege.

19. In fact, bodies in general are a rich terrain for understanding a variety of social issues. However, in addition to anthropology, I think feminist analysis in particular is a very promising field for considering a hermeneutics of the body in research, since feminists often seek to understand social phenomena that take women's bodies as a key signifier. As we see in the case of Nelson's research, her body as read by her research informants—as that of a *gringa*— ends up being one of many manifestations of the discourses of race, nation, and gender that function to define contemporary Guatemalan and Mayan identity. And her body as defined and contested within the research frame is the terrain on which transnational relations of desire between the Global North and South are at play.

The Fulbright Proposal
Statement of Proposed Study or Research

NAME: ALLAINE CERWONKA

FIELD OF STUDY: POLITICAL SCIENCE

COUNTRY: AUSTRALIA

Describe your study or research plans and your reasons for wishing to undertake them in the country of your choice. Outline a plan that realistically can be completed in one academic year abroad. Graduating seniors, applicants in the creative or performing arts, and applicants for teaching awards are not expected to formulate detailed research projects. Graduating seniors should describe the study programs they wish to follow in terms as specific as possible.

The aim of my project is to examine Australian national identity as a site of continuing political struggle and contestation. Defining nationhood has historically been a frustrating process. As nationalism scholar Hugh Seton-Watson commented in frustration, "Thus I am driven to the conclusion that no 'scientific definition' of the nation can be devised; yet the phenomenon has existed and exists" (Anderson 1991).

Up until recently, a paradigm has dominated our understanding in which nationalism was assumed to be a shared and static identity that bound the community together and meant the same thing to all the members of the society. More recent scholarship in the social sciences, however, has begun to see nationalism instead as comprising a multiplicity of meanings and identities. Rather than reading nations as stable institutions, scholars have begun to recognize them as sites in which various groups within society contest their values and identities.

Thus, by examining national identity, I will in fact be locating a significant site in which power struggles play out among groups in society as they compete for prominence in relation to the collective social identity. The nation is a socially and historically constructed category, much like race, culture, and gender; it is shaped by political struggles and power relations in specific historical circumstances. To understand the nation fully, we must examine the way nationality or "nation-ness" has existed historically for a given society and how it has developed through particular social, structural, and institutional arrangements (Anderson 1991). Thus, my aim will not be to uncover the "true" Australian national identity; the struggle for national identity, much like the Gramscian "war of position" (Gramsci 1991), is continual. Instead, I hope to understand the many identities and categories that comprise and often complicate the national one, and to identify the groups struggling for control of national symbols and identities.

Australia promises to be a very productive object of study as the people of this country are actively engaged in a process of self-definition. Although Australia has been substantively independent of Britain for more than a hundred years, there has been a recent movement to withdraw from the Commonwealth on a symbolic level as well. This drive for symbolic independence has left Australians with more "imaginary" space in which to construct a sense of "Australianness." The aim of my research is to analyze the imagined communities of the various groups within Australia; more specifically, I will analyze what it means to be "Australian" among recent Asian immigrants, native-born citizens of European descent, and Aboriginal Australians. I anticipate that this will be instructive about these and other groups, and the power relations that exist between them. Finally, as part of comparing the multiple narratives about Australian national identity (Bhabha 1990), I will also consider the way, and the extent to which, other groups in Australia appropriate Aboriginal culture(s) in a move to identify the "true" or original Australian national identity.

My research will employ an ethnographic methodology, which will include formal and informal interviewing and participant observation. With the help of scholars engaged in studying nationalism in the Psychosocial Studies Research Group at the University of Melbourne, I will identify sites in Victoria that will enable me to make contact with a diverse cross-section of subjects with respect to class, gender, race, years living in Australia, political ideologies, and residential location. Given the questions central to my study, the state of Victoria provides a reasonably representative population; thus my research will take place primarily within this state.

Although national identity is a productive location for understanding the identity composition and power relations of any sociopolitical unit, Australia provides an especially significant opportunity for understanding this phenomenon: national identity is a central political issue being actively debated in both the Parliament and the pubs. By understanding the process through which people in Australia negotiate multiple narratives about nationhood, we stand to gain not only a better understanding of the cultural and political landscape of Australia, but also insight into similar processes occurring in other postcolonial societies.

If you have a preference for schools abroad, list here. Also attach copies of any acceptances you have received from institutions or individuals.

1. University of Melbourne
2.

DO NOT WRITE ON REVERSE OF THIS FORM.

Fieldwork Correspondence

Allaine Cerwonka in Melbourne, Australia
and Liisa Malkki in Irvine, California

To: Liisa Malkki lhmalkki@orion.oac.uci.edu
From: Allaine Cerwonka allaine_cerwonka@politics.muwaye.unimelb.edu.au
Date: Thursday, November 24, 1994 14:36
Subject: war stories from the front lines

Hi Liisa,

Thanks for the brief hello. I get the feeling that your life is as hectic as always. Perhaps Thanksgiving weekend will provide some sort of respite for all the frantic North American academics anticipating the end of the quarter/semester panic. All of that feels very far away from where I sit in the computer center at Melbourne University. My sense of time is really messed up. I'm realizing that a lot of it comes from the seasons and a sort of tempo that gets set up around them. Everyone here is winding down for summer and anticipating greater leisure and a slower pace . . . whereas my body is still expecting the faster pace that usually comes with the autumn and, of course, with the beginning of a project.

As I sit here in front of my screen, I feel very self-conscious about what to write to you. Perhaps my correspondence will take different shape as we go along (this afternoon and throughout the year), but at the moment I feel most inclined toward writing a chatty sort of letter-thingie. When I think about writing anything else to you—such as a report on what I have been doing—I begin to evaluate what I may have to say in overly rigid terms and don't get very far.

So, I am feeling much better about things now that my life is not consumed by trying to find an apartment and then trying to furnish it in an affordable manner. I told you in my last e-mail message that I was learning a lot about the city from that process—but especially at that time—I did not believe it. The whole process left me anxious that my year was slipping away from me.

But alas, it has not. This week I was able to start following up on some things that I kept having to put on the back burner while I made yet one more [furniture buying] trip to the Brotherhood of St. Lawrence (akin to the Salvation Army and simply called "the Brotherhood" by those who frequent it often). I was also frustrated because I would tell people a bit about my project at a dinner or whatever, and would get some very interesting responses and comments about either resources they recommended for doing research here or about their own experiences of Melbourne/Australia/nation—but it would just be a snippet of a conversation (whew!—that was one long sentence. Are you still with me?).

I did not know how to follow up on such interactions, and the setting would make it difficult. I think I will continue to have those kinds of brief encounters as the year progresses—and I will continue to record and think about them in and of themselves—but perhaps they will be less frustrating when I have longer interviews as well.

I have encountered many resources at the university in the shape of other researchers, the "Australian Centre," conferences, journals, etc. I've taken advantage of what I could. My desire is to remain safe and busy myself with that kind of secondary stuff rather than get out there and start to interview. I think I will do three exploratory interviews to see what I may see. By calling them exploratory, I get past the part of me that's saying, "What are you thinking, Allaine? How can you do interviews when you're still fuzzy about some parts of the project?" However, talking to people on a casual basis over the last month has been consistently exciting and has generated a lot of ideas, so I might "have a go at it" (as the locals tend to say). But now I know what you were talking about when you once said that it's all a bit embarrassing and awkward to ask people for interviews in the first place . . . and then to be asking them to tell you about aspects of their lives about which one really isn't suppose to inquire!

I have three people in mind already. Two have already agreed. The first I met when I went to the Remembrance Day ceremony at the "Shrine of Remembrance." He is in his early thirties (Will), and his business card says that he works for the Insurance and Superannuation Commission. When I was at the ceremony commemorating the end of WWI, and those who have served in the military in general, I suppose I was struck by the fact that there were people there who were not school children (I expected them) nor older people who might have served in one of the world wars. I wondered why other types of people would come when it was not a public holiday, nor did the ceremony last more than twenty minutes. So I walked up to a couple of people and tried to start a general conversation about the ceremony and then work around to what brought them out for the occasion. The first set of people had just been walking by as part of their daily exercise, but answered my questions about Remembrance Day and the Shrine and such by thinking back to when they were kids and would come to these things. (They thought more people used to come and made some general comments like that.) I started to chat to Will next, and when asked why he thought other people might have come, he explained that, for him, he used to come with his grandmother (his grandfather was in WWI), had friends who were in the service, and happened to work in the area. We chatted more, and I noticed that he did not seem to want to talk about himself when I'd ask him things like—did he come to these things as a kid, etc. I then started to get embarrassed and rather abruptly told him that I had to go. A few minutes later, he came up and gave me his card and told me that if I wanted to interview him at any stage or needed any help he might be able to provide, that I should give him a call. So I thought I might.

The other person (John) is second-generation Greek and just said some very interesting things about being Australian and Greek. He agreed to meet me if I wanted. Funny that he also spoke of his grandmother. I just found that odd because Seremetakis says so much about her grandmother. When I was reading her book, I thought it was just a peculiarity of hers because I have so little connection to my own grandmother—but having these two people mention their grandmothers in remembering their nation and childhood makes me keep it as a question on reserve.

The third person I am in the process of getting up the nerve to request [. . .] [an interview from] is a man I met who works at the "Brotherhood" (Samuel). Embarrassingly enough, we became friendly because Jim [my partner] and I were in there so often looking for furniture (if you're in there between two and three o'clock, you can get first dibs at the incoming furniture you see). He said he was from "the islands to the North of Australia," and struck me as a particularly interesting person because after inquiring as to when we were going to get ourselves some jobs, he gave Jim the advice that if he wanted to get architecture work, he should link into the American or Canadian community here in Melbourne. It wasn't so much that he was in touch with that community, but rather knew from his own experience that immigrant groups form networks. I'm hoping he can tell me about some of the ones [networks] he's experienced. I think he said he had been here for three yrs.

I regret that this rather haphazard group of potential interviewees does not include any women, and the people are all between thirty and forty yrs. of age. Do you think that matters for this pilot group? If I were to hold off on any of them at this point and try to find someone of a different age and/or gender, I think it would be Will. Certainly there are elderly homes and many clubs that revolve around ethnicity (the Lebanese club, for instance); perhaps I should wander into one of them. I also noticed on my way to the market last week a factory that was getting out (garment industry, I think). I noticed that most (if not all) of the workers were Asian women who spoke English and another language (my guess is Vietnamese) to one another. First-generation Asian women may be difficult to gain access to for interviewing; do you think it would be productive for me perhaps to approach a group after work, or perhaps wait and hope that I can talk to working class, first-generation, Asian women in the communities in which they live? People usually don't respond well to strangers who approach them on the street.

I know this message is going on forever, but I did want to tell you one more thing. When I spoke to the director of the Australian Centre (an interdisciplinary program at Melbourne Uni.), he invited me to a small conference/round table entitled, "Cities Without Citizens? Space and Civic Culture." The group consisted of people from Politics, English,

Geography, History, Urban Planning, the Mayor of Collingwood, and a few others. It was very interesting, and I made the acquaintance of a few people who may be of help to my project. (My experience with these people wasn't entirely as instrumental as it sounds, of course.) But a few people were interested in talking about the fact that sensory experiences make a city, as well. There is a guy from History (Paul Carter) who talks about the suppression of noise in society's memorialization. And another man over in the Urban Planning Dept. seemed like he had a few good references. The conference was a funny experience in some ways. It was a very male academic scene with lots of wood and leather chairs that felt too big for me. Around the table were predominantly older men, each with the distinction of being full professor or Chair of his Dept., with a few women sprinkled about. Against this scene was a backdrop of middle-aged, working-class women discreetly supplying morning coffee and pastries. Nevertheless, I spoke—and that felt great.

So I will close here. Thanks for wading through this bundle of impressions, anxieties, and proclamations. I'd appreciate any thoughts this might have provoked on your end, when you have a minute. Also, if you could print this out and toss it in a folder somewhere, I'd appreciate it. Take care.

Allaine

✛

To: Allaine Cerwonka allaine_cerwonka@politics.muwaye.unimelb.edu.au
From: Liisa Malkki lhmalkki@orion.oac.uci.edu
Date: Monday, November 28, 1994 4:22:22 pm
Subject: war stories from end of fall quarter

Hi Allaine,

What a treat to get such a long letter from you! I've just finished reading it, and am not sure if I'll remember to respond to everything thoroughly enough. Seems to me, however, in general, that you are worried about your "pool" of informants—who they are sociologically. Important considerations, and ones you'll be facing throughout the year there. But it's equally important not to get too, too worried about this. You are still in the initial stages of fieldwork, and therefore should not yet expect to have a whole group of people you routinely talk with. All the ones you describe are promising leads—people who will be informants in their own right, and who will lead you to others. When people give their cards and offer to talk, grasp the chance. Keep track of social networks, see how the "sample snowballs." Now this is important: since you're doing urban fieldwork, it's harder to delineate the "field," "informants," etc. Therefore, systematic/occasional attention to (and use of) institutional frameworks will be necessary and productive. Here, again, think of groupings like "firemen," "cops," "WWII veterans' organizations." . . . If you approach these organiza-tions, it'll usually be necessary to talk with the bosses, administrators. . . . Same with factory workers, say. This might give you the coherence and patterning of activity and schedule that you could find reassuring (and productive). In short, it's important to think critically about the categories of people you are doing research with, while not limiting yourself to members of these categories ONLY. Let me know how it goes . . .

You ought not to feel that you can only write more formal progress reports to me. I like to read what you're up to more generally.

By the way, in the Anthropology and History course, we just read a book you should get your hands on: *The Combing of History* by David William Cohen, Univ. of Chicago Press, 1994. I've put other things in your [university mail]box in the hopes that someone will be picking stuff up for you and forwarding it. Recently, however, I noticed the tag identifying your box has disappeared/fallen off. Should I discontinue with the department mailbox? Do you have a mailing address?

Got to go. Happy to hear you are clearly doing so well, and sounding like yourself (even if a bit nervous!).

Liisa

⚡

To: Liisa Malkki lhmalkki@orion.oac.uci.edu
From: Allaine Cerwonka allaine_cerwonka@politics.muwaye.unimelb.edu.au
Date: Monday, December 19, 1994 13:59
Subject: War stories from the end of fall quarter

As I write this, I'm wondering to myself if you're anywhere near the land of computers, or if perhaps you're not off doing that crazy childbirth thing. It must be any day now. Well, I wanted to get a message in before the due date to say good luck, and I'm sure everything will go well. I'm secretly hoping you'll have him early so that he'll be a Sagittarius.

Oh, speaking of astrology, I'm not a big astrology kind of girl, but on Friday I was staying the night at a friend's house who is. They offered to do my chart because it would seem that twenty-eight (which I've just turned) is a fairly big year. (I think I could have guessed that at this point.) Anyway, the two of them went off and came back to the room with Wayne's Toshiba notebook that his employer pays for, and he popped up the astrology program and proceeded to map out my whole chart. As I sat across the room from Sue, I had a good giggle at the way mysticism and technology have happily conjoined, but also at how the screen of the computer made her face glow as if she were getting a vision from a far off place.

It was also interesting to hear them talk about their lives and spirituality in that much of their interest lies in India as the spiritual center (I guess I had my ears open for links with Aboriginality), but they did talk about being very interested in going to places [. . .] Aborigines [have deemed to be] spiritual places. They spoke as if the land itself was spiritual, and their way of accessing that was not to be taught by the Aborigines directly; [they thought that] perhaps they could access the same spiritual relationship with Australia themselves by going to certain places. I find the energy and tension around the Aborigines here in Australia very interesting, although I am far from being able to make sense of it all at this point. I think there's a lot of confusion and [. . .] [ambivalence about Aboriginality] for many people here.

Things here in the city and certainly at the university have slowed down to a crawl in this last week before Christmas. Shops seem to be the only ones doing business for the next few weeks. I find that a bit frustrating because it doesn't feel like Christmas to my body (ninety-degree weather just doesn't conjure up sleigh bells for me, I'm afraid). But I'm excited about seeing how people celebrate Christmas here and the traditions that surround both Christmas and New Year's. It's funny to see all these cards with snow scenes on them. Interesting mix of those kinds of northern hemisphere images, but then having magazines (*Good Housekeeping* kind of things) talking about how to have a Christmas in a way more appropriate to the conditions in Australia (lots of white in terms of flowers and table decorations).

Jim and I will spend Christmas Eve with my friend Mathilde's family, and then we'll have Christmas lunch (the traditional meal) with my former host family, Max and Roma and the Burgess daughters [my "host family" when I was a high school exchange student to Australia in 1984]. People have been very generous in including us, although I think part of it is done with the hopes of diluting their own family dynamics by having some outsiders.

Since it's vacation time here, and libraries and organizations will be closed until mid-January, Jim and I are going to travel to Tasmania for twelve days (starting January 2.) We're going to fly over and then bike around the eastern part of the island, ending up in Hobart. I've never done an extended bike trip, so I'm very excited. I think it will be a great way to see the countryside as well as to meet more people. Jim tells me that he found on past trips he's made that people often approach him because they're curious [about] where you've ridden from (probably also to find out for sure if you really are as insane as you seem in riding in all sorts of weather conditions). Melburnians are happy to tell us all their stereotypes about Tasmania. People paint it out to be this Gothic place: bad weather, gloomy, English landscape, people with deformities because of all the (supposed) inbreeding. There's also an [historic] convict settlement down at Port Arthur that is supposed to be very interesting.

I don't know if you've gotten out to the movies lately (my guess is no), but the New Zealand film *Once Were Warriors* has just come out here and has gotten very good reviews. It's about domestic violence and the general social conditions of a group of Maori in Auckland. I liked it, although I can't say I enjoyed watching it. It's very disturbing. Afterwards, Mathilde said to me that she's heard people criticize Australian Aborigines on the grounds that at least the New Zealand Maori were a warring people and put up a fight against colonizers; the Australian Aborigines were so passive! Interesting that people should compete about whose indigenous peoples were superior (before being victimized).

I'll close here. I can imagine that you've got your hands full so don't worry about responding to this e-mail, unless, of course, you want to. I'll write again before too long. Good luck with this last phase of your pregnancy and have a nice holiday.

Allaine

To: Allaine Cerwonka allaine_cerwonka.politics@muwaye.unimelb.edu.au
From: Liisa Malkki lhmalkki@orion.oac.uci.edu
Date: Sunday, January 1, 1995 7:10pm
Subject: Re: hi!

Allaine,

Great to hear from you. A Sagittarius it is! Our little boy was born 13 December, and we have both been home for a while now. His name is Elias William Ferguson, and I'd say he's fairly gorgeous. Sleep deprivation is the only drawback in our lives these days. Up every two-and-a-half to three hours day and night.

How was the bike trip? Hope you had lots of good adventures, and that the New Year has begun well for you.

I suppose I should ask you progress-questions. "EEEK!" cries Allaine. I was just wondering which social locations/sites you were thinking of delving more deeply into. You should think of people whom you can return to, over and over, to interview and spend time with, to follow around. That's why certain institutional frameworks can be helpful. But not to worry. When you're ready, things will start jelling.

Have to go. Keep well, Allaine, and write again when you get a chance, won't you?

Liisa

To: Liisa Malkki lhmalkki@orion.oac.uci.edu
From: Allaine Cerwonka allaine_cerwonka@politics.unimelb.edu.au
Date: Tuesday, January 17, 1995 15:46
Subject: Re: congrats!

Hi Liisa!

I am really pleased to hear that you are doing so well on that end. You must feel quite relieved, both physically and emotionally, at this point. I hope you're milking your recovery time for all it's worth (pardon the pun) and getting Jim to do the lion's share of all those boring household things. I read a wonderful novel over this Christmas period, if you are looking for a good read. It's from 1987 (I think) by a British woman named Jeanette Winterson. She's written a few well-received things, but I especially loved *The Passion*. It's a wonderful set of stories about Napoleon's chicken chef and a Venetian fisherman's daughter. I also read a wonderful autobiography by an Aboriginal woman named Ruby Langford, called *Don't Take Your Love to Town* [1988].

I returned from my two-week tour of Tasmania just yesterday. It was an amazing trip and has left me feeling both very fit and relaxed. Tasmania has a great deal of undeveloped land. It was such a treat to be able to bike through so much farm land (I've seen enough sheep for a lifetime by this point) and down miles and miles of deserted coastline. People were very friendly and always came up to us to chat; I suspect that they were a little starved for new faces in some places. I was also surprised to discover that, as cyclists, we were given special status amongst the "Greenies." The environmentalists have a strong presence in Tassie. But overall, I found myself quite glad that I am doing the year in Melbourne. Tasmania is a little too remote, and there is very little in the way of cultural diversity. Most importantly, the caffe lattes are made with Nescafe. Yuck.

I'm excited to be back and feel eager to get into my interviews. I have a letter all set to send out to a few organizations. Six weeks ago I was planning to contact social organizations I got out of the phone book. They revolved entirely around ethnicity (e.g., the Greek-Australian club). I will certainly contact one or two of them, but I have some others in mind as well. I would appreciate your feedback, but I was thinking of starting with one ethnic club, a senior citizen's organization, and a police station. I also ended up meeting the minister of a church in Dandenong at the Boxing Day cricket match. He overheard an Australian friend next to me explaining the rules and decided that he (Richard) was not doing a very good job of it, and took over with the explanations. This led to us talking about my project and him volunteering to help me. Dandenong is a working-class neighborhood that contains many recent immigrants. He said that he has a lot of Pacific Island immigrants in his parish. So, I thought I would add his church to my list.

I've begun to think that it would be useful to establish contact with a gardening organization as well. You would not believe how much people talk about gardening here. I've noticed that people are also very concerned with indigenous plants. The state premier is taking over part of a park in the city to host next year's Grand Prix (car racing). It was very interesting that much of the debate took place around the fact that an Australian gum tree was "murdered" in the process of clearing land for the track. Lots of other imported trees were cut down, but the tears (literally!) were shed for the gum tree. The government argues in retort that they are planning to plant hundreds of gum trees to replace the imported ones that were taken away. These kinds of arguments play into lots of other references to the land in Australia. I see a lot of links between Australia and environmentalism. In Hobart I came across the Australian Geography Society Store that is a chain that looks remarkably like the Nature Company [in California], but all [about] Australian nature merchandise and information. There's another very popular cosmetics company called Red Earth which is a lot like the Body Shop, but uses many images that are used popularly in connection with Australia (e.g., gum leaves, a particular color of red, etc.). This store doesn't claim to be only about Australia, but it certainly benefits from the suggestion.

At this point, the gardens/nature angle doesn't add up to much, but I think it's worth including in my scope. Sometimes the way people talk about protecting Australian trees "which have been here way before Europeans ever came to Australia" sounds a lot like the way people talk about issues relating to Kooris (Aborigines from the southeastern region of Australia).

It's all just swimming around in my head at the moment, but I'm very excited about what I'm seeing and hearing. Themes are starting to develop more so than, say, a month ago even. At this point, it seems like I should see what kinds of things show up in the interviews. Do you agree? Do you think I'm trying to connect with too many different types of organizations at once? I don't want to contact too many at one time in case one gives me a lot of stuff or people to work with.

Oh, I almost forgot. I was reading the paper in the airport on the way to Tasmania, and the leading paper here, *The Age*, is running a series or theme this year called "Australia Remembers" as a way of commemorating World War II. I'll be interested to see what kinds of things come up in that, and perhaps it will make memory more of a sexy topic in general among people this year. [. . .]

Well, that's all the talk about my project that I can stomach at the moment. I hope your Christmas went well. Ours was really nice down here. I was feeling homesick in the two weeks leading up to it, but the weekend went very well. Jim and I spent Christmas Eve with my friend Mathilde's family. They immigrated from Chile when she was a teenager. We went to her older brother and his wife's house with Tilde, her partner, and her mother. They're really great people, and we ate and ate and ate some great Australian seafood. Then on Christmas day we had the more traditional Christmas lunch with my lovely host family— Max, Roma and their three daughters (all in their late twenties and early thirties). Their Auntie Shirley was also there with Uncle Arthur. Again, there was lots of talk about gardening and lots of gardening books as presents (Melbourne is called the "Garden-State").

One thing was funny. They were talking about how you have to lock up good plants or only put them in the back garden (not the front) because it's very common for people to steal plants. I always think of theft as being of things with resale value (VCRs, etc.) or done by adolescent boys (who wouldn't be interested in plants), so I wondered who would be stealing these plants. To be a little clearer, I associate gardening with respectability, and so it's amusing to think of theft as part of the gardening culture. Also (and after this I promise I will stop talking about my project) in one major park (the Fitzroy Gardens), the pathways make out the Union Jack. In the park surrounding the zoo, most of the English imported trees were ripped out within the last five years and replaced by native trees. It's pretty trendy to have an indigenous garden, and it's seen as an environmentally conscious thing to do because native trees will attract native birds back to the area, which will help to restore its ecological balance. [. . .] When I asked a man who works in gardening (I'm not sure doing what exactly; we just started chatting because he's friends with my landlord and is storing plants in our backyard) if people were experimenting with other forms of gardens like Japanese, for instance, he explained that they had not become popular because they were too difficult to grow. "They require a different way of thinking." Gardening essentialism? He had also been to a gardening conference in the United States in the last couple of years, and he said a major question on the agenda among the Australians was, "Is there an Australian gardening type?" Apparently it was not resolved.

Whew, I think I will close here and go get a beer. I will look forward to any impressions you might have about all of this. Oh, by the way, Kathy Alberti has forwarded and will continue to forward my mail. I'm not sure if she has put the tag back on my mail slot, but if not, we have arranged that you can put things into her mailbox with my name on them, and they will wing their way down to Australia eventually. Thank you for the clippings and for the portion of the book you sent. The piece about the Aborigines and [their use of] conference calling was especially interesting. It made me think about some of Eric Michaels' writing [1994] on the ways in which Aborigines are using media technology to continue to strengthen culture, rather than culture being wiped out by it. There is a lot of confusion and nervous energy here around Aboriginal issues. I'm looking forward to hearing what people have to say about these issues in my interviews. I can't really say at this point what is going on with it (other than the stuff that is always said), but I feel a lot of tension and unease among non-Aborigines.

So, I'll talk to you soon and sign off here. Stay well.

Allaine

Afterthoughts

AC: Although I was concerned to get started on the "real" activities of fieldwork, I can now see that some of these early "hunches," surprises, and curiosities in the first couple of months of fieldwork were extremely important for shaping what became the heart of my research. Many of these insights came from talking to people about which neighborhoods I should look for an apartment in, or in hunting around for furniture to borrow for a year. While of course not a *substitute* for the systematic research I did in my field sites and upon which we base most of our knowledge claims, these "peripheral"

activities also provided valuable insights for my dissertation and book. In
this regard, the correspondence shows how knowledge is produced in "real
time" and involves tacking back and forth between the part (hunches, mundane details) and the whole (larger social structures and theoretical framework).

To: Allaine Cerwonka allaine_cerwonka@politics.muwaye.unimelb.edu.au
From: Liisa Malkki lhmalkki@orion.oac.uci.edu
Date: Monday, January 23, 1995 at 1:52:37 pm
Subject: Re: congrats!

Hi Allaine,

What a wonderful long message. I have just a few minutes right now to respond, but I wanted
to say the following, in short order: (1) Your project is taking shape beautifully, and especially
the gardening angle is wonderful. Pursue, is my vote. (2) Anthropological fieldwork is what
you are doing, and therefore regular contact with informants should not just be a goal, but
should be built into your everyday schedule. It's taxing, embarrassing, etc., but you need
the material, and you only have a limited time in Australia. Strike while the iron is hot. (3)
You are right. The organizations/contexts for fieldwork you mentioned are excellent. But
ask yourself, "Why do I want to gain entry to this organization and not that one? What is
my driving question? Why the ethnic club, for example? Do Australians naturally lead you
in "ethnic" directions because one just doesn't study "garden-variety Aussies"?

I'd limit the number of organizations in which you spend more time and to which you
devote more systematic attention. My gut feeling would be to stay away from ethnic clubs
(studied a lot) and to do something more original, like to compare how your research
themes play out in, say, two settings: police station and church (the church you were
offered help in already). The latter might be a good place to follow up leads about the
gardening/nature business. Or, if you want a third, add a gardening club. Something
like that. Remember, gaining entry and introducing yourself is hard; all the rest gets
easier. Also, all other contacts/friends are excellent sources of evidence, and you should
treat them as informants, but having more specific sites of cultural production—more
specific sites for the political imagination of Australia and the Commonwealth is very
useful.

The gardening angle is also promising because it would probably allow you to track down
things about the supranational community, for example, the Commonwealth. English-
ness + gardens + commonwealth, aboriginality + wilderness, the Greens + transnational
political movements, public gardens + citizenship . . . here are some connections that
seem fascinating. Might also get into your stuff about the senses.

Keep well, Allaine, and thanks for the novel tips. I'll look for them after I've finished my current thing, Doris Lessing's *Under My Skin* [1994]. I'm liking it a lot so far. Her biography—life in Zimbabwe and London till 1949.

I enjoyed reading about your travels!

Liisa

To: Liisa Malkki lhmalkki@orion.oac.uci.edu
From: Allaine Cerwonka allaine_cerwonka@politics.muwaye.unimelb.edu.au
Date: Fri January 27, 1995 15:17:45
Subject: back again . . .

Hi, me again and so soon!

I actually wanted to continue the conversation from your last e-mail. I'm really glad you see the potential in the landscape/environment angle. I think there's a lot to it that I can research and that plays into some very interesting larger issues, many of which you mentioned in your last e-mail. In this e-mail I wanted to lay out my plan of attack and chat a little more about fieldwork informants. [. . .]

It's actually very easy to meet people here and to talk about national identity. The people I knew from before are very good about bringing me along to things, and then I find that it's not so hard to start making contact with people independently of my friends. Also, national identity always comes up because once they ask why I'm in Australia for a year, they just assume that I want to hear what they think about Australia. It's kind of funny, but I haven't had to start the conversation in 99 percent of the cases. It's also a good topic, as everyone feels qualified to have an opinion, and they always assume they have something to teach me (which they usually do).

About my sites for the more formal interviews: scratching the ethnic clubs makes a lot of sense to me. Australian national identity as "multiculturalism" is the thing that everyone, especially the politicians, harps on. It seems very stale to me at this point, although I'm sure there are more interesting ways to look at it if one tried hard. But, as for my sites, I've been in touch with the only garden club I could locate, and the president invited me along to the February meeting. She suggested that I say a few words about my topic and announce my interest in talking with people/interviewing. She said that there were quite a few people whom she thought would be informative about such a topic, and she thought that the group would be pretty chatty. We'll see; I hope she's right.

The minister from the church is on holiday, but I sent a letter explaining my project more fully and asking if I could take him up on his offer to help. I ask myself why I want to interview in this site, given my topic. My answer is that this church is in an area where I do not have a lot of contact on a day-to-day basis, so the perspectives will help me get another perspective (more working-class, more ethnically diverse, church-goers). Also, my interest in the connection between national identity and landscape led me to gardening clubs because those members would definitely have opinions and good background information on issues around the Australian landscape. Nevertheless, I also want to talk to people who aren't especially preoccupied with "earthly things;" thus this church group might give me an indication of the way that landscape and nature play in the political imagination of other types of people.

The same can be said for the cops, although they have the added benefit of being a group of people that move around the city and interact with many different types of people, so their view of these issues might be especially interesting. I have sent a letter asking to do interviews at a local, inner-city police station. I'll call and see how cooperative they will be on Monday. But, I also have a friend who is one of the chief advisors for the state's Minister of Finance, and he said that he would contact the State's Police Commissioner to see what could be done, should the coppers reject my initial plea. Hopefully, one way or another, I'll get access to this group.

I'm going to sign off here because a huge storm is coming in, and I need to catch the tram before it hits. I have more to write about other people who, I think, would be good to talk to for background about landscape issues in Melbourne (landscape architects, for instance). Let me know how all this sounds. Can you think of other stuff I want to be doing at this point, things that would be good to look at (books, articles, etc.) as I'm waiting for the tram, etc.? I've looked more closely at the *Imagined Country*, which is a funny book, but says some interesting things about Australia.

I hope you're well on that end. I'll look forward to hearing from you.

Allaine

Afterthoughts

LM: In this e-mail, Allaine's concern about proceeding intelligently is palpable. The uncertainties and structural indeterminacies (Moore 1975) of early fieldwork and the continuous, critical self-monitoring are exhausting. They produce a "nervous condition" during which it is helpful to have someone with whom to talk (see Tsitsi Dangarembga's novel *Nervous Conditions* (1988) for the original use of this phrase). Fieldwork has often been romanticized (and masculinized) as a solitary odyssey and a private, incommunicable test of intellectual strength and character. Yet, to some degree at least, fieldwork always involves communicative, collaborative social processes. While the ethnographer might look first to a disciplinary colleague for conversation, it is also useful to look for intellectual "kindred spirits" among the people one has identified as "informants." I use the term *informants* in this correspondence out of long habit, but I recognize that it is a troubled concept. The term tends to conceal the fact that the people with whom one works can offer more than "data" or "information" in a "raw form," a form to be processed, decoded, and placed in a meaningful larger framework by the specialist. They can, and often do, have critical or analytical insights about the project as a whole. A cautious and conservative critic might interject here, "Aah, but is it wise to divulge the direction of your research to your informants? Are you not thereby unduly influencing their responses to your questions? Are you not contaminating your fieldwork environment?" These are important challenges, and ones that must inevitably be negotiated in context. I do not think that an ethnographer needs to provide her informants with a blow-by-blow, daily progress report on her research by any means. And asking very leading questions is also questionable. In my own fieldwork, I found it reassuring that I had to ask so little, and that people were remarkably unanimous in what they considered important. I was able to feel that the framing questions of my research grew out of the fieldwork context and that I had not simply "imported" them wholesale. But this does not mean that I was an empty vessel when I arrived in the refugee camp (confused, certainly, but not empty).

If anthropology (and ethnography) is, first of all, "an attempt to understand," then talking with one's "informants" at many different analytical levels is surely important. For you to understand, they must also understand (but see Fabian 1995 on "ethnographic misunderstanding"). Throughout this correspondence, Allaine reports on her "informants'" questions about the nature of the project. They were engaging with it as a whole project of knowledge production, and were not content simply to provide unconnected shards of "data" or "raw materials." And in order to get the fieldwork done, Allaine collected much material, but she also offered a great deal to her informants—information about herself and reasons for her being in Melbourne, insights, observations, questions, polite remarks, humour, compassion, friendship.

To: Liisa Malkki lhmalkki@orion.oac.uci.edu
From: Allaine Cerwonka allaine_cerwonka@politics.muwaye.unimelb.edu.au
Date: Tuesday, January 31, 1995 13:06:56
Subject: cops, believers, and gardeners

Hi Liisa,

I just wanted to bleep on your screen to tell you about my exciting morning. As a result of a letter sent last week, the Reverend out in Dandenong (Faulkner) called and said he'd be happy to help set up interviews! He's going to try to make arrangements with a variety of people, from the sounds of it. He mentioned people from the church, [the] Rotarians, [and] teens involved in some of the community organizations. I am psyched. We arranged that we would try to speak again in two weeks, to give him some time to talk to some people.

Boosted by this, I called the Fitzroy police station to follow up the letter I sent to their sergeant last week. I feared the worst when he said he hadn't received my letter, but he quickly assured me that he would help me set up some interviews. Knowing for sure where people will be for an hour [at a time] is tricky, he said, but "we'll see what we can do." Then he volunteered to be the first to be interviewed; so I see him on Friday. John Cash (the Australian politics professor who was at my Orals) predicted that people would often volunteer themselves first. I'm just floored by how inviting the police are! Then on Tuesday I go to talk to the garden club. [. . .]

So, besides that, I have taken up yoga at the Rathdowne Yoga Room, which is just a few blocks away from our flat. I'm amazed at how popular it is! Anyway, I don't know if you've ever tried it, but it's not easy stuff. And some of those positions are a mite bit funny to the observer's eye, but it feels like it should be really good for all the places in the body that academia mashes into knots.

My partner (as the saying goes here in Australia), Jim, has gotten himself an architecture job! He's working for an older firm that is helping to design a few new buildings for a local university. The exciting part (other than having him gone all day, of course) is that the firm is working with a very famous Sydney architect, Glenn Murcutt. Murcutt has built his reputation on doing structures that respond to the environment and "unique" conditions of Australia. Most have been located in outback-type landscapes. I think I'm going to do some more reading about him, as he has recently won an award for an Aboriginal housing project he designed. It's also interesting that many urban architects certainly admire his work but are cynical of the attention he has received because most Australians don't live in the outback; therefore, they argue, his designs aren't quite as reflective of the true living conditions in Australia as many claim they are. Jim, for his part, is excited that he gets a chance to meet with Murcutt every week when he flies down for the project conference.

This message will be a brief one. I hope you're well.

Allaine

To: Allaine Cerwonka allaine_cerwonka@politics.muwaye.unimelb.edu.au
From: Liisa Malkki lhmalkki@orion.oac.uci.edu

Date: Wed, February 15, 1995 14:40
Subject: Re: back again . . .

Hi Allaine,

Sorry to get back to you so late. Got your 2 wonderful communications about fieldwork. YES YES YES: the cops, gardeners, parishioners are, I think, excellent contexts to situate yourself in!! Can't state this strongly enough. You've hit on fascinating, sociologically important, revealing sites from which to explore your questions. And this is really what I was talking about. Informants are everywhere, but there needs to be some coherence, some social/sociological logic to the CONTEXTS or SITES in which you are working. So, two things (in answer to your queries about informants' nature, location):

1. Informants are persons whom you generally have more regular contact with. You get to know them, talk with them pretty often (not daily or anything, necessarily), see them living and working in their own life circumstances/surroundings, earn their trust, learn things about their lives and thoughts from many different angles. Deep (sometimes ridiculously deep) knowledge, thick description. [It's a] very time-consuming process, this developing of relationships with informants—and energy-consuming. This does not mean that chance conversations and casual acquaintances cannot provide valuable material or insights, as well. Simply keep a record for yourself of whom you spoke with at any given time, where, when, how, why, etc.

2. This second point is the one I was really trying to stress. When you come back and write your study into a dissertation and then a manuscript, you need to be able to say something more focused than that you spoke with "some interesting people" in Australia. You need to be able to identify and explain and justify your arguments on the basis of research in specific social locations—because, after all, you can't talk about Australia in general in a serious way. Your informants can, but you as a scholar can't claim that your arguments hold for the whole country. See? You can simply state that in the contexts of which you have thorough knowledge, this and this holds. And from there, other, more general insights might follow. You need to be pretty hard-nosed about this if you claim to do ethnographic fieldwork. And this is, precisely, what you should claim, what you are entitled to claim, and what I (for one) expect from you. I am absolutely tickled pink when I think into the future about your book . . . "a political scientist who did thorough ethnographic fieldwork among Australians in X garden society, Y parish, Z police station on questions of national and supranational identity," etc. . . . I can tell you, I would certainly teach your book in a class on nationalism, or in the one I'll soon do, "Contemporary Ethnography."

So, Allaine, the long and short of it is that you need to think of these contexts as sites that you'll visit on a daily basis and look around carefully in, and work in, and—most important—HANG OUT IN, for the remainder of your time there, and on a regular basis. Important to set up a schedule for yourself to force yourself to get out there and do it.

Enough????? I am very excited about all this, on your behalf, as it were. HOPE YOU'RE WELL IN EVERY WAY.

Liisa

To: Allaine Cerwonka allaine_cerwonka@politics.muwaye.unimelb.edu.au
From: Liisa Malkki lhmalkki@orion.oac.uci.edu
Date: Wed, February 15, 1995 14:40
Subject: Re: cops, believers & gardeners

Allaine,

P.S. I'd limit your field sites to three at the most: parish, police, garden society. Other contacts and interviews can be more casual, accidental. And if you have, in time, to drop one of the three aforementioned because of time constraints or blocked access, I'd keep the cops and then make the painful choice between church and garden society. Logic: This way you'll access two more contrasting social worlds, whereas churchgoers and gardeners might inhabit substantially the same social world, class location, etc. In fact, when you get to know people (your informants) better in these settings, you might find that these two contexts have people in common—that is, parishioners = gardeners and vice versa. But are gardeners likely to be cops? Can't assume that anyway. What you are doing here, then, is identifying and developing your "fieldsites" or "fieldwork settings," and these can't be scattered just anywhere. Starting to make sense? Oh, by the way, could you acknowledge receipt of both of today's messages? I'm having e-mail troubles.

Liisa

To: Liisa Malkki lhmalkki@orion.oac.uci.edu
From: Allaine Cerwonka allaine_cerwonka@politics.muwaye.unimelb.edu.au
Date: Thu, March 2, 1995
Subject: Interview madness II

Hi Liisa,

I'm sending this for the second time because my e-mail system has been screwed up for the last two weeks, leaving me unsure about who has received what from me. I would not have received anything you have sent in the last two weeks, either. Hope all is well on your end.

Allaine

To: Liisa Malkki lhmalkki@orion.oac.uci.edu
From: Allaine Cerwonka allaine_cerwonka@politics.muwaye.unimelb.edu.au
Date: Thu, March 2, 1995
Subject: Interview madness

Hi Liisa!

I just wanted to bleep on to say hello and give you a brief idea of what's happening on this end. My guess is that you're quite busy on that end yourself. Hang in there.

Things have gotten quite busy since mid-January. I'm really, really excited about my project and about the things I have been doing. I'm so glad that I have this fellowship that allows me to just throw myself into this project for the year. It's hard to get to sleep some nights because my pulse is just racing, and I am thinking of all the things people tell me and the directions I see the project heading in. I know this probably sounds pretty nerdy, but it feels really good.

I interviewed the Sergeant from the Fitzroy Police Station. He was interesting [as he talked about] happenings around the city and attitudes toward various groups. But he did not have a lot to offer in terms of the landscape angle. What he did have to offer in this area was not necessarily a consequence of his being a cop. He is willing to help me continue interviewing with other cops, with a little prompting from me, but I do not think that the present direction I am heading in with the project would necessarily benefit from talking with people who move around the city and among various different groups.

I joined the East Melbourne Gardening Club, telling them up front that I would like to do interviewing. I have interviewed three out of the five who volunteered the first night. The last two will happen this week. I am optimistic that I can get more volunteers at the next meeting, too. This has been interesting and very useful. I won't go into the types of things that are coming up right now as it would make this message very long. But in a minute I will tell you some of the ideas I have about my project at the moment, many of which come as a result of these interviews.

I am going to try to get the minister in the outer, working-class suburbs to organize the interviews there next. That will be in a few weeks, I think. Then I was talking to John Cash [my informal mentor at Melbourne University], and he suggested that instead of the cops, I try to find a church or community group contact for the inner suburbs as a way of doing comparisons as well. And I am thinking as I write this that perhaps, in addition, I could try to go to a country town as a fourth site. Most Australians live in an urban context like Melbourne; then all the others (like maybe the last fourth of the population) live in small country towns like the ones here in Victoria. Interviewing there might assure me that this phenomenon is not only an urban/suburban thing. What do you think?

Let me briefly tell you some of the ideas I have had about the issue of landscape/ environment and Australian national identity.

1. I think what I might be looking at is not exactly landscape/environment, but rather Australians' growing preoccupation with things (constructed as) aboriginal or indigenous to Australia. Not only have there been trends of increased reverence for native plant life, but also [the growing use of] indigenous plants for medicines and body products. Further, there are several very popular Australian chefs (and many food companies now) promoting the purity and desirability of Australian food products (Tasmanian cheeses, Queensland seafood, etc.) It's interesting that what are in reality very regional foods and trees are always talked about as "national" species. A local culinary talent, Stephanie Alexandre, says a lot about this and was in the USA in 1992 doing a series of television shows teaching people about Australian cuisine/cooking that uses all Australian products, of course. I pick up a lot of utopian undertones from all these areas.

A popular refrain I hear from people is that they came to love and see the land and forests of Australia after being to Europe and seeing that Europe had cut down all of its trees long ago. The fact that so many people seem to have had this very personal revelation in Europe makes me think it's a social phenomenon, and that perhaps natural Australia is being constructed in contrast to spoilt Europe and America.

2. There's a lot of political talk and contestation around "woodchipping native forests." The Prime Minister is caught between the demands of industry and a growing popular concern for the native forests. It's led by the Greenies, but the paper polls (and my interviews/conversations) indicate a lot of sympathy for green causes among the general population. I think there is an interesting connection between the supranational/environmental movement and the national here. Also, it's interesting to discover how much money the government has put into grassroots attempts to convert areas "back" to their native state of vegetation.

3. The body products of Red Earth, the food products and production styles (which extend to the idea of service and entertaining the Australian way, I imagine), the environmentally sensitive products sold in the Australian Geographical Society, [and] the codes of how to maintain an indigenous garden make me think about the prescriptive quality of this aspect of Australian national identity. They all seem to prescribe new styles of living and ways of ordering one's private space. Further, they are so indebted to market forces. It's like being Australian is in part a consumer activity.

4. I've been thinking about the relationship between indigenous Australia and multiculturalism. It will be interesting to see when I interview in the outer suburbs how much value

this discourse has [there]. I also wonder what the social consequences of this discourse are on the power dynamics of multicultural Australia. I guess my most cynical question is— does "indigenous" Australia (and the lifestyle it prescribes) really have a Euro-Australian priority system and cultural system embedded in it? Perhaps it's a way of providing cohesion (an imagined community) in an atmosphere of volatile identity politics. Perhaps it's a way of achieving a degree of assimilation (a term that is taboo in political discourse here these days) to European values.

5. Finally, I am thinking about the way these discursive practices work in relation to the Aborigines in Australia. I think that through tourism, especially, white Australia has sought to establish a link with Aboriginal cultures, because it's very good for Australia to be seen as both a very young and exciting country, but also very old and offering a unique cultural contribution (like Aboriginal art and culture) to visitors and the international community. These links would also give more of a sense of ancientness to Australia's national identities. However, these links are fraught with difficulties because of the many Aborigines who continue to remind white Australia that their histories are different, and that white Australia must take responsibility for crimes against their people (past and present).

I think the narrative around an indigenous Australia implies the Aborigines, too, without saying it right out. Plus it accomplishes the same things as establishing cultural links with the Aborigines. The land itself is less inclined to remind society of the crimes enacted against it.

Finally, establishing a relationship with the land and nature implies a false unity in Australian society. It ignores the issue of whose land it really is, and that Europeans stole the land from the Aborigines and continue to hold it hostage. I have heard more than one white Australian talk about how white Australians have a Dreamtime, too—that white Australia has a spiritual relationship to the land (born out of hardship and experience). I think this discourse operates to legitimize white ownership of the land and thus serves to undercut land rights claims by Aboriginal groups.

So, when you have a minute, I'd be interested to hear any response to this that you might have (perhaps not mocking laughter). Also, are four sites too many? I think that I will get ten to fifteen interviews from the garden club. If I get the same from each site, how does that sound? I think I will also talk to people in the various stores promoting indigenous products to get the full spiel about how their product is meant to be used and how it's supposed to put one in touch with the earth forces. I already chatted with the manager from Red Earth; it was very interesting. Any other ideas?

Whew. I'm obsessed at the moment. Also, I have regular contact with the garden club. [. . .] I've also gotten to be very social and find that Australians tend to expect to see their friends a lot, so getting out and about gets easier and easier.

Is all this optimism getting you sick or what? Don't worry. Next time I'll be e-mailing you saying that the sky is falling, no doubt. Until then, be well.

Allaine

To: Allaine Cerwonka allaine_cerwonka@politics.muwaye.unimelb.edu.au
From: Liisa Malkki lhmalkki@orion.oac.uci.edu
Date: Thu, March 2, 1995 17:59
Subject: Re: interview madness

Hi Allaine,

Just got this message from you, and also retransmitted two of my latest messages to you. I hope they're not obsolete/useless. In very brief response to your queries, four sites sounds like a lot. Potentially. But see how it goes. Make sure you ask the gardeners about what they grow. And ask them about things like English roses and lavender. Just open-ended questions about this and that. (A most effective interview-technique, that!) I don't remember what else you asked now. Ask me again if questions are not answered here in any of today's three transmissions. I'm so happy you are really getting the taste of doing fieldwork. It is heady and overwhelming and consuming and—strangely enough—it can give you a powerful inner peace to do it, and to know you are on to something, and that you have truly original material. So, this is Empirical Research. Make sure you don't get too exclusively wrapped up in the Aborigine-nation question; it is surely crucial, but these English rose gardens might be somewhere in the landscape, too. I only mean: look widely, without closing off directions [too] quickly.

    Would you let me know if you received these messages? Keep well, and write soon again. Your "letters from the field" are great reading.

Liisa

To: Liisa Malkki lhmalkki@orion.oac.uci.edu
From: Allaine Cerwonka allaine_cerwonka@politics.muwaye.unimelb.edu.au
Date: Tue, March 7, 1995
Subject: Re: re: Interview madness

Hi Liisa,

You asked me to respond right away to let you know I had received your e-mail. I did at last (although it may have been sitting in my mailbox for three or four days). Thanks for all your comments. I haven't had time to digest them properly, but there is one thing that I wanted to talk further about.

Cops. . . . what are we to do about them? You spoke highly of them as a site in your first e-mail message, but that was before you read my message talking about my queries about the value of that site ("interview madness"). So I'm wondering what your reaction is to the issues I raised in that transmission. The trail has cooled off with that site, but I think I could still get in there again with a little work.

The issue, briefly, is that I am unsure why they would be particularly useful as a site, given that I am looking at the intersection of landscape and national identity. It seems that they would be useful as people who have experiences and opinions that come out of their personal lives, not necessarily out of their professional lives as cops. In some ways they would work nicely with the Garden Club, as the garden gang tend to be mostly older women (middle- and upper-middle class) and [the] cops tend to be younger and middle-aged men (working- and middle-class). But perhaps another site would give me more variety in perspectives and might be easier for me to blend into. This is the kind of thing that makes me lose sleep, so do get back to me with your thoughts so we can see this issue through.

I have gone through my initial list of interview volunteers for the garden club. There's a meeting tonight, at which I hope to pick up a few more takers. The word has gotten out about how the interviews went for the first group, so I'm hoping others will be less intimidated (or whatever) by the process. I also feel quite good about things with the first group, as I feel comfortable calling most of them up and having a casual coffee. So, further interaction with them all seems quite plausible. They're a good group, and I've learned a great deal in the last month amongst them.

I will attend church in Dandenong this Sunday. I think you're right about possible overlaps between gardeners and believers, except for class and being "outer-suburban" versus inner-city. That's an important division for people in Melbourne. It sounds like the parish is very active in terms of community volunteer work and such, so there might be opportunities for me to interact with people through those groups. I'll know more on Sunday. (Remind me that this is only fieldwork if I start e-mailing you about the healing power of Christ next time.)

By the way, it's still so damn hot down here. I miss California's perfect (if not smoggy) weather. Every time I turn around it's ninety-five degrees! But so far, outside of friends and family, that's about all I've been missing about the U.S. I love living in an older city. And after all this garden talk, I really have come to respect the priority that Melbourne, at least, has given the parks and gardens. It's been really nice that the garden clubbers have always suggested we do the interviews in their homes. It's funny that it only takes a few queries about the art on the walls or the period in which their home was built, and I score a tour of all the rooms (save the bedrooms) in the house. I see a lot of oil landscapes on people's walls.

Being so social is really exhausting. I think I'd started to become more of an introvert over the last couple of years at graduate school (well, sort of at least). People are quite forthcoming with invitations, which has been nice. I have started to develop a closer relationship with a few people. It is very time-consuming, but you're right about the different type of information that comes from those relationships and interactions. Yesterday, Sue (the oldest sister of my former host family) asked if I would go to the library with her to show her how to dig up research for a novel that she wants to write. It was such an interesting experience because throughout the day I got insight into what she thought the novel would be about and some of her fears about its reception. In a nutshell, she is writing about an expatriate Australian woman who comes to terms with her relationship to her country and her father. This happens through a spiritual experience at one of the old Aboriginal sacred sites at the Kimberlies (Northwest Australia). At one point, after reading a passage by an Aboriginal person in a book on Aboriginal legends (the passage was about how whites have [stolen] and continue to steal the stories of native people), she was exasperated and said, "How long do we have to wait, and how much blood and sweat do we have to put into this land before it's ours too?" I found myself wondering why she imagined that the way for her character to develop a new relationship to the country was through the land and Aboriginal cave paintings. I think I will ask her that when I see her next.

Got to go. I'll try not to get obsessed with the Aboriginality angle of the project. It's very interesting to me, but I am seeing many other things that are interesting as well. Thanks for the encouragement. It helps. I'll keep in touch. Let me know what you think about the cops.

Maybe we should just find a different third location?

Allaine

⚡

To: Allaine Cerwonka allaine_cerwonka@politics.muwaye.unimelb.edu.au
From: Liisa Malkki lhmalkki@orion.oac.uci.edu
Date: Tue, March 7, 1995 15:27
Subject: Re: hot days down under

Hi there! Sounds like you're making excellent progress! Okay, not much time. Rough notes and reactions follow.

Coppers: if you really find yourself resisting working with them, make sure you ask yourself why and [only] then abandon that dimension of your project if you feel like it. I was just thinking—as you indeed observed—that cops would make a good, exciting contrast with the gardening [club].

But how would cops and landscape go together? Here I was in my mind extending the landscape concept toward the new geographers: Soja at UCLA, David Harvey, Michael Watts at Berkeley. A quick, brief introduction into this field is to be found in Watts's commentary in the *Cultural Anthropology* volume (1992?) that my "National Geographic" essay is in. It's got other stuff on space and place as well.

I was thinking also of Appadurai's "scapes" (in Fox's *Recapturing Anthropology*). Police work and landscapes might be related in other ways, too. Urban landscapes of crime, the predictive mapping of criminality onto the city, computerized police maps of Melbourne neighbourhoods in relation to class and immigrancy, etc. Teresa Caldeira's work is key here. This is not to presuppose that all the cops are reactionaries, xenophobes! Among the cops you might very well find churchgoers and gardeners [and all sorts]. "Climate" [can also work] as a metaphor for social phenomena—climate of fear, for example.

But do not do any of this research on my account. It has to be all yours and your call at every turn. I will not be disappointed in any way by choices that are utterly yours to make.

Another observation: You wrote originally (in your research proposal) about interconnections between Australian national identity and the wider world, in the form of the Commonwealth and Asia, etc. I think, as ever, that this dimension is very important to keep in the project. I bet that even discussions of species of plants, gardening habits, etc. would get you into [the] supralocal [social imagination] of community.

Yes, yes: follow up all interviews with "casual coffee" and "chats." These are "evidence"—as real as it comes, and very important. Make sure you are very careful with notes.

Wonderful that you are being invited into homes. I would write notes right after each visit describing the house, its interior, [its] garden, noting down its address, describing the part of town, anything you can think of—what you were served, topics of discussion. If ever there's something really striking, you might ask to take a photo of it (if you know your informants would not mind being asked). And sometimes you should possibly ask to make copies of photos people show you from their albums or whatnot, and get written permission for you to reproduce said items. Easier now than later.

Be scrupulous about keeping track of all addresses, contact information on all informants for the future—for years to come.

Take high-quality photos of people's houses and gardens—you might use photos in your book in the future.

Don't worry about a third location if [the] cops don't pan [out]. That would be my advice. Got to go. More later,

Liisa

Afterthoughts

LM: Photography as an ethnographic technique is a complex subject and much important work has been published on it. There is more I might have discussed with Allaine at the time. For instance, some of the issues I now discuss with graduate students in my fieldwork techniques course are as follows. First, it is important to think about why photographs might be useful as a form of evidence, and to consider the possible social lives (Appadurai 1986) of the images in one's work. Second, ways of looking (Grimshaw 2001 and Alloula 1986) and ways of seeing (Berger 1973) should perhaps be more self-consciously examined before one starts taking pictures. In *Coral Gardens and Their Magic*, Malinowski has an interesting, very honest section on shortcomings in his own ethnographic work (1978, 317–40, 452–62). We can also draw on the benefit of his hindsight and consider how much we do not see even when we look. In the seminar, I link Malinowski's thoughts on photography with Marcel Mauss's essay, "Techniques of the Body" (1973) and Susan Sontag's *On Photography* (2001). (See also Carol Squiers's *The Critical Image* 1990.) Mauss is, to me, a sparkling example of someone who looks well, and of what "observation" can mean at its best in the phrase, "participant observation." Sontag's book is useful in many different ways. When she describes photography as a kind of "soft murder," I think about the ethical challenges of using photographs in ethnographic research. There are many pitfalls, not least of which is the production of spectacles of otherness— whether spatial, social, or temporal otherness (see Fabian 1983; Susan Stewart 1993).

Forwarded To: Liisa Malkki lhmalkki@orion.oac.uci.edu
To: Edna Levy pedandjake@smtp
From: Allaine Cerwonka allaine_cerwonka@politics.muwaye.unimelb.edu.au
Date: Wed, March 15, 1995
Subject:

Liisa,

Me again. After I sent off the last e-mail to you, I wrote to Edna Levy in Israel (working on dissertation there and just had a baby, Gavri). I thought I would forward you that message, too, because I try to explain my project to her, and it might give you a clearer sense of where I am struggling to put together the theory and what I am more comfortable with. Sorry if it is repetitive, but see how you go.

I'll let you know how getting access to the coppers goes.

Allaine

To: Edna Levy pedandjake@smtp
From: Allaine Cerwonka allaine_cerwonka.politics@muwaye.unimelb.edu.au
Date: Wed, March 15, 1995
Subject: Re:

Edna,

Should you really be typing curse words with junior in such close proximity? Glad to see that motherhood has not made you any more ladylike or anything mushy like that. How is little Gavri? It's been so long since we've had a proper chat. He must be walking by now or getting ready to enroll in kinder or some such thing. We received the news release. Both the kid and the hubby are very cute indeed. Have you bonded, or are you ready to sell the little one off because he keeps demanding milk? Do tell me about your life. Do you have more energy? What's postpartum like? Fun? Right. Must be nice to just have to cart your own body around. Any stretch marks or cool battle scars like that? It takes a while for your belly to go back to normal, right? What's that like? Do you ever feel like having sex? (This isn't a proposition or anything; it's just that you're my first post-baby friend, and I have to get the scoop.)

My life is good, but not great. I just sent Liisa an "I don't know what the fuck I'm doing" e-mail. This is it. She's going to finally realize that I never had a clue about this whole dissertation thing. Maybe she won't even write back. Can people resign from one's committee?

I've been doing interviews in a garden club and am about to expand to a local police station (if they don't [. . .] back out). The idea, I've finally figured out, is not to attempt to be representative [of the whole of Australia]. There are a million different national identities in any given nation. I am interested in certain processes, so I have chosen two field sites that are more promising for giving me insight into the particular processes I am researching. The process I want to look at is [the linking of] landscape and national identity.

A couple of finer points. Landscape is used as a narrative in Australia at the moment for establishing what's unique and natural about Australian-ness. The story goes, "Yes, we're a multicultural nation, but as generations are here they experience the harshness and beauty of the land here (form an almost spiritual relationship with it), and develop a unique "Australian-ness." I have been looking at the discursive practices that testify to this narrative and also reinforce it. For instance, there is a popular garden and ecological movement (often sponsored by the government) privileging native plants over exotics. Big hubbub in the paper a couple of years back when the city needed to plant trees to line the central avenue downtown. People were outraged [that European trees were being put in]. . . . "Got to be proud of Australia. Stop looking to Europe for our identity, etc." This narrative comes up in interviews, too. This is only a portion of the dissertation. It shows how there is a process of trying to establish the "naturalness" of Australian identity and the invention of tradition around it (á la Hobsbawm). Reinforces the legitimacy of the nation (especially in the face of land-rights claims by Aboriginal groups) and reflects the assumption that nations and peoples are naturally rooted in certain territories (cf. Malkki 1992, Gupta and Ferguson 1992). I feel like I am witnessing the invention of tradition or of a national narrative as it is just getting off the ground here. It's also interesting to see it pop up at different levels in society, from personal testimony to ad campaigns to government policy. I have gotten insight into a lot of this through more casual participant observation and by interviewing, and [have] continued contact in a local garden club (thought the club might have more insight into gardening politics and fashion).

I am going to interview cops because as a group that moves around the city so much, they have insight into the social landscape of the place. The [usual social] fiction is that identities are stable and disparate. My argument is that they are developed in relation to other identities. So on the national level, I am hoping to show how supranational influences also shape national identity. In part, I will do this by showing how individual groups define their place and identities in relation to other groups. As Malkki says, "Identity is always mobile and processual, partly self-construction, a shield, a fund of memories, etc." (1992, 37). Identity, in this wild and postmodern landscape, is increasingly displaced and decentered. Yes, there has always been migration, tourism, international business, but now the pace of that and the number of people who fall into those categories have greatly increased. Consequently, your location/identity, even if you yourself never move, is usually affected by these dynamics. The story about nationalism is that it is an inherited, stable thing, natural (because it's ethnic or whatever) to a set of people. Or, according to globalization theories, local identity (and the nation as well) are becoming obsolete because of this international flow of goods and people. Well, national identity is asserted more fiercely than ever and does not seem to be going away or [becoming] homogenized. That's easy enough to show; what's harder is to trace how national identities are influenced by other, supranational identities. The multicultural narrative is addressing this movement, but doesn't get at it exactly.

So I think I will try to understand and document this process by exploring how local communities here in Melbourne are influenced by this transnational public sphere. I saw this happening in California when I was teaching for the Taiwanese American SAT prep program. These kids had very complicated identities. They were definitely "American" in their self-identification, but it was no longer that melting pot thing where former identities are expected to be shed. Their daily spaces were both the streets of Irvine, but also (through gossip and parents' businesses) certain neighborhoods in Taiwan.

I will freely admit that this is still at the stage where it hurts my brain to think about it. It's easier for me to see how an Australian culture, rooted in the soil of the land, is being manufactured, but it's harder to see the more complicated ways that identity really is constructed. I get frustrated because I feel like I have been trying to gain mastery over this concept/process for over a year now. I'm in a different place with it at this point, but it's not set quite yet. It's that fucking space/place thing I was babbling about at the Alta [café] last spring.

I think that the senses thing might still have a place in the dissertation, believe it or not. Raymond Williams (one of the early cultural studies figures) talks about alternative cultures/groups that develop despite bourgeois hegemony. He talks about groups or alternative visions coming out of "structures of feelings," which is a response to the world based more on affect (senses or memory could be a part of it, I think). This is how he conceives of resistant or just alternative consciousness in the face of class domination. I'm thinking that structures of feeling might be a way in which communities are constructed/imagined. Anderson only talks about them coming out of print capitalism and administrative organization. But structures of feeling might be the kind of thing that ties people into communities beyond Australia and, vice versa, also a way supranational communities affect national identities (in addition to technology and such).

Work is taking up all my brain cells at the moment, as you can probably tell. Well, I still have a few left over with which to contemplate what a jerk my landlord is. He does not want to do anything about the liquid that is beginning to ooze down our entrance wall. I'm not sure what it is, but it reminds me all too much of a few scenes from *Amityville Horror*. Jim has a higher tolerance/threshold for such things. Boys—go figure. But we might be moving. I won't tell you about it now because I don't want to jinx it.

Besides all of this, life is [going] well down here. Jim is working like a madman to get this building done at the company he's working for, plus trying to do his MA courses. He's a bit grumpy at the moment. I think he thought life in Australia would contain more beer drinking and shrimp on the barbeque.

So, now it's your turn to fill me in on the gossip. Tell Jacob I said hello. I suspect that this e-mail might have been a little too boring and filled with work to keep your attention—but I know for sure that Jacob didn't get through the first couple of paragraphs. I'll try to write more sexy and scandalous news next time. But, alas, there has been very little interpersonal drama in my life in the last month. Hope you are well. Tell me the truth. I miss you both [. . .].

Love, Al

⚡

To: Liisa Malkki lhmalkki@orion.oac.uci.edu
From: Allaine Cerwonka allaine_cerwonka@politics.muwaye.unimelb.edu.au
Date: Thursday, March 16, 1995 12:28
Subject: those brave boys in blue

Hi Liisa,

This is an important point in my fieldwork for organization and reorganization. I had a long think about your last e-mail and looked back over past correspondence as well as rereading some of the stuff from the new geographers.

I am beginning to see much more clearly how some of these bits and pieces of theory can come together in my project/dissertation. It's very exciting, but daunting as well. I have tried to take emotional and intellectual inventory to get a clearer sense of where I feel less in command of the theory or of what I need to find out about through my fieldwork.

1. Coppers are a go. I see the connection with landscape and feel good about pursuing them as my second site. (As an aside, thank you for giving me the intellectual space to draw that conclusion. Many people would not have, had they been in your shoes.) I went to the parish, but found that they were mostly senior citizens and, after having lunch with a group after church, [saw] that their perspective was not that different from that of the garden club (despite some class differences). I contacted the station again and found a new person in charge (Senior Sergeant Deborah Mills; working with a woman in that capacity could be good) who is going to talk to the other Sergeant about what to do about me. I'm worried that access will be denied for some reason, but I will cross that bridge when I get to it. I have certainly learned a lesson in striking while the iron is hot, but I do think that my interviews will be better for the month's work that I have done in the meantime.

2. I have a few uncertainties about interviews (understatement of the year). I am trying to conceptualize the social spaces in a way different from the rhetoric on multiculturalism, but it's difficult. I hear how X group comes to Australia and settles in this neighborhood, Z in this neighborhood; Z can't afford the rents anymore, so they have moved further out of the inner city to yet another neighborhood. Coppers might tell me how the eastern European migrants resent the refugee status of the Vietnamese because of the social services the Vietnamese get, or how urban Aborigines don't seem to them to be mingling with other ethnic groups, but I'm struggling to put that into a theoretical framework. I keep seeing trees and can't make out the forest at this point. What kinds of things should I ask about in trying to work out the processual quality of identity?

3. This frustration is echoed in thinking about the effect of the supralocal on national identities. (Can you recommend any more sources for me to read on the supranational in the local, by the way?) I had a reread of your "National Geographic" article (among other things) and got to thinking about your point about the camp refugees imagining the Hutu nation as a moral community or destination. It makes me think about what Britain or the Commonwealth means to people here in Australia. Is it a moral community or an identity as part of the first world or Europe or something? It still isn't clear to me. England used to be an imaginary homeland of some kind, but now . . . hum. But again, it's hard to think past the narrative of, "England used to be a type of parent to Australia, a colonizing force as well, but now the younger generation just sees England as irrelevant."

4. In looking at practice, yes, there's still a lot that is indebted to England, like gardening style—the "cottage garden" is still the most popular, despite a patriotic push for Australian plants. And there's not a lot of physical interaction between Anglo-Celtic Aussies and Asian immigrant groups (a little more between the first group and Greek and Italian second-generation groups). People tell me how multicultural and how open-minded Australians are to ethnic groups and use the fact that they eat all sorts of ethnic foods as proof of that fact. Discursively, Vietnamese are used as examples of bad parenting by many Anglos ("[They] leave their children in the car while the parents are in the Casino gambling").

5. I am interested in locating the places that different groups occupy in Melbourne and in getting a sense of how the lines of communities are negotiated and contested. So, should I take the opportunity, when presented, to talk to members of different ethnic groups? The cops would have insight into a lot of points of conflict and dynamics between groups, but there's a lot that people deliberately keep from the police and lines of contact that are drawn quite peacefully and thus might not catch the cops' attention. But I am aware of not spreading myself too thin, nor trying to be representative. This is why I ask. I am thinking especially of the Koori population in Melbourne whose links to other areas in the country might be invisible to the cops.

I'm in an opaque space at the moment. Nothing is clear, but there is the hint of lots of interesting things. I feel frustrated at my inability to think these issues through in a clear and fresh way. I need some help at this point. And I'm not exactly sure what I need from you. Direction, confidence, optimism. Whatever you have handy in your bag of tricks at the moment. This all seems very complicated on my end, but it would be great if it strikes you as child's play. Let me hear from you.

"dazed and confused,"

Allaine

Afterthoughts

AC: Coming from political science, which has a stronger tradition of quantitative studies that seek generalizabilty (e.g., surveys, statistical research, etc.), I was concerned in the early part of fieldwork about how I could make larger claims by studying something so particular as a garden club, or a parish. In this sense, the initial phase of my fieldwork was marked by some very deliberate thinking about who I should engage with in my study and why. Within the logic of positivism, conducting research at the garden club was problematic since their preoccupation with landscape would prevent me from claiming that geography and landscape were important to the process by which Australian identity was produced. *Of course* geography would seem important if I conducted my ethnographic research with them. And perhaps I would find that they drew upon transnational (or supranational, as I phrased it) discourses like environmentalism; but what could I claim to know that would be of scholarly importance, even if I did find these things in the course of my research among them? The concern and direction I received from the two political scientists with whom I discussed my research program during the year (see correspondence Cerwonka to Malkki, March 2, and Petracca to Cerwonka, May 2) indicate the pervasiveness of positivism within political science.

With time, I came to see that instead of being able to make such broad claims, ethnographic research done in very particular and deliberately chosen field sites does enable one to take a concept or phenomenon and understand it in deep, rich ways. Instead of knowing what "most" Australians do or believe, I could speak, in the end, to how geography, spatial practices, and supranational communities are involved in the process of imagining the nation.

In some cases, ethnographic knowledge can be combined in productive ways with survey or statistical research in order to make both kinds of claims. Ultimately I *did* claim that the spatial production of identity was a significant process for Australia, and discussed in very particular detail the different dimensions of how the nation is defined and claimed through spatial practice. I was able to make larger claims about the importance of this phenomenon for Australia because, in understanding the practices and attitudes of garden club members about landscape and nation, for instance, I could see parallels in other areas of society. In this case, I also saw the spatial construction of nation in the symbolism used in the Australian Parliament building and in the historical material I gathered about the territorialization of the landscape during the British settlement of Australia, as well as in numerous other contexts.

To: Allaine Cerwonka allaine_cerwonka@politics.muwaye.unimelb.edu.au
From: Liisa Malkki lhmalkki@orion.oac.uci.edu
Date: Tue, March 21, 1995 14:18
Subject: Re: here I sit

Allaine,

It's not exactly child's play, is it? But would it comfort you to know that you are socially a child in your new fieldwork environment according to tenets of classical anthropological theory? No? Well, stay tuned. I'm rushed off my feet right at this moment, but I'll write at more length very soon. Pep capsule: you are doing exactly what you should be doing (including aimlessness + doubts). I always think of pep talks and truth as mutually repelling, but here they are not.
Soon,

Liisa

Afterthoughts

LM: The question of representativeness is one that haunts Allaine's thoughts during much of her fieldwork. I read it as a gloss for a whole, interrelated cluster of worries. In what sense can these sites produce understandings representative of all of Australia? Is that the goal? If not, then what authority and explanatory weight does the urban ethnography in the two sites have? And by what authority does Allaine advance her insights? What is a reasonable "sample" in the ethnographic study of nationalism in an urban context? This question fails to make sense unless it is connected to another: What is the unit of study? Wim van Binsbergen's (1981) work addresses how easy it is to naturalize "the tribe," "the ethnic group," "the nation," "the village," or other like units as the obvious or ideal units of study. These are ways of looking for identifiable "social wholes." "The nation," the "ethnic group," and the like are often socially relevant categories for people, in this case, for people in Australia. We see throughout the correspondence that many of the Australians with whom Allaine discussed her project on nationalism spontaneously advised her to look into ethnic groups and their clubs and associations. She was similarly advised by several of the colleagues with whom she talked. Allaine herself, at times, felt a compulsion to talk to members of different ethnic groups to get a representative sampling, an *array* of the differences that were thought to make up Australia. Much of the literature on the concept of identity follows these analytical pathways. But the delineation of the unit/s or object/s of study is much more complex than that, as van Binsbergen (1981), Gupta and Ferguson (1997a), and others have demonstrated. That certain social categories and groupings that are socially or common-sensically meaningful is important to know, of course, but it does not follow that these should be swallowed whole as *analytical units.*

To: Liisa Malkki lhmalkki@orion.oac.uci.edu
From: Allaine Cerwonka allaine_cerwonka@politics.muwaye.unimelb.edu.au
Date: Mon, March 20, 1995 12:19
Subject: thumbs up

Hi Liisa,

Just a quickie to say that I feel more organized about the theory at this point, which is great. I would still be interested in any suggestions you have for things to keep an eye out for or questions to put to the cops.

Got the okay from the cops recently to do interviewing at the Fitzroy Station (the station I have wanted to do all along). The officer in charge, so far, does not seem concerned about monitoring when I am at the station and with whom I speak. It seems like it will just be whomever I can make arrangements with. That will be very good, I think, and I will try to drive around with some of them. So I start over there this afternoon and continue with the garden club.

Speaking of the garden club, one of the women, Edith, called me up first thing Friday morning saying, "Come on. It's a beautiful morning! Let's go for a walk together by the river!" It's interesting, the different stories you hear when you change the location [in which you meet people]. That's why I think it will be good to just hang with the coppers in the cars on their "beats." Weird work, this is. But fun.

Talk to you in time.

Allaine

To: Allaine Cerwonka allaine_cerwonka@politics.unimelb.edu.au
From: Liisa Malkki lhmalkki@orion.oac.uci.edu
Date: Wednesday, March 22, 1995 at 8:35pm
Subject: Re: those brave boys in blue

Hi there. Here comes a (slightly) more thought-out response to your long and interesting communiqué. Uncertainties about interviews: don't be afraid of having exchanges that look more like rambling, long, multifaceted conversations and chats rather than formal, structured "Interviews." It'd be easy to adopt a very rigid [. . .] interview style with Q & A following in neat rows and columns. Anthropological fieldwork doesn't look like that—or not only. Often the best material comes in strange forms—chance bits, like *objets trouvés* [found objects]. Besides, you are also doing the observation side of the participant-observation process, which means you notice your surroundings and make notes on them—things like where, when, how, why, what, who. And more specifically, you could make observations on such things as the interior decoration of people's houses and gardens, what magazines they subscribe to, what their hobbies are, what they eat and drink, where they shop, what books they read, what they enjoy on TV, where they go out for dinner or dancing, what relationships they have with what neighbors, what they warn their children about, what they fear, what they are worried about (like crime, e.g.) . . . a whole world of stuff, in short. Now, don't tie yourself in knots if you haven't done some of this yet. You can and should be continually changing and adapting your tactics and techniques of fieldwork. So, if you didn't write descriptions of landscape before, you can start now. Or if you remember stuff about interview situations done months ago, write it down retrospectively. And remember: no one but you will see your field notes. They are a private resource, truly a form of wealth that only you have access to. When you make aspects of it public in your writing (in the dissertation, in articles, in your book, eventually) that'll be another matter. No one will ever come and say, "Ms. Cerwonka, your field notes are not up to snuff." It's your own private gold mine that you will be using for years to come. It's in that spirit that you should keep a record, as full a record as possible, of all goings on. Don't rely on your own memory to hold and fix things reliably.

So, about interviewing: decide what you want to know, go about finding it in subtle and considerate ways, listen to things that are not about your topic, because your topic might change (even radically) as you listen more and more. That is, be open to change. "Interviews" with a capital "I" do not necessarily yield a more powerful form of evidence than "conversations," "chats," "gossiping." You can freely mix and match more formal and less formal styles of questioning. Okay?

You asked: what kinds of things to ask to get at the processual quality of identity? Hard to know, but your own notes suggested two things or directions to me. #1: [I saw] lots of talk there about "neighborhoods," but perhaps this is your preoccupation, not your informants'? It just sounded like a lot of people were talking to you about that. Moving in and out of neighborhoods, tracking how their ethnic compositions are changing, that kind of thing. If that is so, why are people investing such cultural energy in that? What might the language or vocabulary of neighborhoods be saying above and beyond the obvious? So, I guess I see a link in what you wrote about social mobility and the spatial politics of neighborhoods. But there were two much stronger angles of view into the processual question: generation and class. Maybe talk about neighborhood is talk about class location and its inter-penetration with ethnic/categorical locations in the contemporary context.

You said the "younger generation sees England as irrelevant..." I think you could really foreground the generational question for both the coppers and the garden club in different, very useful ways. In one case, listen to how people talk about their gardens and cultivating, taking very seriously what they say about the weather and the climate and the natural landscape. Weather is an interesting language. I mean, everyone talks about the weather, and it seems so innocuous, but, really, people manage to get a lot said with this vocabulary. So, listen carefully and take careful notes on it and on the plant varieties, seed types, tubers, graftings, seasons, imported versus domestic strains or varieties of plant, pesticides, environmental hazards. If one were doing fieldwork in Africa among people who are recognizably "cultivators" [not to mention Trobriand gardeners!], one would quite naturally, automatically take notes on such things. Why? I think it would be fascinating if you approached the gardeners' local knowledges about cultivating with this level of anthropological dead-seriousness and ridiculous detail. Who knows what arguments that level of care now will empower you to make later? Eh?

I think the generational shifts of style and "values" that people tell you about may link up in some manner with shifts of terrain in terms of possible class locations. Ask how things used to be in the old days. Open a file, perhaps, on people's remembering of "the old days."

Try to find out what the gardeners say about "what kind of people" gardeners are. Who doesn't know about gardening—or doesn't care? What about gardening for food versus flowers/ornamentals? Do Aborigines "know how to garden"? What do they grow? You are trying to flesh out cosmological maps. (For good definitions of cosmology, see S. J. Tambiah, "Introduction," in *Culture, Thought and Social Action* [1985].)

With coppers, similarly, ask exploratory, mapping-kinds of questions: life-historical questions are always a good entreé because it makes sense to most people. So, for example, ask if coppers are married, have children, what their spouses' occupations are, where they live, what their parents did, what they hope for their kids, what they think of changes in kinds of crime across time. How do younger and older cops differ from each other? Do they go to church? Might be important. What hobbies do they have? What social or other clubs do they belong to? Do they hunt? What are the most interesting or notorious cases they've ever been on? What do they consider the rough beats? What kinds of crime do they get in posh neighborhoods? How has crime type or incidence changed over time? Do they have national military service? Do you see evidence of class resentment among cops— or the gardeners? How does either group talk about the very elite of Australian society? Where have your informants traveled? Where do they go on vacation? What do the coppers think about crime among Aborigines? (Cf., possibly, [the literature that links] criminality and alcoholism on U.S. American Indian reservations.) Where do they get most domestic violence calls from? What areas? (I remember your notes on the Vietnamese.) Do the cops watch cop shows? Which ones? What about gangs, especially "immigrant mafiosi"?

Lastly, you were worrying about being representative. Make sure you ask: representative within (or in relation to) what unit of analysis? The nation? The neighborhood? The city? I think that question is covered nicely with the two sites you have chosen. You cannot do old-fashioned holistic ethnography where you think you are describing the whole society *in toto*. Even the old-fashioned ethnographers themselves got it wrong when they thought they could do that. What you or anyone gets is partial views and "situated knowledges" in Haraway's terms [1991]. And that is very valuable.

Try to tease out more, I'd venture, on this question of "ASIA." How do people imagine Asia and Asians, whether as foreigners or as Australian immigrants and citizens? The social imagination of the "other" could have two axes here in your work: one would be the Aborigines, and the other "other" would be the category, "the Asians." Pursue both axes in both sites (among cops and gardeners).

Another thought: read Balibar on "class racism" in his book with Wallerstein [1991], *Race, Nation, Class.*

The structures of feeling thing sounded very promising! The sensual aspects (Seremetakis and all the work you did before) might also come in handy.

Oh, you might also ask if informants' family members have (distinguished) records of service in the various wars. How does that figure into how people establish pedigree and entitlement? For it sounds like all Australians, especially the whites, feel called upon to establish claims to membership all the time.

Another detail: the younger generation say, "Stop looking to Europe for identity." Remember that a negative relationship or a relation of denial is still a relationship [see Jean Comaroff, cited in Malkki 1995, 317n1; Comaroff 1985].

Finally, I've written this whole thing without the usual niceties, using a lot of imperatives: remember to do this, don't do that, make sure you. . . . Please don't mind that. It was easier to make quick, abbreviated, rough notes like this than to put everything in the form of questions and enquiries. Please add all that later and know that none of this should you use if you don't consider it useful. These are all merely suggestions and ideas that were sparked by reading your communication. So, please: disregard at your ease!

Okay, got to go. Please let me know when you get this monstrously long thing so I know it's not lost in e-mail heaven. What you are doing is so exciting. I am surprised if you ever manage to sleep.

Keep well.

Liisa

PS. Are you keeping copies of everything in some other, safe location? Sending them to the USA, for example?

Afterthoughts

LM: A point worth emphasizing is the importance of being flexible and open to change in one's fieldwork, both methodologically and theoretically. "Be flexible" is so open and general an injunction that it is difficult to identify it as methodological/epistemological advice (See Bornstein 2003). It is, however, a principled and reasoned stance. One does not spend years studying field languages, reading the relevant regional or theoretical literatures, and living and talking with people "in the field" simply in order to prove or disprove the hypothesis with which one arrived. The living social context of ethnographic research is *expected* to transform one's original framing or animating questions. To hold on to the questions posed in one's original grant proposal when the context is continually teaching one how to ask better questions makes little sense in ethnographic fieldwork. This is obvious to most professional sociocultural anthropologists, but it may be useful to underscore for students only beginning their research processes. At issue is an improvisational flexibility.

LM: Above, I also mentioned the significance of generational angles of view in social research, but forgot to follow up on it. This is what I meant to say: we too often regard our "informants" as generic adults, an age-wise un-marked category. When we discuss social categories that fall outside the unmarked one of generic adulthood, like children, these straightaway become a special case, a marked category. That is, their "childness" itself tends to become the privileged object of knowledge. Treating "adultness" as a like object would generally be nonsensical. (And, interestingly, we unproblematically refer to adults as "people" or "persons," but not to children. One does not write, "This person mentioned that the fish have been plentiful this year," when one is writing about a conversation with a seven-year old. One does not write, "These people suffered in the bombardment," when one means that *children* suffered. This is one indication, perhaps, that children tend to be a marked category.) More broadly, then, we are accustomed to conjugating social or categorical difference according to sex, gender, race, ethnicity, nationality, and class, but much less according to age and generational difference. Kay Warren's work on the social significance of age and generational difference in Guatemalan political movements (Warren 2001) shows how productive (and socially salient) this conjugation of difference can be (see also Steedman 1986). Old age, similarly, often becomes a matter for gerontological anthropology, and not for anthropological theory in general (see Cohen 1998).

AC: In her e-mail Liisa lists some of the things that might be recorded in field notes and describes field notes as one's "own private gold mine." Field notes in fact are a fascinating genre of writing. They have received little critical analysis as a form of writing, perhaps because field notes are usually only circulated in piecemeal fashion as support for formal arguments in the polished ethnographic monograph. The tradition within anthropology of keeping field notes private is partially a strategy for protecting the privacy of our informants. This tradition might also be part of the tendency to repackage the ethnographic experience into a more polished form, one in which much of the uncertainty and subjectivity of the ethnographer is edited out (see Pratt 1986 and Geertz 1983). Additionally, in our formal, scholarly analyses, we try to create order from an experience that in many respects created a sense of vertigo for us as ethnographers; thus, a significant challenge to writing done after fieldwork is how to keep a sense of the richness of the social context that is often captured in our field notes.

The following excerpt from my field notes illustrates how field notes can operate as a conversation with oneself which records "evidence," but also where I attempted to be aware about my own positionality in the field. Further, the passage illustrates how ethnographic information is often entangled with one's own feelings, memories, and reading. This example of field notes also captures the layer quality of our analysis during fieldwork, which often includes an analysis of the terms, ethics, and epistemology involved in doing fieldwork. As elsewhere in the text, I have used pseudonyms to protect the privacy of the people with whom I worked.

From Allaine's Field Notes
1 May 1995

I called the station first thing in the morning to see if I could come in mid-afternoon. It had been about two weeks, and I was feeling very anxious about having been away from the site for so long. It is still very difficult for me to get up the energy to go into the station. I hate it that I have to ask permission each time, although no one has specifically said I do. It's just that it would be more awkward at the station, I feel, if I just show up without anyone expecting me. Luckily Acting Serg't Arnolds answered and was very warm and encouraging. He said to just come on in anytime today. I was relieved.

I stayed in the Watch House [operations center of the station] "observing." I want to do more taped interviews, but those are easiest to do with the section serg't's help, and I had already interviewed Arnolds anyway. Besides, it's yet another thing to ask permission for—so it takes more energy than I have right now (I think I may be a little depressed). Ned R—— was just getting off shift in the Watch House (we overlapped about a half an hour) and Paul V—— was coming on. Paul and I went out in the patrol car together with Burns, so I feel more comfortable with him. He's going up to Central Australia and Queensland for ten weeks for his holiday in July with some mates. Bummer. Ned teased me about being interested in seeing Serg't Arnolds the last time he saw me and wanted to know what was going on. I joked back—although this was the first conversation we have ever had with each other. He and Paul were joking about who got banged up worse—I thought they had had a run-in with some crooks; but Ned was hurt in footy [football]. Both he and Paul are into being in shape. I asked Ned about his tattoos (was he drunk when he got them?). He said that they won't give them to you if you're drunk; besides it's better to be clear-headed (I think he meant so you can feel the pain the most and not hide from it). I asked what he thought about "tats" on women. He said he thought a small one on a woman with a really great body was sexy. I thought Ned was a bit of a meathead personally. When he spoke, he seemed younger than what he looks. He's a Senior Constable, so he is probably in his mid to late twenties.

There was a lot of talk among Paul, Ned, a woman constable, Boyd, and Burns about going out the night before. They go out after Sunday shift (ends at 11 p.m.) and then have to be at work at 3 p.m. Paul said they had gone to an S&M club in Carlton. Apparently they watched others getting spanked, but no cops got up there. Sounds as if most people got very drunk. Listening to their conversation reminded me of starting at a new school, where everyone has bonded already primarily on the basis of shared drunkenness—and I just feel very sober and nerdy. The atmosphere is to joke and slag one another off. I try my best, but I feel I am limited in that I don't know the people very well yet, nor do I feel entirely comfortable with that genre of humor. The women seem to join in easily.

Acting Serg't Arnolds called up the Statistical Services Division and ordered me a copy of whatever report they put out on crime in Victoria. It was good to listen to him describe me because he said I was going to be around for the next few months and had authority for this type of information. Cool. I don't feel like anyone is resistant to helping me (although some, like Paul Easton, might dodge my interviews); but they just don't know what to do with me.

One call was to pick up shoplifters in Safeway (Smith Street). They were fifty-five yrs and thirty-five yrs old. They were both Anglo-Australians ("mockie [moccasin slippers] wearers"—meaning lower-class). The cops joked about what a motley-looking twosome they were. There was little commotion made over them. On their way out, Boyd read them the conditions of their bail, which meant they came through the Watch House.

It's hard to describe the tone of these encounters. The cops get this air of being excessively polite, treating them nicer than most of these people would normally be treated by the middle class. It reminds me of when popular boys in high school flirted with or were especially nice to unattractive, unpopular girls (or guys). It was like it was so obvious that it was a joke and an especially "funny" one because the people responded (couldn't help but respond) to their seeming kindness. They act very familiar with them, like—we're all friends here. So when the fifty-five-year-old man went to leave and turned to the door on his right, they said, "Oh, yeah, go through that door." It ended up being a closet with a wall on the other side; the older man smiled sheepishly at being the victim of a prank. The cops all laughed and showed him the real door.

Then the woman came up and was treated with excessive politeness. It reminded me of the woman who turned herself in several weeks ago for stealing from the volunteer collection cup. She had the same air of being grateful that anyone bothered to talk to her and for being treated so nicely by good-looking guys with jobs. She came back to check in with the cops for bail. I think she was secretly pleased to have something to do and someone to be responsible to—finally someone would give a shit about where she was all day.

A drunk guy came in of Eastern European background. One eye was really fucked up (from a previous point in his life). He was very drunk and yelling, and smelling very badly. The woman cop was pissed off because the Richmond Station should have processed him. However, they claimed to be too busy at that point, which forced her and her partner to take him back to

Fitzroy. There was a lot of activity around his arrival. He took a while to say his name, but he had identification on him. The cops started to yell back at him to shut up. They took him to the cell after taking his property off of him. He continued to yell. People periodically yelled back at him to shut up. Serg't Easton told Paul lightly (with his mock impatience for everything) "not to swear at the prisoners." I don't know if that was for my benefit—he seems very aware of my presence. He says, "Hey, there's some multiculturalism for you!" in order to punctuate the criminality of non-Anglo-Celtic Australians. I feel uncomfortable around him because I know he could easily belittle me behind my back. I am an easy target; I get the sense that he looks for easy targets and then despises them for being so easy.

There was a sublime moment when the first drunk was in the cell screaming and cursing, and all the cops were in the Watch House trying to figure out what type of pizza they wanted to order for dinner. It reminded me of Robert Scheer's essay, "Eating Tuna Fish, Talking Death" [1988]. Another drunk came in soon after. He was a Greek man who was also quite dirty. He was not arrested but came into the station on his own. I am told he just wanders into the station periodically and curses out the cops in a drunken stupor. Senior Serg't Bates was there and said that Hughes [the last Sr. Srg't] use to yell the few Greek words he knew at this drunk Greek fellow. I felt some indication that Sr. Serg't Bates was a little uncomfortable with this situation and perhaps told me about Hughes to let me know that other commanding officers condoned such carnivalesque behavior toward the occasional drunk. Only a guess.

Anyway, I was a little uncomfortable with the way that the cops crowded around the drunk from the safety of the counter that kept him on the other side. He was slumped over in a chair (nasty scar on his head) and periodically grumbled loudly. At one point all the cops gathered round and laughed and tried to get him to look up so they could take his picture (that would be for fun, since he wasn't under arrest, and therefore there was no need for his picture). Then Easton started to tease the woman cop, yelling to the drunk that she was single and available. She laughed, embarrassed, and kept telling him to shut up (in a light way that just prompted him more). One guy kept his face very close to the drunk to get him to raise his head for the group gawking at him. Easton warned him to be careful not to get his face too close to the drunk's (safety for the cop as he might get hit or scratched). The whole scene reminded me of a zoo animal or the scene from the *Elephant Man* when he asserts, "I am not an animal." I wondered how much the drunk registered of all of this.

Paul chatted to me about movies he likes. *Pulp Fiction* is right up there. He saw it four times and has the sound track. In that way he is typical of his age (young people at the party at Dave's friend's house all loved it too). Also *Reservoir Dogs* and *Home Improvements*. . . . He asked me about pick-ups, and I said "hicks" drove them in the U.S. He liked the new word and told Serg't Easton when he walked back into the Watch House that he [Paul] was a hick. Easton said, "Are you a Greek hick or an Australian hick?" since Paul is of Greek descent. Paul replied that "a hick is a hick" (which I'd be inclined to agree with . . .). I wonder if Easton says those things for my benefit or if he is obsessed with ethnicity.

To: Allaine Cerwonka allaine_cerwonka@politics.muwaye.unimelb.edu.au
From: Liisa Malkki lhmalkki@orion.oac.uci.edu
Date: Wed, March 22, 1995 12:47:17
Subject: Re: here I sit

Hi. Me again. Thanks for sharing [your letter to Edna] with me. I just wrote you at length a few minutes ago, so no more here. Just say hi to Edna when next you beam something to her. And congratulations to her, too, on her little boy. My Prince Moonbeam is an utter delight. And Aila is a heartbreakingly sweet and conscientious Big Sister.

    Meant to tell you: anthropology probably will have a *wonderful* new hire named Teresa Caldeira. Did I mention this? I really, really should FedEx her dissertation to you. It's about urban violence and police and the "commodification of security" in urban Brazil (São Paulo). She is [quite] Foucauldian, worked with Rabinow, and—get this—our Dean Willy is very high on her. I hope so much she'll come. Here would be another potentially fantastic person for you to work with as you are writing up. So, let me know if you want the dissertation, and I'll contact her for permission. [See Caldeira 2000]. If you do, please supply a telephone number and street address for FedEx purposes.

    [. . .]

Liisa

✦

To: Liisa Malkki lhmalkki@orion.oac.uci.edu
From: Allaine Cerwonka allaine_cerwonka@politics.muwaye.unimelb.edu.au
Date: Friday, March 24, 1995 10:48
Subject: quick hi

Hi, hi.

I wanted to let you know that I received your three messages (one long and the other two shorter). Thanks for beaming through your thoughts/ideas/reactions. I have been trying to keep the interviews as free-flowing as possible. It's usually easier to create such an atmosphere when I meet someone for the second time, but most have talked on at length even in the first interview. I have been meeting again with the [gardening] group I interviewed first and have talked to them about getting together (one on one) for coffee once a month until I leave in Nov. So far, the three I've asked have said fine. I'll also see them at the [East Melbourne Garden Club] meeting once a month, and then I've been invited to come along to the "first Sunday" get-together each month that has many of the garden gang in it, but [also] a few others. It's a social thing held in peoples' gardens. So I'm hoping that through these other types of get-togethers—impromptu or planned—I will see many of them regularly without feeling like I am asking for too much of their time. They like it when I ask to photo their house and garden. It's funny. [I had been nervous about asking them.]

I'm unsure of what my contact with the coppers will look like at this point. I tried to have my first interview with one sergeant last night, but he got called away to investigate an attempted child-snatching very [early in] our conversation, so we didn't get too far. If this is the norm, it might be hard to hang around too much. He didn't invite me to come along, and I didn't want to push for too much when we hadn't established any type of relationship. We're scheduled to have me ride along with him on Tuesday night (11 p.m. to 8 a.m. shift!), so I'm hoping that that happens without a hitch.

Curious thing about the cops. When I talked to Acting Sergeant Burns to set up times, we went into the interrogation room, and he was extremely friendly and open. I did not ask to tape our conversation because we were just setting things up. But without prompting on my side, he started telling me about which groups the cops hate (cue: they're responsible for all the drugs and violence) and laid out some of the other groups they deal with daily . . . such as the "poofters" (gays). I acted casual about all this information—not jotting any of it down in front of him, etc. When I went back for the "real" interview, he was much more formal and immediately asked if I wanted to tape the conversation, and did I want them to supply a recorder, etc. I taped our very brief conversation that was only about safe things like where he grew up, occupation of his parents, before he got called away. Upon reflection, I do not think I will tape the interviews with cops at this point (although I know that might make it impossible to whip out the recorder at another time). It strikes me that *they* are in the position of taping people (in the interrogation room), and their context for that is to use the information people give them against the people they arrest. So I think the recorder will color the interviews too much. Any thoughts about this?

And the woman who worked with the cops down in South America, did she say how she set up her contact with the officers? How much time was she allowed to be in the station? Was she allowed to sit around and observe? I'm still feeling out what the possibilities might be. I thought I'd establish a relationship with this Acting Sergeant before I negotiate to follow someone around the station and "observe their station duties" (Burns suggested this as an activity for me, and I thought it'd be a good chance to talk more casually with them and have them get used to seeing me around). But last night I just felt underfoot, and the possibility of hanging out seemed remote. We'll see.

I'd like very much to take a look at the dissertation on the commodification of security, if you can still send it to me. My address and phone number are as follows: [. . .]

The phone numbers are becoming eight digits because there are so many mobile (hand-held) phones here. Many, many people have them. In addition to business people, you see cyclists with them, teenagers, parents in restaurants talking to the babysitter while they dine. When I was eavesdropping on a group of teens on the public transport, they were having a conversation about what a drag their parents were and how they would really like to leave home. One girl (about sixteen) said, "Aahh, I'd love to ditch my parents, I'm so sick of them, but I just couldn't live without my mobile phone." (I assume her insensitive parents would no longer pay for the bill if she moved out.) Another, more beatnik type waxed poetic about how such materialist things were useless, but did not appear to have convinced anyone in the foursome.

I keep asking people why they think Australians are so enthusiastic about "mobiles." I get the technical answer about certain fiber optics, and [they say] the condensed population makes it affordable to phone companies and thus to people, . . . but a couple of people have suggested it ties into a general Australian anxiety about being out of touch with the world (although they are only calling across town). A [well-known] conservative historian (Geoffrey Blainey [1975]) wrote a book called *The Tyranny of Distance* some years back [which argues that Australia's "distance" has been pivotal in shaping its history]. Those phones are sociologically interesting but, on a daily basis, very obnoxious. It's freaky to be in a restaurant and have phones continually going off. Only the two "younger" members of the garden club (in their thirties) have them. None of the older ones that I've talked to so far.

Anyway, I'm guilty of false advertising because this wasn't a quick hello at all. I'll let you know how it turns out with the coppers.

Allaine

Afterthoughts

LM: The possibility of disquieting links between the interview and the interrogation, ethnography and police work, became very vivid at the police station. As I have written elsewhere, "Examining the differences and similarities between police work and anthropology invites anthropologists to consider themselves in relation to two models: the anthropologist as investigator and the anthropologist as witness. [. . .] Many factors push the anthropologist to try to assume the location of the detective or investigator. [See Carlo Ginzburg on "the inquisitor as anthropologist" (1989, 156–64).]

Anthropologists also routinely look for clues, follow hunches, assemble evidence, and work with cases. [. . .] The anthropologist as witness is differently located. Here, the injunction to know "everything," and to find the key to unlock mysteries is not a central (or sometimes even a meaningful) activity. Trying to be an attentive listener, recognizing the situatedness of one's own intellectual work (Haraway 1991), and affirming one's own connection to the ideas, processes, and people one is studying are more important in this kind of practice. [. . .] These two models represent different modalities of ethnographic authority. It is not essential to do away with the investigation in order to affirm the value of a methodological and political positioning as a witness. And to pursue a caring vigilance, to be a witness, is not to lose concern for questions of evidence or explanation" (Malkki 1997, 95–96).

To: Allaine Cerwonka allaine_cerwonka@politics.muwaye.unimelb.edu.au
From: Liisa Malkki lhmalkki@orion.oac.uci.edu
Date: Friday, March 24, 1995 at 2:37am
Subject: Re: quick hi

Hi back. This one really will be short. All of this sounds good. The once a month pace: you might be able to step up just a bit at the garden club. Don't worry about being embarrassed. I mean, you will be because it's embarrassing. That's ethnographic fieldwork. Take advantage of the weirdness that people (like the cops, perhaps) attribute to academics. It's weird, what you are doing. Play it up, perhaps. Just one more stance for you to think about. Going on the beat sounds great. Then ask that copper if you can do it again, and ask if other coppers would allow you to do the same, and that way you'll develop a "snowball sample" of informants there. You could have a dissertation chapter on nocturnal conversations with police. Which leads me to ask: have you seen the film, *A Night On Earth*? Ask cops and gardeners for advice on how to proceed with aspects of the research, sometimes. That's it for now. I think I wish I were doing fieldwork, too. But I'm not sure.

Liisa

Afterthoughts

LM: I wrote to Allaine, "It's weird, what you are doing." I do not think about research quite like this now, many years later. Ethnographers often worry about appearing odd or socially out of category to the "ordinary" people with whom they hope to work. There are good social reasons for this concern, but one might also pose the issue differently. Instead of assuming *a priori* that the ethnographer is an alien in human clothing in her or his research context, one might ask: What is so *unordinary* or abnormal about social research after all? And who, precisely, are "ordinary" people? Are the categories "student," "professor," "scientist," "writer," "academic," or "university type" not widely recognizable social categories like others? "Doctor," "lawyer," "teacher," and "journalist" are no more or less strange than "university student" or "professor." Yet, ethnographers think a great deal about the acceptable, socially legible presentations of self in the fieldwork setting. In my own case in Tanzania, I worried about the pre-existing bureaucratic and other social hierarchies into which I would be inserted in the refugee camp (Malkki 1995, 48). Would I be yet another white European "expatriate"? Would I be taken as a "UN-type"? Would I be a "young woman," too young to be taken seriously? Would I seem like a very rich white person with my Jeep? I found out that "university student" was socially a good label or persona for me in the camp. Without even realizing it at the time, I momentarily treated my "university student" persona as something I was trying on for size—like a costume for a stage play. Then I realized that I *was* a university student and was unsettled and embarrassed at my own willingness to be chameleon-like in order to "blend in" and make myself less strange. And what was the uniformity into which I would have blended in? "The refugees"? "Ordinary people"?

Ordinary people is a convenient, catch-all phrase in ethnographic writing, somewhat like the term *informants*. But it is a fiction that needs to be troubled. This fiction inhabits field research especially in sites that are different in terms of culture or class from the researcher's own social world, but it is also evident in fieldwork done in one's own society. Very commonly it is a shorthand for an imagined "grassroots." Sometimes it refers to "ordinary working people," "peasant cultivators," "the poor," "the huddled masses," "normal people," "ordinary citizens," "villagers," "African refugees," and so on. It may be an aspect of the ethnographic convention of "studying down." When "studying up," as Laura Nader (1972) has put it, the ethnographer is not thought to be studying "ordinary people" anymore. Who is "up" there? Intellectuals, government officials, politicians, guerilla leaders, the rich and powerful—social categories with institutional protections, or with the socioeconomic means to block access to researchers. And yet everyone should have the means to block access to researchers, to refuse to participate in a project, to decline to be interviewed. That is one of the basic ethical tenets of social research, but it is not reflected in the broad structural dynamics of knowledge production (see, e.g., Donzelot 1979; Foucault 1972, 1978; Piven and Cloward 1971; de Certeau 1984). Social disempowerment makes people more vulnerable and accessible to research, and, indeed, to social regulation, care, and control, and all manner of interventions. If the disempowered are conceived of as the "grassroots," they are often attributed a certain virtuousness as well. They can be studied "despite themselves," as it were, because they are not expected to have the cunning and self-consciousness of intellectuals or social elites (cf. Malkki 1996). They are sometimes, unreflectively, thought to be more "authentic" than elites.

Moreover, the category of "ordinary people" suggests a lack of internal social differentiation, a social homogeneity. It follows that to interview one of them is to produce more representative knowledge than if one were interviewing, say, government officials. This is an overstated and even caricatured characterization meant to highlight implicit fictions—fictions that in any serious piece of research will shatter.

To: Liisa Malkki lhmalkki@orion.oac.uci.edu
From: Allaine Cerwonka allaine_cerwonka@politics.muwaye.unimelb.edu.au
Date: Mon, March 27, 1995
Subject:

Just to prove that I can do a quick hi, and also to let you know I got your message. Nocturnal conversations with cops. I must admit, if that were on the table of contents of a book I picked up, it would be the chapter I turned to first. They're a funny group—coppers. They've got a good friendship network that entails much socializing together. I'll aim to work myself into such circles. It will help that there's a scarcity of women in their station (and profession). When I asked this one guy on Friday whether cops socialized together and then if they drank much, he said, "Well, we're not alcoholics or anything, but I'd say most go out and get drunk about three nights a week." I had to suppress a smile. I await the official okay on the drive-arounds, but I feel optimistic.

It's funny that my fieldwork experience seems to be developing into a weird crossing of *A Night on Earth* and *Fried Green Tomatoes*.

Allaine
P.S. I think I have seen most movies out there that aren't the usual Hollywood rubbish, and even a few more of those than I care to admit.

To: Allaine Cerwonka allaine_cerwonka@politics.muwaye.unimelb.edu.au
From: Liisa Malkki lhmalkki@orion.oac.uci.edu
Date: Tue, March 28, 1995 22:49
Subject: re: Re: quick hi

Hey there.

This sounds really excellent so far. A friend of mine, Roberto [Kant de Lima], who worked with police—I told you about him, yes?—in Alabama said church picnics were a big thing with cops there. Go figure. Roberto works in Rio, an anthropologist. The other Brazilian anthropologist, Teresa Caldeira: our secretary copied the dissertation for you and sent it airmail (not FedEx, after all—didn't seem that urgent).

Are you going to have to go and get drunk with the boys in blue? I probably shouldn't meddle or act like mother hen, but be careful anyway, eh?

Watched the Academy Awards yesterday. So L.A. Great.

Take care,

Liisa

Afterthoughts

AC: Various forms of writing in the field such as field notes and e-mail correspondence informed later writing I did from my fieldwork material. Below is a passage from the manuscript that grew out of my dissertation project that illustrates the fruitfulness of my fieldwork correspondence with Liisa for later writing. The excerpt below also illustrates how many of the things that presented themselves as passing or vague anxieties in the field (such as my sense of being an outsider or my concern about having to protect or inform against the police) were eventually issues I came back to and resolved during the more formal writing I did after fieldwork.

From *Native to the Nation: Disciplining Landscapes and Bodies in Australia* (Cerwonka 2004)

The police officers' distinction between theorizing and "doing" shaped my fieldwork experience among them. Compared with my conversations over sherry with the East Melbourne gardeners, officers at the Fitzroy Station were much more laconic and self-conscious about the information they volunteered for me. It is not an original insight to say that the police erect more rigid boundaries between their members and the larger society or community than do other occupations. Certainly this truism was confirmed by my own experience with the Fitzroy Police. For instance, one of the sergeants took particular interest in helping to arrange taped interviews with individual officers at the station. These arrangements developed into a strange kind of ritual where each interview began with the sergeant "joking" that the junior officer about to be interviewed "mustn't give away the shop secrets" before I was left alone with him or her. This sergeant's anxiety was perhaps the most blatant, but a similar concern that I was going to learn the "shop secrets" manifested itself in numerous other interactions throughout the months I was at the station. I initially assumed that the shop secrets were dark incidents of police brutality and corruption. This may have been part of it. However, after having spent an extensive period of time at the station and reflecting on it while writing, I have come to believe that the heart of darkness the police members were protecting was, in some sense, an empty center. That is, the members were being asked to defend the boundary that I was threatening just by being in the station and seeking to understand them better. I was out of place (wrong country, outside of the academy, a woman among many men, a lay person among uniformed officers) and they responded to that.

Frequently individual officers greeted me with the question, "Are you still here?" which of course caused me to feel a wave of rejection and anxiety each time this ritual was enacted. I wracked my brain to think of how Malinowski would have responded to such a greeting in order to work out what my half of the ritual might be if I were a "real" anthropologist. But alas, each time I just ended up responding with a slightly embarrassed shrug of my shoulders and nod of assent. This embarrassment was confounded by my nickname at the station. All of the officers at the station had a nickname, so in retrospect I should perhaps have taken it as a good sign about how my fieldwork was developing. For men, their nickname was usually a twist on their last name. For instance, an officer whose last name was Dunne would be called "Dunny," which is Australian slang for an outdoor toilet. The female officers usually received nicknames with a little more dignity; Helen would become "H" or Sharon would be "Shaz." Needless to say, neither my first or last name provided the officers at the station with much to work with. As a result, my nickname became, "the spy" or "spy" for short. The move to state the obvious in the form of an ironic joke—I was threatening the shop secrets—was typical in this community. This nickname also seemed to be a way the officers reconciled the boundaries I was crossing and the threat that I potentially posed for them. They found a way to neutralize the threat by literally announcing it. But they announced my infiltration or reconnaissance in ironic terms that lightened it and characterized my threat in overtly dramatic terms (as a threat to national security), not to them as a community or as individuals. . . .

Nevertheless, it was not only the officers whose comfort level was affected by the chasm between academics and police in Melbourne. There were limitations I placed on the intimacy I allowed between the officers and myself. One of the challenges of fieldwork for me was being aware of both a pull to find out "secrets" (those things that people did not want to tell me) and feeling anxious that I would see things that were not connected to my research questions. I was anxious that such "dark secrets" might force me to confront very difficult ethical questions about my responsibility toward fieldwork informants versus reporting violence or illegal activity within the police force.

Therefore, if I am honest with myself, I must acknowledge the way in which I too was invested in protecting the "heart of darkness" that the officers patrolled in many of my interactions with them. I wanted them to trust me, to trust that my stated aim of understanding the ways in which they define Australian identity was not just a cover for a secret agenda I might have to document police brutality or other such things. At the time of my fieldwork, I was also anxious about the ways in which my research could potentially harm them; it was long into the written analysis of my material on police spatial practices that I came to truly believe that there was another story one could write about the police besides a journalistic-type exposé or a romantic narrative about un-sung heroes.

To: Liisa Malkki lhmalkki@orion.oac.uci.edu
From: Allaine Cerwonka allaine_cerwonka@politics.muwaye.unimelb.edu.au
Date: Friday, March 31, 1995 12:07:55 EST
Subject: "Nocturnal Admissions"

Liisa

Ha, ha, ha! Excuse the bad play on words. Whoa! Out with the coppers! 1:00 a.m. until 3:00 a.m. last night! They have this bad habit of calling and canceling because some sergeant in charge doesn't think it's okay, or things come up at the station, but I finally got out with them for a little while last night and have plans to go out with one guy and a different partner on Saturday night.

Liisa, it is such a blast. There's so much blood! There is little to no gunfire here, but lots of drunks smashing each other over the heads with beer bottles and such. And it is great because the cops let me come inside with them and explain things to me as we go. It's also great that for every incident, they ask all the people for their address, age, whether they live alone, and other such nosy stuff that I'm dying to know. That gives me a good sense of which people are mixing together and in what areas of the city.

Neighborhoods are very important here (it's not my imposition). Narratives on each (about what type of people live where) abound. A friend I know from my last trip to Australia [Richard Allsop] was commenting that people really identify with their suburb (even inner-city areas are called suburbs), and feel it reflects something about who they are, but they don't tend to know their neighbors. He also has a "corridor theory"—that people from certain areas only move to certain other areas (like when they grow up and leave home or buy their first home). Coppers will be good for this type of information, for sure.

Funny experience to be riding around in the back of a police car, waiting there while coppers work out a brawl outside the car. I get funny looks, like I am a criminal waiting to be brought to the station. No one so far has said to the cops, "Who is this?"—like when we went to get a statement from a guy in the emergency room after a brawl.

I am so aware during this research of how I manage my presentation of self, and ethics, and respecting the people I am working with.

It's exhausting. I have gotten to a new stage with the garden club where I am stopping in for ginger wine in the late afternoon. I struggle with finding how to combine my fieldwork interests with friendship. Fieldwork often travels the same roads as friendship, and that is difficult for me. For instance, at Edith's the other day, she and Judith mentioned that Dora was in a local hospital for ulcers on her leg. She's waiting for tests and is bored to tears. I went to visit Dora because she is a very nice woman and hospitals suck. But I had this imaginary person in my head saying that I was insincere because I am also hoping to get to know Dora better to learn about the construction of national identity. I am learning that friendships usually arise out of a shared social structure that puts two people together, so it's odd that I would be so involved in their lives without much of a structure in place (garden club research doesn't usually [entail] visits to the hospital). But on the other hand, I am delighted that I have the financial means and the type of professional activity this year that give me the time and allow me to slow down enough to see even the things that are going on for other people (and to respond to them). Also, Margaret's husband died recently, and I sent a card and called several weeks later to see if she needed anything, or company, whatever. But at the end of the conversation, I did not know if she read my call as one from a mercenary researcher or a fellow human being (and it's curious that these are always two distinct categories for me). And I became a little flustered on the phone and couldn't find the words to say, "Margaret, this is about supporting you; not about my needs at the moment." But that's a weird sentence to try to insert into conversation anyway. So, whew! I am being forced to think about so many things beyond national identity. Yes, I am using my field journal as a refuge for many of these confusing and powerful emotions.

And the cops require a whole other set of issues in terms of self-presentation. There are more gender things going on there, too. I am keenly aware of walking a fine line [between] being professional, but approachable enough to socialize with. Then there's the issue of being somewhat feminine, but not becoming a potential sexual interest. You can bet I won't be drinking much on those boozing nights out. I'll pick and choose my venues carefully, once I have a better idea of options available. Picnics sound sweet; but I have a feeling this isn't a picnic kind of gang. The guy that's been helping me out most seems to err on the side of being too cautious, which ultimately I appreciate. If possible, I will try to develop a few "big brother"–style relationships. Men suck when you think about it too much. I saw *Bandit Queen* yesterday. Man, oh, man! That was a hard movie to watch.

I'll close here. I'm so glad I have gone ahead with the coppers. I think there will be a lot there. God, it is such a contrast from the garden club. If I had more time, I could go on a bit about Edith's and Judith's comments (over ginger wine) about sexual harassment, experiences of all-male pubs growing up, their continued resentment of Churchill for his resistance to letting Australian troops return to defend Australia! That was a great conversation.

Okay, I am off. I'll look for the package in the mail; thanks. I'll keep you posted on the night shift. I am simultaneously doing interviews during the day. I'm going to try to do a night shift a week, if that doesn't make the commanding officer too nervous (perhaps he won't notice). I'll be able to go into the station at least once a week beyond that. From there, I'll see what else pops up and how disruptive my presence seems to be in the station during the day. Talk to you soon. Hope all is well up there.

Allaine

Afterthoughts

LM: In her e-mail Allaine brought up a pervasive and delicate fieldwork quandary: what has the presentation of self to do with ethics? What does self-respect have to do with respect for those with whom one works? In the course of fieldwork, the ethnographer often becomes a chameleon and tries to be flexible, open-minded, nonjudgmental, accommodating, approachable, and, of course, polite. This is not just an "act" or a "front," and one (usually) tries to be all these things in any social relationship. But in a fieldwork context, one is always aware that the negotiation of the relationship is at least potentially instrumental. People as informants are in a very real sense valuable for what they can teach us. It is obviously unethical to set out to misrepresent oneself or one's project, but in the micropolitical, quotidian engagements that a researcher has with people, there are countless fleeting moments of uncertainty and challenges to the researcher's own subjectivity: should I disagree openly? Should I insist on more privacy? Am I intruding? Should I admit I don't care about the things about which my informants care so deeply? Why do I try to dress "appropriately" for interviews with people? Am I being honest about who I am? What do they think of me? Who am I? What am I? What am I becoming? There is no one formula that can guide one through relationships with people during fieldwork. Ethics is always at play in the presentation of self, in multiple directions. That is, the ethnographer's relationship with an informant is not authored or defined by the ethnographer alone. Informants, too, continually observe and learn things about the ethnographer as a social being, a person—and decide how they want the relationship to develop, or not.

LM: "Mercenary researcher" or "fellow human being": It is interesting that we so often think of research as mercenary, of knowledge production as something that requires apologies, discretion, dissimulation. But a person is a person, no matter how much a researcher. And knowledge production is not necessarily an unethical, violent, or colonizing enterprise, any more than it is an intrinsically useful or virtuous practice of Enlightenment ideals (knowledge for the sake of knowledge). The question is what one does with research material, and why one wants to know. At the same time, it is necessary to be very aware of the extractive and abusive potential of any form of knowledge production. It would be difficult to forget how much knowledge production has been enabled by colonial and imperial domination around the world, and how social disempowerment and marginality can act to make certain social categories especially accessible to research and other interventions, as was mentioned earlier.

AC: Of course, part of "why one wants to know," as Liisa puts it in her Afterthought, is because for many people, ethnographic research is highly connected to the credentialing process, be it qualifying for the Ph.D. or writing a second book that will secure one the rank of full professor. But "wanting to know" or doing ethnographic research is also about answering questions that engage us. And those questions are often deeply personal, as well as theoretical. Therefore, our engagement in fieldwork is often a combination of credentialing ourselves, intellectual journey, personal commitment, and improvised encounter.

Once we relinquish the idea of our informants as "authentic" or "ordinary people" in a way that is *a priori* distinct from the researcher, we are better able to see how our informants also engage in the fieldwork encounter on a number of levels at once and with multiple motivations, just as we do as researchers. While they usually operate out of a desire to be helpful, plenty of our informants may also be motivated by a desire for company, money, intellectual curiosity, a need to feel important, sexual interest, job security, among many, many other possibilities. Realizing multiple (and sometimes even contradictory) motivations does not necessarily mean that our informants are not "truthful" or "authentic" any more than it means that as researchers we are "mercenaries."

Challenging the categories and moral qualities we assign to people in the field and to ourselves as researchers is a necessary extension of thinking about the link between power and knowledge. For ignoring the multiple investments of those in an ethnographic encounter subtly invites us to continue the Enlightenment fantasy that "truth" (authenticity, "real-ness") stands outside of material or emotional investments, as embodied in the romantic ideal of the informant as innocent, authentic, "ordinary" person. And feeling "guilty" about our personal and professional investments in our ethnographic encounters indicates a sense of failure concerning the way our research is embedded in material relations and is informed by personal, as well as intellectual, curiosities. An awareness of the links between power and knowledge is not an invitation to try to escape that link. Rather, it is a challenge to make intellectual decisions and ethical choices that come out of defensible goals (which might include, for example, a desire to write a book, to gain a Ph.D. or to answer ethical research questions).

"Defensible goals" is certainly a slippery category, and I am not in a position to provide an exhaustive list of what those might be. Often ethics are context-specific. But societies (and smaller professional networks like those of academics) engage in on-going discussion about ethics. Such discussions give us as researchers a forum for understanding the ethical merits or problems in our "desire to know" and, hopefully, challenge us at every stage of the knowledge-production process.

AC: I wrote: "fieldwork often travels the same roads as friendship [. . .]." Should one shy away from friendships in the name of "objectivity"? Should one work only with informants whom one considers friends, or whom one likes? My answer to both questions is no. Ethnographic training entails many lessons in "objectivity" and "critical distance." Much of it is useful. But challenges to the ideology of objectivity are perhaps even more useful. As I mention in my essay "Nervous Conditions," Joanne Passaro has remarked about her study of homeless men in New York City, "For most people the essential question was whether by doing fieldwork in the United States I was 'distant enough' to produce adequate ethnographic knowledge. Whether I was 'close enough' was never an issue" (Passaro 1997b, 153).

To: Allaine Cerwonka allaine_cerwonka@politics.muwaye.unimelb.edu.au
From: Liisa Malkki lhmalkki@orion.oac.uci.edu
Date: Fri, March 31, 1995 16:05
Subject: Re: "Nocturnal Admissions"

Hi. It is such a treat to get these reports from you! You're just popping and crackling like fire over there. In case you were still wondering: you are now engaged in honest-to-goodness, Real-and-Authentic-Anthropological-Fieldwork, and you are better prepared for it than many [. . .] anthropology graduate students. That's because you have throughout been very professional about the groundwork, the homework, the self-questioning, the thinking through about tactics and ethics. (You might keep notes on that stuff already, by the way, for a section in the dissertation subtitled "Tactics and Ethics." In anthropology dissertations anyway, there usually also is a section called "Fieldwork Settings [and Methods]" or some such.)

It's a very tricky question, this friendship and fieldwork link. I would not put it as an opposition anymore, though I used to. I realized over time, over many years of keeping in letter contact with my informants, that for them the dissertation and book were a small detail of a human link they had with me. I had some say in it, but so did they. I realized recently that I've known a lot of my informants for a decade already. That's a big chunk of a human life. Not trivial. Ergo, perhaps the informant-researcher relationship is not trivial either. I think some of your misgivings come—very reasonably—from the expectation that the researcher has to remain pure and uncontaminated by too much emotion/subjective stuff. I know I felt that. But that may come from a somewhat positivistic, unexamined expectation that social situations can approximate laboratory situations. And of course they do not. When Dick Hebdige was here giving a talk, he said something that really stayed with me. Fieldwork should be less about this lab-like procedure of [managing] data and informants and more about "caring vigilant testimony" [Hebdige 1993, cited in Malkki 1997, 94ff.]. I thought that was reassuring and useful. You are perhaps in that kind of relationship, as well, with some of the informants, friends, and acquaintances that you were talking about.

But there's no getting around the fact that everything that happens around you is a potential source of inspiration and raw materials for you. You can't even help it, unless you just leave the project! Anyway, you are not being a greedy, heartless, insincere, mercenary person. You have a social location that the people around you know about: you are a researcher and a university student studying things in Australia. Try those things on for size! All this said, you should always back off if you feel it's proper. No good having stuff lodged in your memory that you regret many years later.

I can't even begin to say how exciting and intriguing this police research is to read about! It sounds amazing. (If stuff, themes, observations come up that are not strictly about nationalism, commonwealth, community, etc., best to save it, write it down. Who's to say you'll always be writing about nationalism? Your Australia research will be a rich vein to mine for years to come, for all sorts of stuff.)

More to say, but got to go. Elias is hungry.

Take care,

Liisa

Afterthoughts

AC: The following excerpt from my field notes provides more insight into the ways in which I was trying to work through my ambivalence and sense of ethics involved in a research methodology that overlapped with some of the characteristics of friendship. Rereading this entry, I am also struck by how

I was thrown off balance by the new and unfamiliar patterns of emotional distance and intimacy I experienced as an ethnographer.

From Allaine's Field Notebook
April 26, 1995

My (second) interview today with Mary included a discussion of her marriage (her husband had died several years previously), her family, and, strangely enough, the emotional trauma of sex on her wedding night. Much to my surprise, I found myself embarrassed at discussing sex with someone over eighty years old. I feel a responsibility about what is being taped or recorded in notes—what I am being told as friend, researcher, etc. It is interesting that I am told things that few friends know about my informants' lives. Why? Is it because I am an outsider? It is also interesting that a different person/interviewer might elicit different stories. Do I invite these stories on some level?

I am so tired. I feel like I don't have the emotional space to register/process all this stuff (so many intense conversations!); nor am I completely willing to, because I'm not sure I can deal with the emotions. I fear they might take over, and I have a lot of "work" to do.

I have also been thinking about the level of "friendship" (?) my relationship with garden club members has reached. People do not impose on me yet. For example, Lloyd did not ask me to help when he went to paint his recently purchased beach house "because it would not be right." But such codes of etiquette also keep me at a safe distance. The people here are not indebted to me, while I feel constantly and enormously indebted to them. Connection to Nietzsche—debt as connected to power and memory? Asking for help is an important stage in friendships. I discussed this issue with Lloyd; he was floored at the idea that he might ask me for help and explained that he would not want to impose. Perhaps that played into the dynamics with Margaret. It was unthinkable for her to ask me for any help after her husband's death. But for me, helping would be an indication that others accepted me on some level and could perhaps also even up the imbalance of their always giving to me. It would also "normalize" the relationship more, so I am not just the interviewer/researcher. But perhaps they do not want to let me be something else. I get mixed signals. And perhaps it is that I am younger, and they are used to giving to young people.

There is something mercenary about ethnography. The lines between researcher and friend are blurred, which allows for much more rich information and better understanding because our theoretical insights are informed by the material world. But are informants/interviewees really aware of the way their stories and opinions are always heard within the context of my project? Contextualizing ideas makes the researcher more responsible insofar as their theories/arguments are better informed by ethnographic insights. But are we being completely honest in this situation? Do these people understand that *everything* interests me?

Talking with Mary saddened me today and made me aware of my own vulnerability in these interviews and in fieldwork more broadly. Vulnerable in that they elicit memories and emotions in me that I don't want to have to deal with right now. I feel like the pain and experiences of these people are catching on my clothes like burrs might during a walk through the woods. I marvel at the things I see, hear, touch, and smell as I walk. And when I reach a clearing, I am surprised to find that I have gathered up parts of the woods with me as I went. I don't have the control of the scientist to simply take off my rubber gloves at the end of the experiment and emerge unchanged. But as I reach the other side, I suppose I have also changed the composition of the forest I have passed through, if ever so slightly.

But today I am tired and raw. I am flustered and frustrated by the pieces of lives I feel. I want to lie down, but when I do, all the words and fragments of experiences I have gathered up from people in my field sites are still there.

To: Liisa Malkki lhmalkki@orion.oac.uci.edu

From: Allaine Cerwonka allaine_cerwonka@politics.muwaye.unimelb.edu.au

Date: Wed, April 5, 1995

Subject: Re: re "Nocturnal Admissions"

Hi Liisa,

Thanks for the last e-mail. It was really good to hear your experience with some of the ethical/emotional issues I wrote of last time. I think Margaret must have registered the weird quality of our conversation, as I received a very nice note from her early this week that reassured me that she did not take offense at my call. I suspect it's easier for Margaret to take care of others than to receive it for herself.

The garden club relationships are going very well. People are used to seeing me zipping around the neighborhood streets on my bike. People are starting to invite me out to do things (going on a tour of extinct volcanoes of Victoria next month!) and tell me to drop in for tea when I am in the neighborhood. The relationships are also starting to extend to people's children and grandchildren. They all seem quite aware of and comfortable with the fact that I will be around until November. All [of] this is very satisfying.

The copper scene is still in a nascent stage. The senior person I interviewed before has left, and I have not had an extended conversation about my research with another senior officer since. I have gotten the okay to do interviews and observe from many sources now, but no one seems to want me to tell them how long I will be around. The most senior person (Bates) read a brief description of my project when I wrote him a letter to get special permission to go out in the cars. He had no problem with anything. I'm a bit puzzled that no one seems all that fussed about my being around. I have the same anxiety that I did with the garden club that someone will at some point soon say, "What are you still doing here?" I do think that there hits a point—at least with my project—when people begin to realize that the research takes more time than just a few interviews here and there. I hope that the coppers respond [like] the gardeners and think that it's okay for me to be around for a while. I did not tell the first senior sergeant that it would be many months because I don't think I was aware myself of what I wanted from them. And now that I think about it, it's hard to get people to okay many months of contact without knowing what my presence will be like in the station. But the lack of clear definition makes me uncomfortable during this phase . . . that and the fact that I do not know the people very well yet. Perhaps they assume it will take a while—I did say I wanted to interview a lot of people and observe around the station . . . but I doubt it.

Saturday night went very well. The sergeant told me before we went out that I had only been approved for this night, so I would not be going out again. I doubt that that was a restriction that the outside inspector placed on my research. I think Burns only asked for one night and does not want to have to go through all the trouble to get it approved again. Perhaps he assumes he would be the person I would always want to go out with. Anyway, I will leave the car thing alone for a bit and see what kind of resistance there is, and from whom, around this issue. I made sure people knew I thought it was extremely helpful.

It's funny because both the Senior Sergeant and Arnolds, after feeling more comfortable with me, said that Americans have the reputation for being pushy (so what else is new?), so I feel like I have to avoid filling that stereotype. I am hoping that they said that because they didn't think I belonged to that camp. So, I will be doing observation in the station and one-on-one interviews with people when possible. The station observation is really good because people like to sit around and talk, and they seem to feel comfortable saying what they think about Australia, different immigrant groups, whatever, when others are around. They certainly aren't worried about me thinking they are racist; they just tell it like they see it (or so it seems).

The guys (Burns and Paul V——) on Saturday night kept apologizing that it wasn't busier so I could see more action; but the down times were great! We just cruised the area, and they talked about who hangs out where, what kinds of cars they have, what kinds of jobs they like going to. It was very funny. We actually actively tried to avoid being called to traffic accidents (no, it's not the blood or tragedy, but the paperwork involved that they hate). They love car chases! It's funny that they call the people on the streets that they arrest, "crooks"— it just seems like a kid's word. We had dealings with drunks on the nightclub strips, women calling up complaining about being followed home and harassed, rich people calling up to complain about the party next door, an Aboriginal guy stealing a woman's jacket, a trendy student locked out of her car, cruising the homosexual nightclubs (which led to a conversation about homosexuality—it's bad—lesbians in the police force—which is okay by them—and the increase in Asian homosexuals), going to the various places the cops thought the Aboriginal ("Abo") guy might be, talking with owners of clubs about Aborigines who steal ("Oh, we don't let any of them in here any more; they only make trouble"). The list goes on.

Then there are all sorts of interesting ways these two dealt with constantly being abused and taunted by people on the street as they drove by. My emotions were just all over the place that night—empathizing with the shit the cops take, feeling bad for the way that Aborigines [and gays] get treated by cops, leery of the way women's complaints got brushed aside ("Oh, they were just flirting with those guys at the club and then got mad when they followed them home"—and started banging on the women's windows, I might add).

I really, really hope that I can go back out in the car. It's very exhausting, however. What a weekend. I went into the station during the day. Then went to a dinner party and joined up with the cops on their patrol at 12:30 a.m. We were cruising and hanging at the station on and off until 6:30 a.m. Then I had a garden club get-together that afternoon. I went from a night of eating disgusting greasy food and coffee to quiche and champagne in someone's garden. The most difficult thing right now is getting it all written and recorded.

That said, I'm going to go and see if I can put some time in at the station observing today. Did I mention that the package you sent arrived today? Thanks; I'm looking forward to having a look at [Caldeira's] experience. There are few people to whom I can talk about this stuff at the moment. It's interesting that some of my friends from my last trip to Australia are absolutely disgusted that I would be talking to the police. At least it keeps me from being tempted to talk to them about what I actually learn from the police.

So long for now. I have a feeling this has turned into a mighty long message. Hope all's well there.

Allaine

⚡

To: Allaine Cerwonka allaine_cerwonka@politics.muwaye.unimelb.edu.au
From: Liisa Malkki lhmalkki@orion.oac.uci.edu
Date: Wed, April 5, 1995 14:37
Subject: hi

Hi there. Another interesting communiqué! I'll steal a few moments to reply now. First, very useful for you to know that one social set—the friends—gets disgusted with you for talking to the police. Then you know you've crossed a major social divide. It's a divide those friends can't easily travel, and won't. Same with the cops, of course. Fieldwork is about precisely that kind of socio-spatial travel. Probably best—ethically and otherwise—that you're doing what you're doing: that is, not allowing the cops to become a spectacle at the hands of the other group. (I'll just call them the friends; I mean the people you met last time you were in Australia.) After all, the coppers are your informants. Of course, the friends could be, too. Might be worthwhile to record their impressions and reactions to your cop-work, and then to try to extend that at some later point. Actually, maybe not. It's very good to be focused and rigorous about precisely what social settings you want to explore in depth over a longer time.

Recording things: it is very tiring, but field notes are your most important resource— so, take lots and lots of them. When easy, tape. When possible, write down important comments *verbatim*, because otherwise you can't quote them *verbatim* later. You'll just have to paraphrase. But that's okay, too. Direct quotes are liveliest, and often best evidence.

Also, it's useful to get any kind of documentary evidence or any kinds of "artefacts" broadly defined when opportunity knocks. Do the cops have a library, an open archive? Do they have annual reports? What kinds of documentary accumulation? What public service brochures or such? Remember, you'll also be teaching about this work and giving presentations, and then visuals can be useful to have. Ergo, photos by your informants or by you are useful. Are you taking photos of gardens, plants, interiors, people? (You don't have time for EVERYTHING, of course, but I figure my role is to think of these things in response to your e-mails, and you can take them or leave them.) You can also ask to borrow people's photos, as I think I mentioned, and get reproductions made. Also keep track of ADDRESSES OF ALL INFORMANTS AND THEIR UNCLES!! ANY KIND OF TRACKING INFO FOR FUTURE YEARS (for vol. 2, of course). You never know if or when you'll want to retrace steps.

Re: the lack of definition of your location and status at the station. Not to worry too much, though I think worry is inevitable. The more information and insights you are given, the hungrier and more desperate you get. You don't want to be cut off and closed out before you're done. So, yes, important to tread with care as you're doing. But sometimes, given the way institutions think, the people at the station *don't want* to have to make a formal, official decision about where you fit; it's easier for them and more productive and enabling for you to keep you in limbo, and to keep your role ill defined. Am I being clear? That way they don't have to acknowledge [formally] that there's this weird, out-of-category person hanging about.

As for length of stay: it'll dawn on them, and perhaps by that time they won't care, and you'll be more familiar to them. Anyway, people don't track time so carefully in many instances, [especially] if it doesn't concern them and their time very directly. You can also say (if asked): "My stipend is for X months. Then I have to go back, but I am really worried because I am not sure I will have learned enough about Australia in that short time. There's so much to know, and it's complicated for a foreigner like me to get a sense of the lay of the land . . . and the first months I just spent acclimatizing." That is, you turn around the question from the start and make them marvel at how short your time with them is! Because that it is, in some respects. And then you ask if you could write to them from the States if you've forgotten to ask them something or want more information, or want to send them a draft of a chapter for their comments. Mail contact for me with people in

Tanzania and Burundi was INVALUABLE. It was regular and informative, and letters became the backbone of my [. . .] postscript in the book.

About note-taking: I found it useful—indeed, necessary—to come home after a day of talking with people and to spend hours and hours with field notes—going over and amplifying and filling in anything I might have managed to write in the course of the day, and then, in addition, to write more observations, impressions, memories, to describe the context I was in and also fleeting, highly perishable information like my sense of the mood of a conversation, the atmosphere of a social setting, . . . anything to make it all memorable and retrievable for you. And remember not to censor yourself in note-taking; they're for your eyes only. No one need ever see them. They're your raw materials, your wealth, like I said before. And they'll be the thing that keeps you honest over the months and years that you'll spend working with this material. The mind does funny things to memories; they're very mobile and changeable and vulnerable to tampering.

By the way, to return to an earlier point: if someone at the station gave you permission to do XYZ, write down who, when, where it was, so you can say: "Oh, but Tom already said it would be alright." Being specific helps with credibility.

The extensions of relationships with garden club people sound exhilarating, exciting! How wonderful!

Derrida is having a conversation with Spivak just now at HRI [University of California Humanities Research Institute]. It's Jim's turn to go and hear a talk and mine to watch Elias. I got to hear Judith Butler. Another thing: don't worry about reading theory, "keeping current," or even reading Teresa Caldeira's diss. right now. What you are doing is vastly more valuable and necessary. And I promise you: I'll let you come and peruse my bookshelves when you're back to satisfy yourself that you didn't miss much while gone. Not that I'm so current. (I don't have the money to be so current!)

Elias is needing a change. Talk to you soon again.

Liisa

Afterthoughts

LM: In her e-mail Allaine wrote about friends who were disgusted with her for talking with police. I replied that fieldwork requires and empowers such forms of "socio-spatial travel." In *Anthropological Locations: Boundaries and Grounds of a Field Science* (1997, 5), Gupta and Ferguson usefully refer to this kind of socio-spatial travel as "location-work": "It seems most useful to us to attempt to redefine the fieldwork 'trademark' not with a time-honored commitment to the *local* but with an attentiveness to social, cultural, and political *location* and a willingness to work self-consciously at shifting or realigning our own location while building epistemological and political links with other locations." In insights grown from recent feminist theory, they critique conventional modes of spatializing difference and also the "sites" of ethnographic knowledge production:

> Fieldwork reveals that a self-conscious shifting of social and geographical location can be an extraordinarily valuable methodology for understanding social and cultural life, both through the discovery of phenomena that would otherwise remain invisible and through the acquisition of new perspectives on things we thought we already understood. Fieldwork, in this light, may be understood as a form of motivated and stylized dislocation. Rather than a set of labels that pins down one's identity and perspective, location becomes visible here as an ongoing project. [. . .] We would emphasize, however, that [. . .] shifting location for its own sake has no special virtue. Instead the question of what might be called location work must be connected to the logic of one's larger project and ultimately to one's political practice. Why do we *want* to shift locations? *Who* wants to shift? Why?" (Gupta and Ferguson 1997, 36–37)

To: Allaine Cerwonka allaine_cerwonka@politics.muwaye.unimelb.edu.au
From: Liisa Malkki lhmalkki@orion.oac.uci.edu
Date: Wed, April 5, 1995 14:46
Subject: Re: Sat. night with the coppers

Hi, Allaine.
Did you get my long reply to yours entitled "hi"? I sent it to someone else by accident! Then I tried to redirect it. So let me know. . . . Liisa

To: Allaine Cerwonka allaine_cerwonka@politics.muwaye.unimelb.edu.au
From: Liisa Malkki lhmalkki@orion.oac.uci.edu
Date: Monday, April 24, 1995 at 8:59
Subject: animals

Hi. I was just thinking as I was watching a nature show on Australia and marveling at the classificatory weirdness of animals there that animals might be a really good point of entry in interviews, re: nation-landscape-moral community, etc. If it's troublesome for whites there to claim Australian Aborigines as national ancestors (since they argue back), it's less problematic to appropriate emus and kangaroos as signs of self. Just a detail that might get people talking.

Hope you're doing well,

Liisa

Fax from Allaine Cerwonka in Melbourne, Australia to Mark Pertracca, Doctoral Dissertation Advisor in Irvine, California

Melbourne, Australia
2 May 1995

Hello Mark.

I hope this fax finds you well . . . your carefree, happy-go-lucky self (ha, ha). I trust that teaching is going smoothly and you're stealing some time away from all those requests for recommendations from undergraduates to do some of your own research. J—— S—— tells me that it actually looks like you're going to let his dissertation fly. Your standards are slipping; what are you doing letting that postmodernist/nihilist freak graduate on us?! Just remember how to access this kinder, gentler side of your personality for when my dissertation lands on your doorstep, eh?

I have come in from the "field" to fax you as I received the annual, end-of-the-year call from the department for graduate students to account for their worth. I am going to e-mail Dorie directly and give her a general idea of what I've been doing, when I will come back, and, alas, what I would like for support when I do return to Irvine. I assume that the department does not want anything detailed re: my project—just to know I am doing more than drinking Fosters and watching cricket all day. But I also thought that this was a good time to touch base with you and let you know where I am at in relation to my project. I would be very interested in any comments, questions, or suggestions about my project thus far. Liisa Malkki has been giving me a lot of help over e-mail about the tactics involved in fieldwork and helping me to identify what types of activities are best suited to answering the questions I have set out to address. Over all, I am happy to say, I feel very positive about what I am doing and optimistic that some interesting things will come out of the information I am collecting this year.

Okay, so . . . in my dissertation proposal, you will recall, I talked mainly about the way in which supranational identities play in the construction of national identity. This question interested me, as national identity is thought of as stable and as derivative of elements within a territory (ethnicity, language, shared customs, and so on). Post-structuralists instead argue that identity (national or other) is far from stable but is a result of social narratives and structures. Analysis of this kind has even been done about Australia (cf. Gibson, White [1981], Kapferer

[1998]). I see my looking at supranational influences further chipping away at the naturalizing discourses about nations. My work will illustrate that identity is relational and fluid, but it will also demonstrate the way that national identity is constructed out of relations that are external to its borders.

When I left California, I also had a few other issues about which I was curious (questions that came from reading in the area and from preliminary interviews with Australians in California). One was the role that the senses play in constructing/maintaining imaginary communities (I see this as being potentially an example of Raymond Williams's "structures of feeling" [1977]). I was also interested in how Aboriginal culture is appropriated by non-Aboriginal Australia in attempts to establish national identity. And lastly how social relations intersect with geography. How are social relations organized spatially; how do discursive practices delineate the nation? What groups are constructed outside of the nation (and how) despite living within the geographical borders of Australia?

Fieldwork: I have chosen "Landscape and Identity" as the lens through which I am going to analyze these issues. This was not a random choice but made after being here for two months and noticing the way in which people talked about things indigenous to Australia. These included plant and animal life, the landscape and harsh beauty of the continent, "natural" products of Australia (wine, timber, cheeses, herbs, seafood), Aborigines. On multiple levels of discourse in Australia, things [and people] "natural" to Australia are privileged over imports. It is more than just a "buy Australia" push—quite often discussions about native products get conflated with issues of having pride in Australia, fostering a national identity, etc., without getting linked to the economy and employment. There has been a native garden movement, a culinary push to define the "Australian cuisine," government sponsorship of replanting of bush areas (tearing out "exotic" plants and replacing them with indigenous plants), consumer products made from only local (Australian) ingredients, and so on. I will talk about the way this narrative intersects with my original questions in a moment.

First I must say a word or two about how I am researching these issues. My methodology is ethnography, so I have chosen two social sites where I have been conducting most of my formal interviews and participant observation. However, in addition, I move in many other circles (without conducting formal interviews or maintaining the level of consistency that I do in each of my field sites) that provide me with continual information. I also gather statistical and policy information from government, academic, and news sources. Finally [I] have been talking to and collecting the written work of Australian academics.

My two field sites are an inner-city police station and a garden club. I chose the garden club because I thought that the members would be more attuned to the way indigenous plants intersected with national identity (the native garden movement was one of the bigger areas where these two discourses were entangled). I continued on with this group after testing the waters because of opportunity for continual contact. I have also discovered that their diverse life experiences provide me not only with a spectrum of interesting perspectives, but also insight into the way "indigenous" products in Australia have been privileged in other spheres (medicine and architecture, for instance). This group is middle- to upper-middle-class, predominantly over sixty, and predominantly female. Please remember that ethnography has no hope of being "representative." The power of this methodology is that I am collecting very detailed knowledge about two groups of people and from there will analyze, with authority, the process of identity construction in these two social locations. Nevertheless, I believe, through linking my work to other theoretical and empirical work, I will also be contributing to what we can say more generally about the processes by which national identity is constructed.

The police station proves an interesting contrast in that the members are predominantly male, and many come from lower-middle-class backgrounds, although all would be firmly part of the middle class now as a result of their jobs as police. This location provides a second area for interviews and observation from which to theorize about identity construction. The police, however, are also in [a] unique position to move across many different sections of society. In this way, they have valuable knowledge to share about the social landscape of their Australian city and in particular the climate of social relations between and among groups of diverse ethnicity, class, and sexual orientation. They have knowledge as to which spaces different groups [inhabit] and under what conditions. They also participate in the reproduction of narratives about what is Australian or not and what type of people do what type of things. (Certainly garden club people also propagate narratives about various groups and about being Australian.)

Some Things of Theoretical Interest. I will touch on some of the ideas that have come out of my research thus far.

1. I see the discourse on things indigenous to Australia as a way of naturalizing national identity in Australia. Anderson talks about the way modern nations establish their legitimacy through claims to ancientness (e.g., the English claim they are part of Viking culture and their nationhood evolved into what it is today). Australians are aware of the newness of their nation (1991).

However, the naturalizing discourse suggests that Australia is a unique and valuable place because it produces things of value (wine, cheeses, wildlife, etc.), and it is a land where nature is overwhelming, sometimes in its beauty, sometimes in its cruel harshness. This narrative continues the "Arcadian" dream of Australia being a type of utopia, but it also establishes Australians as a unique breed, formed through endurance and appreciation of this unique natural landscape. Social practices such as the native gardening movement reinforce the notion that the truth about Australian identity lies in its native trees and animal life. The state has endorsed this (and exploited it in choosing to construct the capitol building in

Canberra, for instance) through sponsorship of the "rejuvenation" of bush areas. It also plays on this theme in tourist promotions. Finally, this conception of a natural Australia is compatible with the image that Paul Keating (Prime Minister) lays out for Australia in his insistence that Australia is an independent country with an independent identity (see *The Age*, March 22, 1995). This is an inherently conservative vision about national identity in Australia.

One question that remains open is how this narrative intersects with the multicultural discourse about national identity. I am more aware at this point of how it plays into the political relations between white Australia and Aborigines. This discourse comes at a historical point (the last fifteen years) when Aboriginal groups have been most active in their claims for land rights. Thus, a discourse and practices that establish a "natural" relationship and appreciation between non-Aborigines and the land mass of Australia would serve to undercut Aboriginal claims to be the true (legal and moral) owners of Australia. This narrative also gives legitimacy to those pushing to pass a referendum in Australia making the country a Republic (completely independent from England). The perception that life in Australia creates a unique character challenges the monarchist supporters' argument. It plays down claims that Australia's cultural and legal traditions are derived from the British system.

A final aspect to my thinking about the topic of a naturalizing discourse about Australian identity has to do with the way this discourse produces identity. "Common sense" dictates that national identity reflects the character and perceptions of a group of people. [I argue instead] that the many consumer activities that play upon this theme of the purity and uniqueness of the land in fact construct Australian-ness. The advertisement of products such as Red Earth (body cosmetics), Jacob's Creek wine, and Country Road clothing promotes both the "naturalness" of their products as well as suggests that their products are either more Australian than their competitors' or that using them will situate the buyer in a privileged Australian subject position. Red Earth uses only Australian ingredients and helps one benefit from the natural truths/ingredients of the land, while [in their advertisements] Jacob's Creek wine bottles sit in the foreground of a peaceful, outback scene with the red sun setting on a classic Australian country home. And finally, Country Road sends out magazine-style ad booklets that tell the story of an Australian Christmas or of a weekend in the country, where the clothes are made of natural fibers ("naturally Australian" as their ads claim . . . although given that much of their production and materials come from Asia as well as Asian-manned sweat shops in Australia, it must be the wearing of the clothes that is "naturally Australian").

This is by no means a complete analysis of the semiotic mechanics of these products and advertising. Rather, I am giving brief examples of the way advertising and consumptive practice also serve to delineate what a true Australian life is like at this historical moment (although the ads suggest a timelessness to their image of Australia, of course). Further, these products tap into the narrative about nature/landscape and Australian identity. Thus, these consumer practices combine with other social practices (like gardening and governmental policy) to construct what is a dominant narrative about Australian identity. What I want to stress here is not that I have "unearthed" another narrative about Australian national identity to add to those of which we are already aware. Narratives change. My point is that in analyzing this particular narrative, we learn about an important process involved in identity construction. In particular, we learn about the way various levels of social practice work to produce Australian-ness and that this happens within a narrative that is purporting to describe what is most ancient and natural about Australians.

2. Social Geographies. In both field sites, as well as in other groups, I have been listening with much interest to how people group themselves and others, and how that can be mapped spatially. In describing the physical layout of Melbourne, people tell me a great deal about what are important social categories and about the relations between groups. I see it as productive to question these local categories in order to understand relationships within the nation, as most (if not all) of the categories of people who exist in Melbourne exist in Australia at large. Perhaps there is more tolerance toward Aborigines in Melbourne than in the Northern Territory, for example, and thus what I learn about those relationships here would not be true of a different region. That is not a problem; I am not trying to find out the "truth" about relations between Aborigines and non-Aborigines, but I am interested in being able to say something about the process of identity formation. By examining the social relations between groups in Melbourne, I expect to be able to give insight into how identity is formed relationally, for instance, or how social relations divide up space, often along very different lines than national borders. I want to be able to discuss the way that geographical space in Australia (Melbourne in my examples) is given an identity as a place and reflects the hierarchical power relations among the groups that live within the national borders, as well as between them and groups external to Australia's borders.

Given this end, both the garden club and the police have been very useful in understanding how community is formed from the demarcation of space and through "clusters of interaction" (Gupta and Ferguson 1992). Thus such knowledge is shared through conversations about which neighborhoods have which types of gardens, what kind of people do not garden, grow veggies versus flowers, etc. It also exists in descriptions of why it is desirable to live in one section of the city versus another, or where various types of crime happen, or which areas of the city are changing in character and why. While most people assume their description is a statement of empirical reality or common sense, it usually reveals a perspective on their social world and [gives] insight into the process by which it is made meaningful to them as participants. (Which isn't to suggest that it doesn't reflect empirical reality or common sense on some level.)

One example is the way that "Asians" are talked about. "Asian" is used in very sweeping terms in much of the discourse I have been privy to. It refers primarily to first-generation immigrants, regardless of class or country of origin. Perhaps this shorthand has been possible (without striking most people as erasing many important differences between Asian immigrants) because most of the immigration from Asia has been in the last ten years from [countries poorer] than Australia. Perhaps that is what makes it easy for many Euro-Australians to talk about all Asian-Australians as Asian (implying just off the boat and not a permanent part of Australian life yet), poor, uneducated but appreciative of being in Australia, used to worse conditions in Asia (because they came from warring countries or overpopulated countries and thus can endure several families living in one apartment, or [can] commit violent crimes). This popular perception ignores that there are many immigrants who arrive from Asia (Hong Kong especially) with enough money to allow them to take a place among the middle class, as well as the fact that there is a population of Chinese-Australians who have lived in Australia since the gold rush in the late 1800s.

So, where do Asians fit into the imaging of Australian-ness? The Asian community (there actually are many) is usually called up as an example of the latest group to enter into the multicultural society of Australia. In the narrative of multiculturalism, they are included in Australian-ness, following the immigrant path that the first British and Irish settlers laid and that was then continued by the Italians and Greeks and the Jews. Time after time, the proliferation of Vietnamese restaurants and shops in Victoria St. is used as testimony to the success of multiculturalism. Asians are commended for being hard workers and making their shops succeed, much in the way the Greeks and Italians did in the 1950s.

However, Asians also figure as the Other to what is seen as Australian. They disrupt the Australian way of life and "social evolution" with the choices they make. They do not respect the "quarter and an acre" tradition—buying a house for the immediate family as soon as possible. They defy common sense by living in housing commission flats (gov[ernment] subsidized housing), with many families to a one-bedroom flat, sewing illegally at night for local clothing manufacturers (sources tell me Country Road is one of them, ironically enough). Instead of using their money to move out immediately, they send their children to private schools and buy expensive cars. Furthermore, Asians are assigned responsibility for violent crime, increased drugs in Australia, and gambling addiction.

The truth about these conceptions is not what is of most interest. Rather it is interesting for our purposes that national identity, as I have observed it in my field sites, is experienced through the construction of Asian-ness. However, "Asians" and "Australians" (discursive categories) are not symmetrical opposites in this narrative space, nor does the Otherness of Asians seem to rotate around the axis of race. Thus at this point in my research, I begin to examine how the Otherness of Asians functions for Australian-ness. Is there a consistency in the characteristics denounced as Asian? How do these dynamics configure in (and possibly reflect) Australia's international relationship with Asia? In short, what might be structural factors playing in these discursive practices?

Interestingly, the senses also seem to function in the delineation of community in this example. Sensory experience marks what is Australian (such as the smell of eucalyptus or cut wheat), versus what is non-Australian or foreign. Although it is acceptable to eat in Asian restaurants, my interviews reveal little interest in shopping in their markets. People refer to the odd smells of their herbs and raw food, the clutter, the confusion about how to use the food. I am not seeking to condemn Anglo-Australians for their attitudes. Instead, what I find interesting with this example is how the senses serve to construct the lines of community. Asians are foreign because of the smells they produce, the strange appearance of their foods in their raw form. Thus, Victoria St., the location of both these shops and the popular Vietnamese restaurants, serves [as] an example of how Asian-ness remains exotic in relation to Australian-ness. It is an acceptable place to venture for an exotic, multicultural culinary experience, but contact that would require a more sustained interest in and understanding of Vietnamese culture is, at best, [not] forthcoming.

3. Supranational influences. This is the idea that makes my brain hurt the most at the moment. In some ways, saying that Australia's identity is influenced by external forces is the most obvious and accepted thing one could say about its identity construction. People will tell you that of course it has been influenced by Britain because it was originally a colony. The influence continues because it is part of the Commonwealth, still receives English and Irish immigrants, and has a culture that was formed by immigrants that came solely from the U.K. People will also say that Australia is a multicultural society, so it is simultaneously unique and is a mixture of influences brought [by] immigrants that have come from all over the world.

But there's something that strikes me as static in all of this. Multiculturalism, to my mind, doesn't get at the volatility [. . .] of national identity. It suggests that all the parts blend into this Australian whole. I think it also suggests that all the parts make up a whole whose boundaries coincide perfectly with the national borders of Australia. It doesn't take into account the way that media, communication, and transportation technologies, plus the vast increase [in the] mobility of people in terms of tourism, refugees, immigration, guest workers, and international business have created a transnational public sphere that can't help but change the way local and national communities are constructed. Australian identity cannot help but be influenced by these global changes and in ways different from the colonial and melting-pot models that are offered up so readily.

I have some things in mind in relation to this, but I think I would rather wait and discuss them with you when I have some clear examples from fieldwork for you. I think one thing that makes this issue a headache is that it is difficult to see things in a different way when there is a strong, popular explanation about it. But, yes, I am also keeping myself open to the possibility that I am just dead wrong about this supranational thing. Time will tell.

So . . . this has been much more in depth than I had planned but it's hard to limit what I have to say. There is plenty I left out, if you can believe. Comment if you feel inclined. If I have left you speechless, perhaps you can just let me know what was said about me in the faculty meeting (I realize that might not happen for a month or so). I hope this description has not made you worry.

I really think it will be okay.

Allaine

Fax from Mark in Irvine, CA
to Allaine in Melbourne, Australia

DEPARTMENT OF POLITICS AND SOCIETY

SCHOOL OF SOCIAL SCIENCES

IRVINE, CALIFORNIA 92717

May 13, 1995

Ms. Allaine Cerwonka

c/o Dept. of Political Science

University of Melbourne

Parkville, Victoria

Australia

FAX 61-3-9344-7906

Dear Allaine:

Thank you for your long and informative letter. My apologies for not getting back to you sooner. There's so much work here to be done, I rarely have any time these days to spend with my family, never mind locate a microscope to read your letter. Anyway, here's a brief response to a range of points made in your letter of 2 May.

1. Liisa Malkki is very impressed with the work you are doing and has told me so on more than one occasion. Thank goodness there's someone who can really help you. It seems you are becoming a real anthropologist—great, I'm sure there are even more jobs for anthropologists than there are for political scientists in

American universities (ha-ha). Seriously, though, Liisa is very pleased with your progress, and therefore I am relieved.

2. You should be in very good shape for a departmental allocation of TA support. I will make that point to S——— in writing. There's always the possibility of some problem or issue being raised; but I'd be guardedly optimistic about the prospects of getting another year of support out of the department. We've yet to have the department meeting on this subject—it's always best to make everyone as miserable as possible first!

To the research.

3. I wonder how amenable the process of identity construction—as you have defined it   is to general theorizing. Is it so case-specific and contextual that generalizations cannot be made across cases? You've not said quite this, but I wonder about it from what you did write.

4. It would seem the Aussies are intent on "going native." But what does "native" really mean in a country dominated by immigrants?

Isn't a garden club a rather "elite" (if pleasant) site for doing this kind of "ground-level" research? I would have thought a corner tavern more appropriate. Perhaps these are the "informal" sites you mention but do not explicate. What are the socioeconomic characteristics of the garden club women you are studying? I hate to sound too Marxist—especially to a post-structuralist—but might not their class (leisure) have something to do [with] the freedom they have to worry about native plants?

5. One problem with the garden club vs. the police station site selection is that class overlaps with gender as a key variable. The police station is filled with men, lower- to middle-class; and the garden club with women, probably from middle to upper classes (and old to boot).

6. You can't use the police as a lens [through] which to view the rest of Australian society. That would make no sense in the context of your methodology. All you can presumably do, given this ethnographic approach, is analyze *how* they see/view Australian society—not what they see. To put this a different way, the police are not (and cannot be) research assistants or research surrogates. Make sure to read the book by John and Jean Comaroff on Africa in this regard.

7. What does it mean to "naturalize" national identity? This means, contrary to Schlesinger's view of America, that Australia is a place, not a people. Australianness constitutes a connection to place, not to an idea (compared to Schlesinger's [1992] notion of Americanism as an idea).

8. Advertising can create as well as respond to demands. How do you know Red Earth isn't creating a demand for natural, native products, rather than responding to a discourse about the naturalness of Australian identity?

9. What is "the important process involved in identity construction"? The use of mass media to sell commercially produced products for profit? Is this identity construction (here comes Marx again) the creation of a false consciousness about what it means to be Australian? (i.e., "real" Australians use Red Earth, drink Jacob's Creek, and wear Country Road.) Sounds like capitalism investing itself in the process of identity creation—the question is this: does it work? (How are sales?)

10. Your observation about the construction of community invokes a wide-ranging political and philosophical literature (beyond the anthropological stuff) about which you should be aware.

11. Without Asians as a point of comparison, there might not be Australian-ness? Having an "other" is very convenient that way—especially since Aussies might not want to [see] Aborigines as others because of an obsession with place and past.

12. What is the Australian "whole?" Again, per Schlesinger, is it a place or an ideal?

Thank you for taking the time to write such a long and truly informative letter. Sometimes writing a letter is a good form of therapy and a way to get important ideas down on paper (without being on paper). At some point we need to have a "what are you going to do on the job market" conversation, but that can probably wait until your return.

J—— S—— defends his dissertation [this] Wednesday. All should go well.

Best regards,
Mark P. Petracca
Associate Professor

Afterthoughts

AC: There are a lot of aspects of fieldwork that foster "nervous conditions" for the researcher. There is a lot of anxiety and insecurity that runs through my correspondence with Liisa, especially in the first months of fieldwork in Australia. And it is clear that although there is much goodwill between Liisa and myself, even a form of friendship, there is a hierarchy of authority in my fieldwork that exists between us. It is instructive to think about what creates the nervous conditions that are reflected in my e-mails. My anxiety was not generated by the prospect of making my way in the foreign country of Australia or making friends, for instance, since I had already lived for a year's time in Australia at a previous point in my life. And although my respect for Liisa as a scholar and person was firmly established in the early days of our working relationship, my anxiety was more complicated than simply a case of wanting to please Liisa.

Much of my anxiety was a product of the fact that I was trying to make sure my choices and fieldwork fit with anthropology. In this way, much of my conversation with Liisa was a conversation with a discipline—its expectations, mores, assumptions, etc. And of course my situation was further complicated by the fact that I was not an anthropologist and therefore did not have the benefit of the informal socialization that students experience in graduate anthropology programs. In fact, I was a guest worker or refugee, depending on one's perspective, in anthropology. And as is evident in the exchange of faxes between my political science advisor, Mark Petracca, and me, I was in fact having a correspondence with two disciplines and trying to reconcile their different assumptions and cultures within my research project.

On her part, Liisa was training me in the practices of a discipline (anthropology) that she herself was challenging in certain ways. In her essay "Tradition and Improvisation in Ethnographic Field Research," Liisa discusses the shared interest we had in interdisciplinary work. And while she certainly facilitated my desire to do interdisciplinary research by helping me undertake an ethnographic study for a political science dissertation, she also found herself weighing up her responsibility toward me as a mentor. She notes that she was concerned not to make me an "experimental doll" for her interest in interdisciplinarity, for fear that I might incur costs in my home discipline or find it especially difficult to find an academic job. In this regard, the correspondence between myself and the various academics advising me (Liisa, Mark, and John Cash) captures some of the ways mentoring relationships are overdetermined by the institutional frameworks a faculty member represents and those into which the student is being initiated. And our exchanges point to the way these dynamics are at times a part of what is being negotiated and a part of what is at stake in conversations about fieldwork decisions.

To: Liisa Malkki lhmalkki@orion.oac.uci.edu
From: Allaine Cerwonka allaine_cerwonka@politics.muwaye.unimelb.edu.au
Date: Thursday, May 18, 1995
Subject: update

Hello Liisa.

It's been a while. How is it all going over there? It's spring semester in Irvine, and it's frightening to think that I will be back for fall semester. So little time!

I want to touch base on where I am and bounce a few ideas off of you as to what I want to do at this point. I have been in touch with Mark Petracca, by the way, to give him an update on my work. Parts of it mystify him, no doubt, but I think he is comforted by the fact that you think it is under control. Thanks for telling him as much when you have seen him. He's given me some feedback in writing that helps me in anticipating how others in political science might respond to various parts of it.

I have also been talking with [political scientist] John Cash about where to take my fieldwork next. So some of what I have in mind comes out of that conversation as well. It's hard to pinpoint exactly why, but I feel like I am at a point where I need to take a look at the big picture again. So, how to structure the information to follow? Bear with me.

1. Gave John Cash the description I wrote for [Mark] Petracca. He thought that my fieldwork was leading my theory. I was pulling in theory as I needed it to support what was coming out of my interviews. He suggested I position the work in a framework better. In my dissertation I should have:

1. A chapter on political science explanations of nationalism and my response to that body of work coming from a more postmodernist/post-structuralist position. This could be dropped in publishing, and the base of it might be salvaged from the literature review I did on nationalism before advancing.

2. A chapter planning out the general approach I am taking (and methodology). He suggests that sketching this and the next chapter out now might help me in thinking about what is going on for me in my fieldwork at the present time.

3. A chapter that provides a global sketch of the principal discursive form in the construction of national identity in Australia. This would include class, supranational agents, gender, race, multiculturalism, environmentalism-nativism. Also, in this, state that structural changes in Australia (like fuller entrance into the world economy, changes in foreign relations with Asian nations, flooding of the dollar, changes in tariff structure) have given rise to fresh attempts to define what it means to be Australian. Finally, lay out that by analyzing the discourse of environmentalism-nativism, [I am identifying] a relatively new imagining of Australian-ness. We can see some of the mechanisms involved in the production of national identity in general and get insight into the conditions under which Australia is imagined by various groups.

Allaine

Afterthoughts

AC: My two political science mentors, Mark Petracca in California and John Cash in Australia, each provided comments on my project midway through my field research. Their concerns about the relationship of my ethnographic material to my theoretical arguments illustrate some of the interdisciplinary differences that the correspondence reveals.

In his faxed response, Mark raised concerns about generalizability in my empirical research. He wrote, "I wonder how amenable the process of identity construction—as you have defined it—is to general theorizing. Is it so case-specific and contextual that generalizations cannot be made across cases?" He further inquired, "Isn't a garden club a rather 'elite' (if pleasant) site for doing this kind of 'ground-level' research. I would have thought a corner tavern more appropriate. . . . What are the socioeconomic characteristics of the garden club women you are studying? I hate to sound like a Marxist— especially to a post-structuralist—but might not their class (leisure) have something to do [with] the freedom they have to worry about native plants?" (see fax preceding e-mail May 18, 1995).

Mark's questions reflect the dominant expectation within political science for generalizability in empirical research. He correctly identifies some of the attributes that would make it impossible to generalize from a garden club— the club members' gender, class and love of plants all rendered this group distinct, rather than representative of the "common Australian." When Mark suggests I might have more productively used a corner tavern as my field site, he also refers indirectly to anthropology's tradition of studying marginalized rather than privileged people in pleasant surroundings. From the supportive tone in his letter, it is clear that Mark raises these questions in a generous spirit to prompt me to identify how it is that I can make compelling knowledge claims based on my research. What can I claim to know about Australia and national identity on the basis of a year spent among two very particular groups—gardeners and police? As the correspondence documents, Mark raises questions that I grappled with myself in the first phase of my fieldwork.

The empirical tradition within political science (survey methods and statistical analyses) emphasizes generalizability. In the context of this epistemic paradigm, the gulf between the specifics of a field site ("sample") and the expected universalism of theory can only be bridged if the members of one's field sites are representative of the larger population or, at least, of an important subsection of it (working-class people, women, Aboriginal Australians). Of course ethnographic studies cannot be generalized to the larger population. Rather, they do more than simply provide detailed (thick) description of a particular context in so far as they develop theoretical insights from the empirical material in relation to existing theories and other studies.

However, my Australian mentor, John Cash, raised other important questions about how one uses theory. The contrast between the ethnographic approach I was taking and John's expectations as a social theorist (trained in political science) provides another glimpse into what is particular about ethnographic knowledge production in so far as fieldwork *does* lead theory and is supposed to do so. In an e-mail message to Liisa, I recount John's concern. I write, "He thought that my fieldwork was leading my theory. I was pulling in theory as I needed it to support what was coming out of my interviews. He suggested I position the work in a framework better" (May 18, 1995). In a sincere effort to help me, John recommended I use theory as a framework through which I could interpret the ethnographic evidence from my field sites. In contrast, ethnographic knowledge production draws on theory to interpret cultural phenomena as they are encountered. The ethnographic material is the basis for constructing new theoretical insights, as well as for generating deep empirical knowledge about a particular context at a moment in time. Paul Willis describes this distinct approach to theory as "principledly eclectic," explaining,

> My own view is that ethnographers should have a healthy independence [from theory]. I'm not against any of the theories actually. I've learned a great deal from all of the theoretical revolutions at the Centre, and I learn a great deal from the incredible range of Bourdieu's work now. . . . The problem is if you're, for example, just a Bourdieu disciple before the fact of fieldwork, it's even *harder* to do creative fieldwork; you would be using a Bourdieuan system and looking for exemplifications and illustrations. . . . The commitment of the ethnographer should in some way be to his/her topic and set of small "p" politics and priorities. Being principledly eclectic, rather than putting all their eggs in one basket. . . . You should only use a theory if it creates illumination, casts light on things, helps you present a phenomenon more fully *in itself*. (quoted in Mills and Gibb 2001, 411–12)

The correspondence as a whole documents a process at the heart of ethnographic knowledge production—"pulling in theory as I need it to support what was coming out of my interviews"—that challenges the conceptualization of theory as a "framework" to interpret what we see in society and to generalize from it. It also reveals how interdisciplinary research might appear as incomprehensible or dangerous from the perspective of a single discipline because it deviates from discipline-specific epistemological assumptions and methodological orthodoxies. Given that my dissertation project has been validated by several outside sources (a political science award and a book contract), we can reasonably assume that the anxiety of my mentors was not prompted by poor quality in my work. Their concern and my own "nervous condition" during the fieldwork might instead be read more structurally— as a sign of the epistemic borders I was crossing with my interdisciplinary project, thereby challenging discipline-specific ideas about theory and its relationship to empirical materials. In this way, it also reveals subtle but important differences between knowledge production in ethnography and in other disciplines.

To: Liisa Malkki lhmalkki@orion.oac.uci.edu
From: Allaine Cerwonka allaine_cerwonka@politics.umwaye.unimelb.edu.au
Date: Monday, May 22, 1995
Subject: Re: greetings

Hi,

I'm still here, soaking and poking, although I must admit that I try to be selective about the things I actually poke. Shit, I only have about four more months here. I feel like things are always moving and that I have a lot of ideas about where I am taking my research. But I also have this uneasy feeling that there are so many little details that are not worked out. And there are so many things I would still need to get through fieldwork before I could say anything definitively. But I have not got the whole picture put together yet, and by the time I do, I'll be many miles away from here.

Things with the garden club and with the cops are going well. I have seen a little less of the garden club people because I have been putting in quite a bit of time with the cops. But I see them both and continue interviews. With the garden club, I have been visiting and getting involved with the delivery of notices. (They hand-deliver to mail boxes thirteen hundred notices a month, and approximately thirty people come to each meeting! And they cut out and paste a picture of a flower on each notice!) [I have also been] going for little day trips with a few members. There are about five people I have in mind to interview at the moment, and I am planning on sending out a call for more volunteers at the next meeting. I got a little burnt out on those interviews for a while. I felt like I was asking the same questions and getting the same responses. I feel like I have some new ideas again for this group, fortunately.

I am pleased with the way things have shaped up with the cops. I still leave each stint at the station (usually three to four hours) with cramps in my stomach from nerves. I don't think I will ever feel especially comfortable in that social setting, but I think I have become more normal to them. People say to me less often, "Wow, you're still around!" (Always makes me feel good, that comment.) I have been observing in the Watch House, which is the main information center and socializing center of the station. That gave me a good feel for a lot of people and for the social logic of the place more generally. Last week I started interviewing people more systematically. It works well because the sergeant just keeps pulling people who are in less vital duties off to the side for me to interview for half an hour (which usually turns into forty-five minutes). I get a lot done each time I am there.

We have yet another commanding officer there who is working with the understanding that I have been okayed to do just about whatever I say I want to do. He's also someone I can relate to a little better, so it's easier for me to ask him for things. Consequently, we have sent out a new request to let me go out in the patrol units at his discretion. If that's okayed, then I'll be back on the streets! I would go out with sergeants because they have the cars (rather than the van which can only take people in the cage in the back, which is reserved for crooks). Sergeants just go to the cases that are more complicated. That has benefits in that I will see [fewer] car accidents, but also disadvantages in that there is less down time and cruising around aimlessly. I'll see how it goes if I am reapproved and take it from there.

I think doing the formal interviews is helping the people in the station feel comfortable with me. I act like a researcher with my recorder [and ask] questions straight out about Australia and political issues. They don't even seem to mind when I drift and ask them questions about their taste in music or whether they garden (which a good many do!).

I made an embarrassing little *faux pas* when having a casual conversation with one of the sergeants. I was asking him about the process of administering the crooks once they arrive at the station. He told me about charging them, etc., to which I replied, "Oh, I see. And then is it at that point that you take them down to the interrogation room?" He stared at me blankly and then broke out in a laugh saying, "Well, we prefer to call it the interview room. This isn't South America yet!" Freudian slip, I suppose. But it was that very same sergeant that was concerned to convince me several weeks later that I did not hear a woman's scream coming from the back of the station. I don't think the police are bashing people up in the back of the station, but I have gleaned a few tidbits here and there about unofficial practices that are a little depressing. It's funny what people will tell you if you sit around long enough.

Now about where I want to take my fieldwork at this point.

Oh, by the way, how are you? Listen to me. Me, me , me. That's all I can think about. Thanks for the gardening book cutout you sent me. It reached my mailbox this morning. Kristen Maher told me you were very helpful when she went in to chat with you about cognitive mapping some time back. I'm glad she's further enthused about the topic, as it will give me another person to talk with about these issues when I return to Irvine and am tearing my hair out trying to work all this stuff out. Summer is around the corner for you. I envy you; it's starting to get rather damp and dismal around here. I hear that Deborah Mindry had her baby. Wow. I can't believe that three quarters of the women I know at Irvine are having babies! And you're all so damned happy about it. I won't recognize the place. Living with my architect friend, Jim, is quite nice, but no babies for quite some time. He's quitting his part-time architecture job here (mainly because it always requires full-time hours) and is just going to devote himself to his MA work for the rest of the year. I can't image what this year would have been like without him here. He's gotten used to my incredible highs and lows of this year, I think, and has been such an incredible support throughout.

Now, about my fieldwork. I spoke with John Cash recently. He suggested that I do some interviews in a third location. He suggested a group that is involved with some creative enterprise, perhaps, which might involve coming up with an Australian form of their work, but a group that would be tied in with international trends/communities. He suggested people who are part of a local film-making program here in Melbourne, or perhaps architects. I think it could be good to interview some architects because, yes, these issues of internationalism and Australian design are certainly alive in that community. But in addition, I think they would be people that would also be sensitive to their experience of their environment and might give me some more information about postmodern geographies in Australia. I thought I could [interview] some landscape as well as regular architects. They are a better group for me because Jim already has a list of local ones from his job-hunting days, and I have a sense (because of him) of where this community meets, etc. But, he is not involved in the community outside of working for one of the companies, so my interactions with people would not have to be mediated by him.

Time is an issue, of course. I thought that I could limit my garden club interactions a little, as there is already a structure in place for me to access them. I can continue to see them all at the monthly meetings and plan to venture into the neighborhood once a week. I could drop in for coffee or have a formal interview with two to three people on that day. Then the rest of the time could be divided between the cops and architects. What do you think? I think this group could also give me insight into the extent to which business has moved into Asian markets and what types of attitudes exist about such things.

My guess is that my interactions might be more formal with this group: interviews and attending talks, functions, etc. I don't think observation of an office is very realistic. I would like to move on this fairly soon, but would like to hear whether you think it would be a mistake or not. So drop me a line and tell me what you think.

On that note, I am going to close and head off. I'm back in the "interrogation room" interviewing the coppers tomorrow. I went on a day tour with some of the garden club people last week. It was on "extinct volcanoes of Victoria." They are very extinct (six million years old). But we had a nice day (the museum sponsored it), and did a lot of climbing and "bush walking." Hope all is well on your end. Nice to be back in touch.

Allaine

Afterthoughts

LM: Allaine uses the phrase "soaking and poking," an expression for ethnographic methods coined by political scientist Richard Fenno in his study of the House of Representatives (see Fenno 1978). This expression became a shared joke between Mark, Allaine, and myself following Allaine's comprehensive exams, when Mark introduced us to the phrase. The image of soaking and poking is ambivalently humorous because it parallels the term, *participant observation.* It captures something of the old and now outmoded ethnographic ideal of "total immersion" in the research context. At the same time, I think that the joke was an expression of what in anthropological theory is termed a "joking relationship"—a potentially tense, conflictual, social relationship that is eased through joking. (In classic ethnographies, a joking relationship often exists between people who are socially proximate and yet might have to observe ritual avoidances. Or the joking relationship is an alternative to ritual avoidance.) In our case, the tension came from the challenges of methodological and theoretical translation between the intellectual traditions of political science and anthropology—and from both Mark's and my worries concerning Allaine's vulnerable interdisciplinarity.

To: Liisa Malkki lhmalkki@orion.oac.uci.edu
From: Allaine Cerwonka allaine_cerwonka@politics.muwaye.unimelb.edu.au
Date: Wed, May 24, 1995
Subject: Another thought

Me again.

I have been thinking, as always, about the structure of all this madness, dissertation stuff. I think I'm in a bit of a manic phase again, I must warn you. But hopefully it's just too much caffeine.

Could it be that social geography is the key concept around which this all comes together? (In my mind there have been a lot of different theoretical themes this could be organized around, but I am beginning to be especially partial to geography.) I can now see one way that the senses fits into postmodern geographies. I was reading some more of Soja last night and thinking about some of the information I need to collect about what happens in various parts of the city. Some of this I get through interviews, but in the other stuff, like manufacturing or housing statistics, I need to flesh out the picture. I was then reading through a local architectural theory magazine where Paul Carter was talking about "soundscapes" and a new museum project that he has organized that incorporates the sounds of history. This was good because he talks about sound needing to represent simultaneity and not just [take the form of] these kitsch historical (individualized) personal narratives that museums sometimes use. Anyway, that made me think more about how the senses fit into the construction of place. I think that in collecting geographical information about Melbourne, as a way of understanding the social construction of space, I need to think about how sensory details also shape space.

For instance, when I was talking to Judith, the garden club secretary, about delivering leaflets to the next suburb over, she explained how a road that has been expanded in the last five years, Hoddle Street, acts as a divide between the two communities and keeps people from coming into East Melbourne (although they still deliver the leaflets). And as you walk in the area, the noise is so loud that it repels you and causes you to go in one direction or the other (Richmond or East Melbourne).

I would think that things like a predominance of one language versus another in a given area might shape the area (like the dominance of Vietnamese on Victoria Street). I also recall a newspaper article talking about the Western suburbs and the smell of a chemical leak. One woman was quoted in the newspaper article because she lodged a complaint about the bad smell. She said that initially her complaint met with resistance by people who believed that bad smells (chemical and other) were natural to the Western suburbs. (The Western suburbs have traditionally contained working-class communities as well as industry.) Yet, it turned out to be quite a dangerous chemical leak.

I don't want to get bogged down in examples, but hope that these few give you a sense [...] of what I mean. Perhaps you have seen how the senses could fit into postmodern geography before, but the light just went on over my head. I am not sure what will come out of taking note of this other dimension of space as I piece together the city, but it can't hurt. We have emotional responses to sensory impressions, which sometimes show up in interviews, but there are a lot of objective sensory divisions out there that I think would be legitimate for me to describe, as one might [describe] what type of industry or transportation shapes a space. I think the presence of languages and smells might be one way in which the supralocal exists within/shapes the local; I have my eyes open for others. It's difficult to access people's sensory experience of place in interviews. When it happens, usually it's serendipity.

I still think that architects would help with all of this, as they often have to take into account the feel of a place when they are constructing an addition [to a building]. Furthermore, they might have a sense of what type of new housing is going up in different places around the city and who it is targeted for.

Well, I am going to spin off this screen. That's it! No more caffeine for a while! Two nights ago, I woke up and realized that as I had been sleeping, the word *Landscape* was just floating across a scene of a rural landscape in my head. I hate it (and love it, of course) when I can't shut my head off.

One more thing. I am not sure in all of this [...] how [...] discourses about the land and indigenous products [...] and the supranational environmental movement link to [...] Melbourne spatial politics. Oh, I read a while back the article by Ulf Hannerz [regarding] how modernism has shaped Swedish national identity, and that was useful for my thinking about the environmental movement and Australia. (It was in *Cultural Studies* a while back [Hannerz and Lofgren 1994].) Also, there's interesting stuff written about Canada that I find useful in relation to the environmental stuff (Alexander Wilson's *The Culture of Nature* [1992] was useful, too). As you can see, I haven't given up reading entirely. I can't. I think I started a little behind the eight ball in terms of reading in all these areas when I started my fieldwork anyway, but I also find that it helps me continually fine-tune what I am looking at and how I should approach it all. Otherwise, I find that I get lost in the details of the interviews and can't find the big picture as easily.

So, that's that for the moment. I hope I haven't overwhelmed you with information at this point, mainly because I suspect that I'll be lobbing more your way before too long. I hope you're well and your own projects are coming along. Will you be in Irvine this summer, or will you use this as a chance to get away for a while? Talk to you soon.

Allaine

Afterthoughts

LM: About reading. Anthropology graduate students are often told not to worry about "reading theory" during fieldwork. I have given this advice often enough myself, faithfully, just as I received it years ago. (Moreover, I have never met an anthropologist whom I know to have carried a fieldwork manual into the field.) This conventionalized distinction between "field-work" and "reading" might benefit from critical questioning. Once, at a reception, shortly before leaving for Tanzania, I asked a professor of mine what I should do about "methods" in the field, as my training in that di-rection had been altogether light. Swirling around his dark red wine and smiling absently, knowingly, he replied: "Hmmm . . . you may wish to take the corpus of Dostoyevsky with you." As it was impossible to admit that I failed to make the connection, I still don't know what he wanted to tell me. Did he mean: "It's not a matter of taking a manual or how-to book with you; you will learn as you go"? Did he mean: "If you are imaginative, you will know what you have to do"? Or did he mean that fieldwork is like a spiritual, moral journey of ethical challenges, a test of character? (cf. Hayes and Hayes, "The Anthropologist as Hero" 1974). It certainly is a test of character, but so too is any enduring commitment to serious work, in any circumstances.

Looking back on the conversation, I see something more. Perhaps neither he nor I noticed at the time that built into our exchange was the primitivist assumption that fieldwork is a matter of going "far away" to a place alto-gether "different" from the world of universities, intellectuals, well-stocked libraries, and archives. I was preparing to live in Mishamo refugee camp in the sparsely inhabited Rukwa Region of Western Tanzania. My professor had done fieldwork in a much more classically "remote" place. His book from that work was one of the first ethnographic monographs I ever read as an undergraduate, right after Evans-Pritchard's *The Nuer*, about people in the Sudan. Neither of us, as far as I know, had fieldwork experience in cities, or in the wealthy countries of Europe or North America. I was going to a refugee camp with no universities or libraries, although I did meet numerous intel-lectuals there. Some anthropologists do continue to work in places without universities, or regular electricity, or running water, or public transportation. But growing numbers of anthropologists work in urban environments, whether in their own societies or elsewhere. Many in the latter category find occasion, at one time or another, to feel inadequate or to have to explain why they do not work in "remote" (read: exotic, primitive, colorful) places. If there is a default mode of anthropological knowledge production, it might be the expectation that fieldwork involves traveling "far away" to a very "different" place where knowledge comes in "raw" form from persons ("informants"), not from "cooked" theoretical texts. If one is going to work in a place where books and other like materials are not readily available, then it is, of course, sensible to think about what reading to pack along, and one might equally well decide not to worry about "keeping current." If, on the other hand, one is planning fieldwork in a place where libraries have the funds to exist, that is a happy circumstance. But why should it follow that the peoples without libraries and universities are more "real" or "authoritative" sources of anthropological knowledge than those in wealthier or more urban contexts? The most important point, however, is this: whether or not one "reads theory" in the course of fieldwork does nothing to alter the fact that ethnographic field research is always already a form of critical theoretical practice.

AC: Although Liisa wisely cautions me about being too anxious about keeping up with the latest publications, it was advice that I did not follow. This passage illustrates nicely the usefulness of engaging with theory specific to one's project throughout fieldwork, a luxury possible in urban fieldwork. And it shows the process of tacking analytically between the details encountered in my field sites and the theoretical ideas I sought out through reading. While we read and write extensively about our topics before commencing the fieldwork, our topics often shift in ways we could not have anticipated at the outset. Continuing to engage with theory and other scholarly writings during the research process helped me to make sense of the new direction and better enabled me to take full advantage of the opportunities my field site offered.

To: Allaine Cerwonka allaine_cerwonka@politics.muwaye.unimelb.edu.au
From: Liisa Malkki lhmalkki@orion.oac.uci.edu
Date: Thursday, May 25, 1995 at 7:28:34 pm
Subject: Re: another thought

Allaine,

Thanks for your two messages. Miscellaneous notes follow.

I really liked your note that cops are sometimes gardeners, too. Maybe you should talk more with them about that; that is, you're right in not trying to construct a fiction that these are totally unconnected social worlds.

I think I mentioned Cosgrove and Daniels, *The Iconography of Landscape* [1988]. You might have written about it already. I'm not sure. Just a resource, as might the anthropologist Jack Goody's book on flowers be. I hope to get it from the library soon, as I haven't read it. Goody is very creative and intelligent in his older work, so perhaps this will be good also.

If the architects present themselves as a useful or necessary third research site, perhaps you should follow up on it. But, I can't help myself, I have to give advice! It's important not to let the third site become something that allows you to escape the pressures of the sites in which you have deep investments already. That is, if there's still work to do, angles to explore with the first two sites, then the third should not eat away the time and energy you'll need to complete everything. This said, if it promises to be interesting and productive to pursue the architects, I'd go with it. Another related issue (related to the question of what's the best use of your time): sometimes downtime is best, taking a week away from the fieldwork. Then you return to things fresh.

You said you were feeling manic now. Chances are you'll also be taxed by the mere reality of returning to the U.S. and to U.C.I., too. The shock of familiarity: maybe it's a kind of culture shock. What I wanted to mention is this: in anthropology programs, a period of post-fieldwork adjustment is expected, and people are left to collect themselves for a while. In political science, there is no institutional tradition of ethnographic fieldwork. Therefore, your advisor and committee might not be aware of the magnitude of things you are going through. This is just an aspect of different regimes of knowledge and different institutional histories. [. . .]

It might also be hard to talk about your "findings" right away when you come back because all that will only really materialize when you are in the thick of writing. My answer for the longest time was, "Umm . . . " It is hard also to try to introduce these complicated, embarrassingly concrete, often subtle and fragile, webs of knowledge and memory into a disciplinary setting in which the language of scholarship is different. But (more advice, damn it!) you should not allow yourself to be made to doubt your material, nor should you ever belittle your fieldwork or writing, in jest or otherwise. The belittling tends eventually to get under one's own skin. Now, I should be clear about this. I am not anticipating any problems, nor do I really know any of the people you are working with. I assume they would be supportive and nurturing. My only concern is the translation problem. You have done ethnographic fieldwork, in a way, been an anthropologist, for the past year, and you are in political science, and are likely to have a life-adjustment period when you come back. I hope this is not too confusing.

Yes, it's a good idea ([even] necessary) to collect as much documentary evidence as you can while you are there, "on site," as it were.

Postmodern geographies and the senses is an excellent connection, and not at all as obvious as you seemed to think.

I just saw Ian Chambers has published some articles on topics that might be interesting to you. One of them [is] in the *Australian Journal of Cultural Studies* [1985]. Critical theory is trying to get him to come here for a while. Lyotard left U.C.I. for Emory, so the Humanities have extra money to bring in someone else. Also, there's a new *Journal of Material Culture* being started by James Clifford and others. Might be useful for you.

Soundscapes and scentscapes as places where the supralocal inhabits and shapes the local. All this is very interesting and compelling. [. . .] I wonder if a useful interview angle here might not be to ask people about their childhoods and memories of childhood. Often childhood memories are animated by things like the smell of an adult, the texture of skin or cloth, the taste of some food or drink, the smell of salt in the ocean, whatever. This might lead them back to talking more about sensory matters. I'm [still] reading Doris Lessing's autobiography, *Under My Skin*, right now, and there's a lot there about these kinds of issues.

Another thing that I thought very insightful in what you wrote was the link between nativist romanticization of aboriginal worlds and closeness to nature, on the one hand, and the supralocal environmental movement, on the other. (Ecotourism must figure somewhere in this link, too.)

Another interview direction that might yield relevant insights: you might ask people you've already interviewed about how Australia has changed from when they were children/younger, or since their parents' day. Or how has it changed since the loosening of the ties to the UK, say? People are always, I think, tracking and monitoring gradual changes, transformations, alterations in their life worlds. It goes with a personal sense of keeping order or keeping track. You keep track of "world events" and shifts in the political climate, treaties, wars, newspaper stories about this and that, new presidents and administrations, or particularly significant national celebrations or dates. Perhaps you clip particularly significant front pages or headlines for your records or scrapbook. But you also keep track of more personal histories, like which of your friends are having kids or losing their jobs; or you notice how your body changes over time; or perhaps you track changes in climate (you might be convinced that the weather used to be different when you were a child). Or you notice yourself relaxing about certain aspects of your life that used to torment you as a teenager. Or you gradually add entries to your curriculum vitae.

Well, Allaine, what do you make of this? It's a very long-winded way of thinking and writing about the everyday sense of the presence of change in people's lives. This is something that very easily lets someone reminisce about landscape, the senses, and memory, perhaps. Or not.

Liisa

To: Liisa Malkki lhmalkki@orion.oac.uci.edu
From: Allaine Cerwonka allaine_cerwonka@politics.muwaye.unimelb.edu.au
Date: Thursday, June 1, 1995 18:09
Subject: Re: all this

Hi. Good to hear from you!

Thanks for all your suggestions, observations and cautions. I have decided not to pursue
the architects for interviews because I can't be sure that I'm doing it for reasons other than
escape. There's a lot of interesting stuff going on in that field in terms of writing about space
and place that I will continue to collect. And perhaps they as a group might be easier to
get material about the senses and space from, but I think I will continue to see what crops
up in the garden and on the crime beat. I was beginning to feel like I just couldn't think of
another thing to talk to the Garden Club folks about. But then I searched out some reading
on landscape and whatever I could find that looks at the social relevance of gardens; that
helped me see new angles. I have been going back and photographing some gardens I did
not do initially, and that has been good. It has allowed me to pull the tape recorder out
again with them while we walk through their gardens. It's cute how modest they are about
it, telling me that really I should take pictures in the spring, etc. I appreciate how they are
willing to go through this all when it's a bit strange to have this woman coming around
and asking so many questions about things that seem so everyday to them. I think there
is also the issue that they are aware that much of society says the things that they do, like
garden[ing] and meet[ing] with friends, are not important, so it's hard for them to allow me
to take it seriously and see it as worthy of intellectual inquiry.

　　When I was visiting Dora in the hospital a month or so back, I met her son-in-law who,
along with her daughter, is a doctor. He thought it was very nice, if not a bit peculiar, that
I was visiting his mother-in-law, and as an effort to make polite conversation asked me
about my research. When I told him that I was interviewing members of the Garden Club
as a means to understanding how national identity functions, he got this superior smirk on
his face and said, "Well, you realize of course that the ladies from East Melbourne are, shall
we say, a unique group. You aren't going to talk to people from different ethnic groups or
anything like that?" I didn't feel like he was condescending toward me (or didn't care enough
to pick up on that angle of it), but felt very uncomfortable about his manner toward Dora. But
that episode was interesting because it comes into my mind when I am put in the position
of reassuring the Garden Club members that they really have knowledge that is useful to
me. I don't find myself in a position of needing to reassure the cops about the usefulness of
their knowledge. With them it is a matter of making them feel safe that I will not ask them for
certain kinds of information (which I am guessing is stuff that they do that they shouldn't).

One last thing about the Garden Club. I have been thinking about them in relation to geographical questions. Certainly as older women, they must experience the city in a very different way from armed male police. I don't know at this point what their spatial experience is, but it's on my agenda to learn. I am hoping they will find it easier to talk about the senses because of who they are and because the interviews take place in the private sphere. I get some information from cops, but it's patchy and hard to access.

A [. . .] breakthrough with the cops yesterday. Finally, I went out and had beers with a few (about ten) of them after the shift. The suggestion has been made a few times, but it's never been in a way where I could seriously take it up. So at last I went out yesterday afternoon when the shift ended. I was pleased that the Constable who asked me was the person I had interviewed that afternoon as well. That made me feel like it had been a positive experience for him, and it sent out that signal to others as well, which hopefully will make it more of something people want to do rather than are told to [do] by the sergeant. There's always the "joke" by [the one sergeant] to the person I've interviewed, "You didn't give away the shop secrets did you?" I am not sure if there really are some secrets that they have been successful in shielding, but they are kidding themselves if they think that it's not [. . .] obvious that they [work outside of the official rules in many of their policing practices]. I think secrecy is a burden that is hard for people to carry over an extended period of time. And indeed my knowledge of some of other people's secrets is [taxing] at times.

But I am very glad that I have had this experience with the cops, because it's easier for me to see that it's not a black and white situation. I still don't support the abuses of power I see, but I have better insight into the context out of which these choices are made by various police. It makes me a lot less patient with university friends here who are quick to dismiss and caricature the police.

Some of the most interesting moments of conducting fieldwork have come when police members seem to want to tell me things about these incidents. The expectation/paranoia (as I read it) is that I will ask and then publicly denounce the police (in combination with their professional culture, which rigidly defines an inside and an outside in terms of professional loyalties) about these abuses of power. So I am careful never to ask. That makes it even more interesting when they want to tell me. Yesterday, while I was observing at the station, this sergeant brought up the subject twice that he couldn't do an interview with me that day because he had an internal investigation interview about an incident in the station last week. When he brought it up the second time, I figured he wanted to tell me about it, so I asked a bit of a general question and got told quite a bit. It's funny that they almost can't conceive that really I want to write about national identity and not about police abuses. What would be most interesting is if I am totally mistaken and this stuff isn't the "shop secrets," and it's something completely different.

One last thing. Very interesting the feeling I got when I walked with Rob into the pub where the rest of the gang were. I could easily sense that I had walked over an important line and they were a little unsure about [whether] it was safe. All conversations stopped for a moment. Luckily some of the clerical staff were there (all women), and they were excited to talk to me (will work my way upstairs to them and also interview them). One guy is very hostile and asked me in the hush of conversations: "And have you brought that little book that you're always writing in with you?" I told him yes, but that I was far more interested in having a beer than working. The thing that helped me not be intimidated by him and project his hostility onto the whole crowd was the notion that he was just acting out the anxiety that everyone felt a little bit—just playing his structural role. (It's nice when using theory can help us feel less rejected and personal about this stuff; but sometimes it's easier than others.) I'm hoping he'll mellow out a little. I was invited by a few people before the afternoon was out to also come along to a farewell party at a local pub on Tuesday night. Don't worry. I am perfecting the art of drinking my beer really slowly. But I am starting to get a few flirting vibes here and there. That will be another interesting thing to negotiate. Overall, I think it's very helpful that I am female in this setting. I noticed that the internal investigators (who are the other people that put cops on the wrong side of the tape recorder) also wear plain clothes, but luckily are middle-aged men. I think my gender and youth (relative) help establish me as something other than the people who reprimand cops.

Well, I could go on for a long time, but will spare you some of the gritty details. Jim and I are planning to go to Sydney and Canberra for ten days some time this month. I will appreciate a little space from my daily routine and environment.

Allaine

Afterthoughts

AC: This incident in which the son-in-law of an informant was concerned that the social group I chose to study (elderly, women gardeners) was not representative enough of Australian national identity illustrates nicely the way even laymen take the principles of the "hard" sciences (generalizability, objectivity, being representative) as the norm for knowledge production. This is one example of how the scientific paradigm within the social sciences continues to haunt the process of knowledge production.

LM: Yes. This son-in-law also seemed to assume that "different ethnic groups" are the ones with "culture," while his mother-in-law was just a garden-variety old lady. He seemed further to assume that ethnographers should study difference (as he saw it) and not sameness, that is, not a social relationship where differences in and of themselves do not motivate the relationship. His reaction was also telling about how he saw Allaine's citizenship, her class location, her kind of whiteness.

LM: At this point in her fieldwork, Allaine frequently confronted her responsibilities in her knowledge production in relation to things like "shop secrets" and possible abuses of power at the police station. Some research situations involve complex negotiations in one's own thoughts as to what can be written about and what can be known but not made public. This is yet another dimension of ethnographic fieldwork as a form of ethical practice. It seems wise to err always on the side of caution and consideration for one's informants, but there is no universally applicable formula for treating sensitive material. Another common analytical pitfall is that the ethnographer comes to think of her will to knowledge in particular ways in difficult research circumstances. It is all too easy, in other words, to fall into the notion that one will study and write about something in order to reveal and denounce it. But does ethnography as a genre of writing and knowledge production really amount to writing an exposé, to exposing hidden or unjust things? One can well imagine circumstances in which an exposé would be tempting, or even ethically or politically important, to write. One can equally well see why an ethnographer should be extremely cautious about this. Why? First, texts have social lives, and it is impossible to foresee the political or other uses to which one's ethnography may be put. This argues for caution, and for humility about one's own power to know and to predict. "Do no harm" is a principle that has to be honored through time, not just during fieldwork. (Several of the people I interviewed in Mishamo refugee camp asked to be named in my study; I did not dare honor their wishes, and I am now relieved to have made that decision.) Second, the price of writing an exposé may have to be paid, not by its author, but by other researchers who will try to work in the site of the exposé. Governments can regulate research access in the name of national interest and sovereignty. Here is a good reason for seeing one's knowledge production as a social practice, rather than as an individual, private odyssey. Yet, sovereignty is such a troubled and often damaging principle that there is little reason to accept it as sacred. There is ample room here for painful judgment calls, and for thinking about the ideal that ethnographic work should be socially and politically engaged or "relevant." Third, I think of a passage in the anthropologist Cora DuBois's stock-taking essay, "Some Anthropological Hindsights" (1980, 9): "First, anthropology is a philosophical humanism; it is not a pure or social science as the word 'science' is now used. It is rather a science in the earlier sense of the word, as it was used in the past century: an attempt to understand." I like this part of Du Bois's vision of the field (even if I disagree with other aspects of it). If ethnography involves an attempt to understand, it must involve trying to understand both the things and people one admires and also the things and people that one recoils from in distaste or shock. And the more one understands, the harder it is to construct a one-sided account peopled by "good guys" and "bad guys." In a social context constituted by categorical hatred and genocide, the challenges of understanding and of representation become perhaps particularly acute. In my own case, I studied in appalling detail the anatomy of hatred between Hutu and Tutsi. But the social logics of that categorical hatred could not become my own analytical tools. It would have been awful in that situation to set out to write an exposé on "the evil of the Tutsi." Similarly, in Allaine's research, her analytical questions did not centre on whether the police in Melbourne were guilty of abuses or not. She wanted to know things, not in order to disapprove or denounce, but to understand, to understand how things ticked. A nice illustration of this is to be found in James Ferguson's 1994 book, *The Anti-Politics Machine*: One does not go through the trouble of performing vivisection on a frog in order to refute, denounce, or "disapprove" of its liver or spleen; one wants to find out, in a more exploratory spirit, how it all ticks.

To: Allaine Cerwonka allaine_cerwonka@politics.muwaye.unimelb.edu.au
From: Liisa Malkki lhmalkki@orion.oac.uci.edu
Date: Thursday, June 1, 1995
Subject: Re: all this

Hi. More great notes from the field. I'm off to a faculty meeting in four minutes, but just wanted to say thanks for your message. What you said about how the older white women at the garden club and the armed policemen move in very different social geographies/spaces was evocative and put me in mind of... let's see, I think it was either Vron Ware's *Beyond the Pale: White Women, Racism, and History* [1992], or Gilroy's *There Ain't No Black in the Union Jack* [1991]. I think the latter. Gilroy described the frail, white, elderly woman living alone in the city as the embodiment of endangerment, the flipside of the imagined, overgrowing criminality of black men in cities—something along those lines. Oh, I see I'm out of time. Got to go. Have a good holiday. I'll talk to you soon.

Liisa

To: Liisa Malkki lhmalkki@orion.oac.uci.edu
From: Allaine Cerwonka allaine_cerwonka@politics.muwaye.unimelb.edu.au
Date: Tuesday, June 6, 1995 15:33
Subject: g'day

Unfortunately, our trip to Sydney isn't for a couple of weeks. But that's actually fine by me, as I feel so excited about the stuff that's coming out of my fieldwork right now. Just thought I'd bleep on to share some positive energy, even if this is a brief note. I have to scoot out soon and go to a pub where a police farewell for a few coppers is being held; then I have to somehow get down to the garden club meeting by 8:00 p.m.

I spent the morning with a couple from the club talking about their garden. I have been getting some great stuff from these tours, and people just glow to be asked about their gardens. Much is said in people's explanations for why some things grow well in Australia and others don't, why people need to use more chemical sprays and stuff to fight off bugs than they did in the olden days. I also find it interesting how the gardens are tied into people's sense of self and self-esteem. Also, the circulation of cuttings (and when it's appropriate to ask for or take a cutting from someone else or not) is very interesting! It reminds me of *The Gift* (Mauss). It was interesting that when Dora was in the hospital, the thing she stressed out about was the fact that her garden had been dug up by a gardener whom she eventually fired and was lying there empty while she was in the hospital (ties into issues of control in my mind). So, one of her close friends went over and planted it for her. It was an interesting channel for friendship, and, I thought, a really lovely way of caretaking of Dora by Judith. Actually, talking about that makes me think a little more about the double meaning of the word "caretaking" in this instance.

On the cop front, I am feeling much more legitimate in the questions I ask and am gaining access to all sorts of delicious details. I got a great lesson in the computer system of the station last Friday. It was fascinating for me that they have various ways in which to access information. They can call something up by type of crime, fingerprints, name, license number, and others. The most interesting category for me was that they can call something up by geography. Not just that they can punch in someone's address, but they also have details about what area a person hangs around in, who else hangs around there, what type of crime has happened there, who else lives with them, who they were dating last time the police had information about them.

All of these details give the police an amazing spatial overview of the people of the community and of course enable them to better control the spaces in which people move. (So, for instance, when an Aborigine turns up in Northern Fitzroy, they can jump to the conclusion that he or she is there to burgle a place or for other wrong-doing because they are out of their so-called appropriate place.) And, indeed, space is transformed in relation to time. The police's reading of normal Aboriginal space at 2:00 a.m. has to do with a certain constellation of pubs that are open in the district at that time and who they know hangs out at which ones, and where they are in relation to the known Aboriginal hostels. Similar maps are constructed for various groups that the police want to track, of course. It's also interesting how members of the force are regularly walking into the station, frustrated that there is no such address of the place that the "crook" gave as their home address. I guess you could say that a whole series of fictional geographies are improvised as a way of resisting power's control of space (de Certeau's "tactical raids of the weak").

This is so much fun right now!
Gotta run. Talk to you soon.

Allaine

P.S. I also discovered that police love talking about the first dead body that they ever saw, each trying to outdo the other in gruesome detail, of course. I also had a great conversation on Saturday night with a few late into the night at the station about what is funny to cops and what is not. They claim that cops make fun of everything as a way of [getting] release from the seriousness of what they see. Seems that this is true in my experience, except when it comes to incidents involving children as victims. Will listen for if this includes all children or no. Bye for real this time.

To: Allaine Cerwonka allaine_cerwonka@politics.muwaye.unimelb.edu.au
From: Liisa Malkki lhmalkki@orion.oac.uci.edu
Date: Wednesday, June 7, 1995
Subject: Re: g'day

Hi again!

You know, I feel like I'm reading your book already. Every couple of days I get to read another chapter. (Not that your messages are that long!) It's very exciting and interesting. The spatial monitoring by computer at the station is what one always imagines goes on, but then dismisses as a nutty, paranoid idea. So often here in the U.S., at least, one gets an image of cops as blunderers. Not all the time, but it's an underlying theme, perhaps— say, in media coverage of police work in the O. J. Simpson trial. (Oh, by the way, do the cops there follow the trial? Here, it's "gavel-to-gavel" week in, week out, as I think I wrote you already.) In contrast to the U.S. image, in German and sometimes UK police shows and news coverage of actual life (and maybe elsewhere in Europe), police are more often seen as whole organizations, first of all, and not just as individual hero figures, and they are portrayed, too, as technicians and professionals rather than as John Waynes. Just impressions. I'm just interested to know whether this computer resource is much used here.

Another thing I found really compelling in what you said was the way in which you described how Dora's friend planted her empty garden while Dora was in the hospital. You had, I think, a very nice way of seeing the gesture (a keen but compassionate eye). Well, now you're probably embarrassed!

The Jack Goody book, *The Culture of Flowers* [1993], looks interesting for you, by the way. I just checked it out of the library. Another thing of potential interest: a collection named

After Identity, with essays by people in the intersections of law and cultural studies. And I think I mentioned the new *Journal of Material Culture* edited [by] James Clifford, et al.? Don't worry about being out of touch with new literature, by the way; what you're doing is far more important. And when you come back, you can peruse people's bookshelves to see what is [not] new.

My book should come out any day now. What a lot of work that was! I mean just the production process, long after the writing is done. And so many places where it can go wrong. [. . .] Of course, I could have been more energetic about hounding them about all these details. You just sort of assume that since they're a press, they have the know-how. But actually, Chicago was quite professional. I'd publish there again. (Good for you to keep track of good and bad publishers, and not just in terms of prestige. [. . .])

The new social science tower [at the University of California, Irvine] is coming along very fast; we should be moved in in less than a year. This will mean proper offices for graduate students finally, I am told. Hope this plan won't evaporate.

Got to go. Great to hear from you!

Liisa

⚡

To: Allaine Cerwonka allaine_cerwonka@politics.muwayc.unimelb.edu.au
From: Liisa Malkki lhmalkki@orion.oac.uci.edu
Date: Tuesday, June 20, 1995
Subject: Re: greetings

Hi Allaine,

Two references: first, I ordered [my own copy of] the Goody book on flowers, and it looks promising (for my bedtime reading, but perhaps for you, too?). The other thing I saw is titled *Writing Women and Space: Colonial and Postcolonial Geographies* edited by Alison Blunt and Gillian Rose [1994]. It has a chapter by Louise Johnson on "Occupying the Suburban Frontier: Accommodating Difference on Melbourne's Suburban Fringe." This seems to have discussions on "place making at Roxburgh Park." Know of this? Next chapter is also on Australia: land, gender, and indigenous people in settler Australia. Oh, actually, chapter five, too: "Colonizing Gender in Colonial Australia," by Kay Schaffer [1994], associate professor of women's studies at University of Adelaide. The other two authors are at Victoria. That's that for now. Hope you're doing splendidly.

Liisa

To: Liisa Malkki lhmalkki@orion.oac.uci.edu
From: Allaine Cerwonka allaine_cerwonka@politics.muwaye.unimelb.edu.au
Date: Wed, June 21, 1995
Subject: Re: references

Hi Liisa.

Wow, what a great feeling to have you recommend things that I have already gotten to over here! At last perhaps I am on top of the mountain of literature that surrounds my topic. So, yes, I have had a look at the three chapters from that collection on postcolonial geographies. At the moment I am reading various chapters in *Mapping the Futures*, which has some good stuff in general, but some Australian cultural studies people, too. I also have Goody's flower book by my bed. It's been good for me in thinking about the material from the garden club especially, but it's a bit dry so it's perfect for late night reading.

I feel pretty balanced in general with both field sites. At last I feel like I am at a point where I am giving them both the energy they require, rather than always feeling like one has been ignored, repressed, resented, or whatever. This Zen feeling should last about two days, since I am taking off for Sydney on Friday and abandoning both my babies.

My computer terminal has been temporarily shifted here, so I am writing from the desk of one of the office people at the university, not an environment conducive to reflection. Therefore, I will bleep off without saying too much of anything. I guess I just wanted you to know that things are going well. A good chunk of the days I am even calm and happy.

While I am sitting on the train up to Sydney, I am going to think of how to describe my project in a way that warrants a talk with the central map man for the police in my district (a collection of inner-city neighborhoods). Talking with people about what they do with the information they have on crooks has taught me that after it is entered into the computer and the paperwork is filled out, the information is collated and analyzed by an officer over in the District Information Support Centre. I would ask the commanding officer of the station to make a call of introduction for me, but he is already chasing down my request to go back out in the cars. I have found a posture for asking questions at the station that feels okay for me and seems to strike a chord. It's one of awed curiosity at how complicated it all is and the various things they have come up with—formally and informally—to organize it and be effective in their jobs. I have also had some very interesting conversations with people about special squads they have worked on in the past—gambling and vice, armed robbery (better known as the "stick-up" squad), homicide, rape. These assignments make for amusing and interesting stories. I have found that going to the station at night usually leads to more personal and comfortable conversations with the members. Not surprising. And they seem quite comfortable with a rather one-sided conversation where they tell me a lot about their opinions and experiences and don't notice that I have not said a lot about myself. Perhaps it is because our relationship is framed by the research or perhaps men feel comfortable talking about themselves to women.

Several of the garden club members have told me that they will miss me when I am gone. That makes me feel good. Jim and I are staying in Canberra for four days on the way to Sydney. While there, we are going to get together with [a] garden club member's niece and her husband. But [there's] also an interesting question in the back of my mind: why is it important for me that these relationships are reciprocal and function as friendships? One easy answer is that I know the rules or mores of friendship. Ethnographic research is a relationship that requires constant thought on my part as to what is right, effective, fair, etc.

A couple of passing questions I don't think I ever answered. I would be quite sure that U.S. police have as sophisticated, if not more so, ways of tracking people. Also, the O. J. trial does not seem to interest people in either of my field sites. On the one hand, people seem to believe at the station that things that happen in the U.S. will happen in Australia in five to ten years. But then, they don't seem to be interested or aware of the issues in the U.S. anyway. But it's interesting that they don't expect the same accusations of racism or whatever as police departments in the U.S. have had to deal with.

Well, I will close. Nice to hear from you. I will be back in Melbourne on July 3rd and I will bleep back onto to your screen not long after that. Take care.

Allaine

To: Allaine Cerwonka allaine_cerwonka@politics.muwaye.unimelb.edu.au
From: Liisa Malkki lhmalkki@orion.oac.uci.edu
Date: Friday, June 23, 1995
Subject: re: references

Hi there,

I hope this is still the address to reply to. I have to say that sometimes, reading your letters, I wish I were doing fieldwork now. I could even see myself doing fieldwork in a police station. But then I remember how taxing it is, and I say NAAAH! Do you ever ponder how accidental all the directions of this work are in some sense? You had that bit of experience with police work in New Zealand (wasn't it?), and we talked about good potential sites, and you refused to work with real estate agents (more accurately, you ran away screaming), and here you are, rapidly getting deeper and deeper into a social world that will mark you forever in ways that cannot yet be visible, perhaps. It will never leave you. I actually like the idea that I never really transcend anything or leave anything behind. Sartre put it beautifully in *Search for a Method* [1963], something about how surpassing [*dépasser*] is a matter of going beyond and, at the same time, conserving. We read this Sartre book [as a foil for Lévi-Strauss] in the Structuralism and Post-Structuralism seminar. I also liked Denise Riley's book, *Am I That Name?* [1988] about the historical emergence and twists and turns of the Woman category. Okay, one more reference (in case I didn't pass this on yet): *NowHere*. I think I did tell you about it.

We just passed midsummer's eve. Longest day of the year. Very special and beloved time in Finland and those parts.

Keep well,

Liisa

To: Liisa Malkki lhmalkki@orion.oac.uci.edu
From: Allaine Cerwonka allaine_cerwonka@politics.muwaye.unimelb.edu.au
Date: Tuesday, July 4, 1995
Subject: Back from vacation

Whew, that went by quickly!

Jim and I arrived back from Sydney on last night's train. We spent the first few days in Canberra, the nation's capital. Jim was keen to see the new Parliament building (a big deal in international architectural circles), and I thought it would be good to hear the official story about the nation. The building was quite amazing, and I thought it was quite amusing how the tour guide kept mentioning how ordinary folk work there (farmers come in and work as tour guides on the off season), and how each year during the wool auction at the capital they let the merino sheep graze on the grassed roof of the parliament building. It's such a contrast to the U.S. where we usually emphasize the majesty and dignity of our federal institutions. A friend put me in touch with a friend of hers who works as a journalist in the building, and we got a great behind-the-scenes tour of the building as well. It was good that in both Canberra and Sydney we met up with Australians living there, through Melbourne friends, and got a better flavor for some of what's happening in the two cities. But I found that I actually wanted to avoid contact with many people when away; I needed a rest from all the interaction that fieldwork requires.

And Sydney is just a wonderful city. The harbor is amazing, and its presence is felt even when you get away from it a bit; the hilly topography of the place delivers water views when you least expect it. We treated ourselves to a pair of symphony tickets, which allowed us to enjoy the insides of the Sydney Opera House as well. I think I could quite happily live in Sydney.

Several times this year I have remembered what you had said about forgetting to put Tanzania down when listing the places that you had lived. I wonder if there is something about fieldwork that is less conducive to feeling like one actually lived in the place [in which one] spent at least a year [rather than, say, working for a living in that place]. Having lived in Melbourne before, and feeling after that experience that I had truly become a part of things and attached to the place, has perhaps given me a better sense of how fieldwork is [different] from just living in a place temporarily. On the one hand, I feel very much in the thick of things. I have a better sense of what is happening in different areas of the city and know more people from diverse backgrounds than the average citizen here. No surprise, given that that is my research goal, I suppose.

But I don't feel "at home" here this time around. I think part of it is a result of constantly being a bit out of my element. What I mean is that I spend most of my time with people and in places that don't necessarily reflect my values or direct interests. And, although I am sincere with the people with whom I spend my time, I am less bold in my opinions and in general exercise my personality a little less than I might if I weren't conducting research at the same time. I find that this actually limits my attachment to this place, interestingly enough. I think the most taxing thing for me about fieldwork (well, one of them) is not getting [my] worldview [reflected back to me and therefore validated] in the way that [it is] when I spend time with people whose interests or lifestyles are more similar to mine.

Perhaps this has been a mistake, but I haven't engaged with people at the university here all that much. I have found doing so difficult because my schedule operates around the schedules of the two field sites; that has not left me with much time to be consistent in relationships at the university. I have met plenty of people and had some great conversations with people doing work here, but it's hard to develop a relationship out of chance encounters. So, I feel thirsty for colleagues and friends with whom I am not always a bit cautious about what I say [regarding] what I experience on a daily basis in my field sites.

There are so many different layers to fieldwork. Issues multiply and intersect in exciting ways. I am forever in a state of trying to work out what I am doing with my methodology and why, and on top of that, the fieldwork and research is very often about me as well. Fieldwork is about me in that it requires a lot of integrity and self-justification for what I am doing and why, and the issues—like identity and feeling a sense of place—end up being issues in my life as well as the lives of those in my study.

On a more practical level, I think I told you that I would be returning for the beginning of the fall quarter. I will continue in both field sites until the beginning of September. I would like to take the several weeks in September to pack up and ship my stuff properly, but also to sit with the experiences and information I have collected here over the past year. I want to see what sense it makes at that point when I have pulled away from the daily interactions, but am still connected to Australia and my life here. I do this in anticipation of feeling disoriented once I touch back down in Southern California. That seems unavoidable, given how disorienting life in California always seemed in the past when I returned from a week's holiday to the East Coast. It's a funny place, but god do I miss the weather there.

Well, I am off—back into the gray rain. The day will not be a loss, as there is a garden club meeting tonight and they always leave me giggling because the people are so kind, if not a bit nutty. Tonight is ferns.

Thanks for your last e-mail; I enjoyed it very much. You had not mentioned *NowHere* before. Do you know the author? Take care, and I will be in touch.

Allaine

Afterthoughts

LM: In this letter, Allaine again expressed very powerfully the kinds of "nervous conditions" that fieldwork can produce in the subjectivity of the researcher. Different informants and contexts "hail" or interpellate one in different ways, and sometimes one is so busy adapting oneself to the circumstances that one's sense of self comes to seem ephemeral, indistinct, and even distorted. And here, too, the ethics of self-representation involve continual challenges. What are the boundaries of polite agreement and accommodation? Or those between honesty and silence? These are challenges in any life, not just in fieldwork, but they are often thrown into high relief by the critical practices of ethnography. Here, it helps to think of fieldwork as life *tout court*, as opposed to a marked, extraordinary, liminal state set apart from one's mundane realities. This was brought home to me by my dealings with the United States Immigration and Naturalization Service (INS). When I applied for Resident Alien status (or the "Green Card") in the United States, one of the many forms that was required asked me to list, year by year, all my countries of residence since birth. As I had lived in numerous countries in Africa, the Middle East, and Europe, this was a long itinerary. But there was one year that I just could not account for. Finally it occurred to me: I had forgotten my fieldwork year in Tanzania. I had done "fieldwork" in Tanzania; I had not "lived" there. This lapse of memory was sobering: I saw with embarrassing clarity that I had unwittingly framed my work in Tanzania using the rather primitivizing model of classical fieldwork as a year marked apart from ordinary life. I had been a school child and student in Khartoum, Nairobi, Teheran, etc., and had "lived" in those places. But I had not "lived" in Tanzania. Needless to say, I no longer think of fieldwork in these terms. Fieldwork is simply another form of living and working in particular contexts, along with many other people also living and working there. And one can find oneself out of category anywhere, say, at Thanksgiving dinner with one's relatives. (For wonderful discussions of fieldwork, travel, and forms of dwelling, see Clifford 1997, and Gupta and Ferguson 1997b, 31–32.)

To: Liisa Malkki lhmalkki@orion.oac.uci.edu
From: Allaine Cerwonka allaine_cerwonka@politics.muwaye.melbuni.edu.au
Date: Friday, July 7, 1995
Subject: Back in the saddle

Really, this is a short e-mail . . .

Hope you are well. Since it's summer and you are free from teaching obligations for a while, I expect that you are pretty content at the moment.

I've bleeped on your screen because I remember you said for me to get people's permission to use their photos or the photos I take of their gardens in my book. Certainly I have gotten their permission, but it has been verbal permission. Is that a problem? The reason why I have left it at a verbal level is because the interviews with the garden club (which is where all the photos have come from) take the form of a social visit. There is a graciousness on their part to these encounters, and it felt a little too business-like to produce written consent forms. But if you think a written document would be necessary, I could tell them that publishers insist on it. What do you think? I do tell them that I want to take the pictures for research purposes, and would they mind if I use them for a book I'd like to produce out of this study. No problem there, but legal contracts are a little incongruous with tea and scones in the living room.

I have reentered both the garden club and the cop station. I was delighted to find such a warm welcome at the garden club. I also made another request at the end of the meeting for some additional people to be interviewed for my research. Several of the women I have been friendly with rounded people up for me and insisted (to them) that they help me out! It was great and made it much easier. Then another man, Frank, whom I have seen a few times, came up and gave me a piece of paper with seven dates [on] which he would be free to do something with me this month (we had talked about going to the races together and taking a trip down to the beach). It was funny and very sweet of him.

But what really surprised me was that several people at the copper station asked where I had been over the last couple of weeks and said that they had missed me! The warm and fuzzy side of cops. The senior sergeant has also (finally) gotten me permission to go out in the cars again since I have been able to show that the university (Melbourne) has me covered for liability. I will use the fact that I only have two more months left to try to get out in the cars a lot. I also called the map guru for the district, and he was quite willing for me to come on in next week and learn more about the makeup of the district and how the police regulate it. So, all of that is encouraging. There's also a pool hall night next Wednesday, where my police station is playing the next station over. I was invited, so I guess I didn't give away my true geekiness at the last cop function. I just wish I knew how to play pool better than I do. Had I known what fieldwork would entail, I would have spent my undergraduate days in the bar challenging the locals instead of going to classes.

Well, that's all for now.

Allaine

To: Allaine Cerwonka allaine_cerwonka@politics.muwaye.unimelb.edu.au
From: Liisa Malkki lhmalkki@orion.oac.uci.edu
Date: Monday, July 10, 1995
Subject: Re: Back from vacation

Hi. How did the ferns go? I bet you'll become a real gardener when you return here. You know, when I first got to this strange California, that was my great solace: gardens public and private, nurseries, garden shops, gardening. I lived in San Juan Capistrano and taught a hellish-large course with a [. . .] crew of Teaching Assistants at the University of California at San Diego. I commuted by Amtrak and bus. Very stressful. I'd get off the train at the Capistrano train station and walk or drive straight to the nurseries. There were a couple of good ones. I suppose you know of Roger's Gardens here in Corona del Mar? We should go one time and have coffee there when you get back.

Your plans and timetable sound good, by the way. As for contacting the university people, it's probably been best and most effective for you in terms of maximizing your productivity (can you believe these words?!) not to spend huge amounts of time getting to know them. That can swallow up time that would otherwise have been spent at the station or in the garden club. However, it is a good idea to connect now. [. . .] Talk to the Chairs of the Political Science and/or Anthropology Departments and other colleagues who might have a relevant interest. People (scholars) living and working in places they might consider "peripheral" never want to [see] that well-funded, high-powered U.S. researchers are coming through, getting acclaim from work done in their backyard, and by-passing them. But, even more important, I would think that there are a lot of regional specialists and others, too, who would be very interesting to talk with. Often, researchers also give a presentation of their research results as a courtesy, before they leave. Have you been asked to do this?

I'm sure I said this one hundred times already, but make sure you have contact addresses and ways of tracking people for later correspondence. Having photos of them would also help you keep names and faces straight. Group photos, perhaps? Also, photos of neighborhoods, cityscapes (maybe even buy postcards), houses, gardens, the police station, would be great to have not only for possible book illustrations or dust jacket covers, but also for teaching purposes [and as ethnographic evidence]. When you are lecturing on this, slides or other images [might] help to draw people in.

Another detail touched on earlier: it's important to be prompt about writing thank-you letters to all informants. In addition to considerations of politeness, it eases your relationship with people into a new mode: writing, corresponding. People in the U.S. routinely underestimate the power of the pen, while the rest of the world still writes personal, handwritten letters. Here, it's so easy to pick up phones that work, e-mail, and so on. Anyway, letters can be a prolongation of your fieldwork ("EEEEEK!" says Allaine), and your informants may end up putting things in letters that they might not have thought to express in conversation. I did this with almost all of my regular informants and now have a very extensive collection of letters—letters that were invaluable as I wrote the long postscript to my book. I quoted from them a great deal. Also, the contact with the people I had just spent a year with became important to me in ways I could not have anticipated. I was lonely and out of place in California, and letters from them, writing to them, were a lifeline and a comfort. My heart or spirit or whatever one says was still there in Africa, while I was bodily here, confronting things like freeways and computers and the absence of a street scene, of pedestrians. (I was unaccustomed to all three.)

Have to sign off now. Keep well, Allaine. I'm very proud of the work you've accomplished.

Liisa

Afterthoughts

LM: Thinking back, I have experience of many academic settings around the world in which scholars worry about being peripheral in some manner—Australia, South Africa, Japan, many countries in Europe. The only countries where I have not seen evidence of this worry have been the United States, France, and England. Yet, high-powered work is being done all over the world.

Researchers with good funding and wealthy universities behind them sometimes—whether consciously or not—treat their fieldwork sites in a predatory manner. In one case, a U.S. scholar who worked in what was then an Eastern European country and spoke the language of that country used the work of his European colleagues and his own fieldwork material as if they were interchangeable—just raw materials for him to collect, translate into English, analyze, and publish. Those European colleagues who often published in a language other than English did not fail to notice how their work of analysis became raw material that fed the fame of the U.S. scholar. Obviously, this should never happen. In Tanzania, during my own fieldwork, I depended on several international and nongovernmental organizations for many things. By the time I met the director of one of them, several researchers had come through and gotten help from his organization. He was disgusted with all of them, saying that once they had gotten what they wanted, they never shared the results of their research, never even sending copies of their work for the organization's library.

To: Allaine Cerwonka allaine_cerwonka@politics.muwaye.unimelb.edu.au
From: Liisa Malkki lhmalkki@orion.oac.uci.edu
Subject: Re: Back in the saddle
Date: Monday, July 10, 1995

Hi again. About the permissions for photos: if it's easy, get written permission. Otherwise you can get it later if you have addresses for everyone. (My last e-mail, written a few minutes ago, was about this. You're way ahead of me.) If there's a very key photo, get permission in hand, I'd say. If it's taken by you, there may be less of an issue. I know the University of Chicago Press was extremely unbending in these matters, and they are the ones I have had dealings with. Maybe other presses are more relaxed about copyright; but better safe than sorry.

The voice of Mother Hen: remember to exercise reasonable caution even in these last weeks, even though you are now very familiar with these places into which you've knitted so much of your life and energy. I mean things like going out in cop cars, going around to parties, etc. You know. I can just tell, you're making faces.

It will be excellent to have you back here.

Liisa

To: Liisa Malkki lhmalkki@orion.oac.uci.edu
From: Allaine Cerwonka allaine_cerwonka@politics.muwaye.melbuni.edu.au
Date: Thursday, July 13, 1995
Subject: drinking with the boys

Hi Liisa,

Well, your words of caution were spot on. Don't worry. Nothing bad has happened, but I did spend a very long evening with five drunken cops. I went in on Sunday night just to observe and got invited to go out with the guys that were getting off shift at 11:00 p.m. and were partaking in the station ritual of drinking to celebrate the end of night shift (a week-long hell shift that people have to do about once every five to six weeks). I was not in the mood to start socializing but didn't want to miss the opportunity.

It might have been different with a different set of people. Unfortunately one of the people was Wayne, who is the one who has been a bit hostile to me in the past (or very suspicious). He's a bit of a group leader, although fortunately there was a sergeant of higher rank with us as well. I think he is a bit sexually attracted to me because he was very determined to get me drunk so they "could find out what I always wrote in that little book of mine." And unfortunately they get all their drinks for free at the nightclubs they frequent, so he kept showing up with another round of drinks for everyone. Well, I may not have learned how to play pool in high school, but I did learn how to stay sober in the face of stupid men who think it's fun to get women drunk. I tried refusing the drinks, which wasn't received very well (strong tradition in Australia of boohooing "wowsers" who don't know how to have fun). And of course there was the element of it that they perhaps wanted to see if I was a normal person and would make myself vulnerable to them by acting stupid when I was drunk. Luckily they all scoffed down their drinks and didn't notice that half of mine got poured into empty glasses on nearby tables and spilled on the floor. Wayne did see me accidentally run into someone and my drink end up on them (didn't mean that one), and at the end of the night put together that I wasn't very drunk at all. What was so uncomfortable about the thing was not so much hanging out with these guys, because I found ways of joking and relating that went well. But it was just having this person be so obsessed with what I did and "could they trust me." He jokingly (ha, ha) referred to me as the spy at various times during the night. It just reminded me of being in high school and knowing that someone is putting the moves on you because they take responsibility for your demise and then are the one to be nice to you when you puke. He's married, but of course no wives come out on these nights.

I had some very interesting conversations with a few of them. Sad that they do not seem to be able to express how they feel during the day at the station, but once the lights are lowered and they have a bit of beer in them, they'll tell you anything, I am beginning to believe. I heard very interesting tales of [. . .] (because they knew the person was a crook but had nothing else on them) and people's philosophy on violence (very liberal in its use), and I witnessed a very cozy relationship with the owner of the club, who, they tell me, is very involved in organized crime.

None of this is terribly surprising I suppose. But during a conversation with Wayne about his concerns with my being at the station, he said, "Look, if you hang around us for long enough, you will see things that could get us into trouble. You already see things because we forget you're there. What will you do if the internal investigators want you to tell them what you have seen in relation to a certain incident?" I said that I did not consider myself to be an actor in this police world. I want to observe and then try to understand what I see. Issues around corruption are not the focus of my work. He said, "So you would tell them that you didn't see anything?" He didn't wait for an answer, and I am still thinking about that question. I guess it has haunted me because just through conversation and observing these guys during off duty hours, I have the sense that if they let down their guards or if I followed them around too closely, it wouldn't be long before I saw quite a bit of stuff. I can deal with seeing them get drinks for free and hear[ing] stories of things in the past. But I don't think I would like to be counted on by them to protect them in a case of physical violence against someone or who knows what else.

It was a surreal night. So I am having these really intense mini-conversations with a few of them (individually), and then I am standing alone for a moment, and one of the younger ones walks up, on the brink of tears, and says, "Somewhere in your book you should say that I am the most hated cop at the station." (I would think that he was having me on, except that I can pick up that people don't really like him.) I assured him that although I could not speak for others, I certainly liked him and thought he was a hard worker. He said, "I am just too much of an Irishman." (I'm still trying to work out the logic of that one, but it seemed to make sense for him.) I wanted to laugh at how defensive this set was about my presence, but, yet, as soon as they had a moment, and, believe me, without much prying on my part, they talked a lot about some really heavy emotional stuff.

I was talking with someone about being a cop in general, and he asked if I thought he was jaded, because he would quit the force when he thought he had become insensitive to the stuff around him. He went on to say how he thought about quitting many times, but there's not much else you can do except to become a security man if you leave the force. I asked what he liked about the job. He said, "The uniform. It's like wearing a magic suit. I could walk up to that table now and tell them to leave, but they wouldn't care because I am just a normal person. But if I had on the uniform, they would leave without any questions asked." Well, those types of remarks certainly make me sleep easier at night, no? It was interesting that a woman police officer said a similar thing earlier when we were alone at the station. I asked her about how safe she felt in the city, and she said if she has the uniform or even just the gun, she has no fear, but if that's gone, she feels no more safe than any other woman. She even feels unsafe in the central train station (a place I would feel relatively safe actually).

Whew. There's more I could write, but I am at risk of being late for a dinner appointment. I did not go to the pool night on Wednesday. I was too spun out over some of the personal dynamics of Sunday night. I am still looking forward to getting out in the cars, and I will eventually go out on selected social events. I wouldn't want another one of those nights, however. I will be very careful. I am not proofreading this, so excuse the typos and weird sentence construction. Take care. Thanks for your last two e-mails. They were quite cheering. I am really quite fine at the moment, morale-wise. Overloaded emotionally, but fine in general.

Allaine

To: Allaine Cerwonka allaine_cerwonka@politics.muwaye.unimelb.edu.au
From: Liisa Malkki lhmalkki@orion.oac.uci.edu

Date: Friday, July 14, 1995
Subject: Re: drinking with the boys

Ouch. . . . That sounded like quite a night. I hope it didn't end up having any troublesome after-effects or—how do you say it?—ripple-effects at the station? Socially, there's all sorts of subtle restorative work that needs to get done after communal/collective drunkenness, don't you find? That is, when everyone's sober again, you have to work to reassure people that you're not laughing at them, that you still have regard for them, that you didn't take advantage of their feeble state, etc., etc. And in the meantime, when you're doing fieldwork, all this does end up going into the field notes. Difficult.

You know, I think you could tell the cops who worry about what you know that you are ethically and morally bound not to misuse what they tell you and what you see, and also to protect their anonymity as informants. I think it'd be a real problem to cooperate in any kind of internal investigation at the department. You can't reform police practices, and that is not your job there. This is not to say that it's OK to close your eyes to abuses of power and corruption, but the fact remains that these cops are your informants. This you should make very clear to them. You're not doing an exposé (in journalistic terms), nor are you doing an investigation (in police terms); you are doing ethnographic fieldwork. This might seem hopelessly narrow and confining, but it has great value, I think.

This is the kind of high-stress stuff that will maybe inhabit your dreams and subconscious for quite a while after you return. I mean, you might not even feel all the stress now; it might "flower" later. How cheering. That is what happened to me anyway.

What if you ended up writing two books instead of just one? One on Australian-ness, another on police work. [. . .]

Oops, got to go. Stay well, Allaine. I'll write again soon.

Liisa

꧁

To: Liisa Malkki lhmalkki@orion.oac.uci.edu
From: Allaine Cerwonka allaine_cerwonka@politics.muwaye.melbuni.edu.au
Date: Sunday, July 16, 1995
Subject: re: Re: drinking with the boys

Hello. Yes, you're right about the restorative work that needs to be done after that kind of night. It can be a couple of weeks sometimes before I see a given person, because there are several different shifts over the course of the day, and so it's easy to miss people. I noticed that a guy who had been very drunk at the last party and had talked to me in that state was very bashful when he saw me next. I noticed that others tease people about their behavior, and that serves as a kind of bonding. I have just been friendly and conscious not to be any more formal than I had [been] before the drunkenness. It's interesting to me that in this social world of police work, where people feel insecure about the internal machine turning on them and investigating them, and [where] there is so much social hierarchy with little overt emotional support between individuals, people [nevertheless] make themselves so vulnerable to each other by getting very drunk together. As I think about it, I guess that the big issue of loyalty to the boys and the nicknames [are] a big way of supporting each other. People have said that it's the "boys" that make the job for them, and especially sergeants get almost sentimental about the fact that they consider their first responsibility [to be] to take care of their men (which includes taking them out after work and seeing that they have a good time).

It would be interesting to do a book on the police. I feel like I have just scratched the surface of their world in a lot of ways, however. It has taken quite a lot of time to have them get used to me and to develop relationships with individuals, and it has taken time for me to adjust to being with them. And all of these processes are ongoing, of course, but I feel like I am at [a stage] where very interesting bits about their world are becoming visible to me. But it's a fascinating location; I also think that there are aspects of it that are confusing for the members within it, in addition to being novel to outsiders.

I also bleeped on to tell you that I rented a car yesterday and enlisted the photographic talents of a friend. We traveled around the various parts of Melbourne that are interesting for my study and took some (hopefully) good pictures. Diane recommended slides because they are good for presentations, and they can be converted into quality prints for publication. It was a great day, and [it] was great to have someone who has lived in Melbourne her whole life comment on places around the city. It was funny that when we went over to the Western suburbs, she was very surprised that it wasn't as depressing as she was sure it was. She even wanted to drive around more to find "the really bad parts that are here somewhere." A few days ago, I also went and met some people in the community center of the housing commission flats near the police, because it is a place where the police spend a lot of time and talk about quite a bit. It was good to get their impression of the city and of the police. (I just said I was doing research on national identity and did not discuss my relationship with the police.) I was not surprised to hear people talking about how the police are slack in responding to their calls and insensitive to them when they have been victimized by the drug dealers, but it was then interesting to hear people talk with each other about various police they deal with and ridicule one that they find very effeminate. (I [had] not ask[ed] them about the police at all.) I find it amazing to have the public "policing" gender behavior among the police as well as them doing it internally. I'll talk to you again soon.

Allaine

Afterthoughts

LM: Allaine's idea of traveling around Melbourne with a knowledgeable friend and a camera was a productive one. Another graduate student, Amy Stafford, noted that she used "walking tours" with her informants to help her think about issues of space and place, and the social meanings of given built environments and of the category of "nature." Michel de Certeau discusses how walking through a cityscape produces narratives that are literally part of the construction of place (1984; see also Cerwonka 2004 for her discussion of the construction of Fitzroy through her car tours with the police). More generally, it is often easier for people to talk to ethnographers if they are talking about something they see together, instead of just answering questions narrowly directed at them. For example, if the ethnographer and the person being interviewed are talking together about a news event, or fertilizers, or whatever third presence, that conversational moment forms a triangle of sorts: two people discussing something external to both of them. But when the ethnographer fires off very direct litanies of questions at the interviewee, that person is "targeted" in a binary relationship in a different way. Both modes of talking have their uses, of course, but it may be important to be self-conscious about the existence of such different modes.

To: Liisa Malkki lhmalkki@orion.uci.edu
From: Allaine Cerwonka allaine_cerwonka@politics.muwaye.unimelb.edu.au
Date: Friday, July 21, 1995
Subject: musings on method

Well, I am back in the cars!
I went out last night and saw the less sexy side of police work. Lots of report-taking on burglaries in people's homes. It was fun to see what people have in their houses, but my patience started running out when "Fang," the pathetic watchdog for the yuppies from hell, kept jumping up on my pants and getting me dirty. I know, I am not sounding very [nice]. The down times of patrolling are actually quite good for me, as we just drive and walk around the district, and they make comments about it all as we go. It was most interesting to go up in the high-rise housing commission flats (nicknamed by the police "the caves"). Lots of comments about the smell of the food Vietnamese people like to eat. Neither would touch anything directly in the buildings, either (like elevator buttons). Also interesting to see the million-dollar view these people have because [the flats] were built in the late sixties when no one wanted to live on the edge of the CBD, the central business district (and the resentment [today] that this property should be used for low-income housing). Now people would kill for this property. I also went to the community center at the housing commission

flats last Friday and talked to the people in their security committee (I think I told you about that in my last e-mail a little). Interesting to walk through the halls after listening to their descriptions of drug dealers and junkies in the laundries, but also of their sense of pride and ownership in where they live.

I had a profound experience earlier on in the week when I went in to observe at the station. A drunken woman was arrested for shoplifting two packages of cheese and some butter from the supermarket. There was only one woman cop on, and so the sergeant said that she would have to do the search before the other two male cops could question her. Someone jokingly suggested I watch the search because the woman (to be searched) was quite overweight. I asked the sergeant seriously if he would mind. He agreed and instructed Rene to do a *strip* search. I knew from my other days at the station that permission from the senior sergeant is needed for a strip search, and proof of cause is needed before he'll grant it. (This all came about a year ago when a gay night club was raided and more than two hundred gay men [were] strip-searched by the police in a single evening. What's that all about?) I suspect that the sergeant wanted to make the search worth my while to observe and perhaps wanted to see if I would squirm.

I don't think there was malice on his part toward me in it, because he is very friendly and helpful toward me in general. So in Renée and I went, her with rubber gloves in case she needed to touch the woman.

I think this incident was a mistake in judgment on my part. I was impressed that during the search the woman said, despite her drunkenness, "This is really degrading, you know," and went on to try to make jokes [directed toward] the woman cop about having bigger boobs than Renée, etc. (The woman cop was very cold in response; maybe because it was true?) I feel quite bad about having participated in that scene. I do not think it was necessary for me in learning about national identity. What I learned about police-"crook" power relations was certainly no surprise, and I don't think justified in the face of how my presence added to this woman's degradation. [I've been thinking] about what made me interested in observing the scene, even once I knew it would be a strip search. I think I got caught up in the excitement of being allowed more and more access to station life. There's this lust for more access and knowledge, almost for its own sake. [And during the night shift there is an air of festivity at] the station when someone is brought in. It breaks up the boredom of sitting around staring at each other; I think I also got caught up in the excitement of a person to "process." The experience taught me that the person is talked about [at the police station] in such a way that it is really easy to forget that he or she is a person. I was consequently caught up short when I was shut in this little room with a very vulnerable naked body that was stripped down, and she was told to lift her breasts to prove she wasn't concealing anything beneath them, all for two packages of cheese and some butter.

I was taken aback by the way one of the two male police constables interacted with the woman as well. They were much more gentle with her than Renée was. But the one kept constructing her as a desired object and put on this caricature of a courtly man. The "shoppy" (shoplifter) said that she wanted to take a piss. The guy reeled back and said, "Now that's not a very ladylike way to talk." And later when she returned [to the station after being released] because she couldn't find where they had put her keys, everyone started to yell for her to go home (most of which was behind the glass wall and she probably didn't hear) and joked to Al that his girlfriend was back. He went out and said, "Darling, you just go on home and make me tea (dinner), and I will be home shortly." She said she'd cook for him over her dead body. People in the back said, "Yeah, and slip into something more comfortable." I felt like the "joke" of Sam's behavior toward her [was] that she was obviously (according to their priorities) so undesirable that his "flirtations" were hilarious.

I think I will mostly try to go out in the cars for the last month. The men are chattier in the cars, perhaps because it is dark and they can face forward and not look directly at me. Really an ideal set-up for a conversation about personal things, I think. The sergeant at the station seems quite easy about my going out now that permission has come through.

I must end here as Terry Eagleton has come to Melbourne and is speaking at 4:00 p.m. Melbourne University has a number of faculty doing social theory and cultural studies, but they don't tend to get many rock star theorists coming through. Plane trip is too unbearable, most likely. Oh also, there is a good chance that I am giving a paper at their national political science conference here in late September. It will be for the social theory panel. John Cash wanted me to do it on the theory behind my methodology. I think that would suit me well at the moment. A lot of my experiences in the field are fresh in my head, and I would like to organize them a little; I think they would make good points of illustration for my argument about what it is that I am looking at and why I chose to go about it in the way I did. I planned on using September to let some of all this settle a little, so I think writing the paper about it will be a good way to process some of it before I leave the field. Kathy Alberti [Graduate Counselor, University of California, Irvine] has been wonderful, of course, in helping me make arrangements to miss the first week of courses [in my capacity as a teaching assistant] so I can give the paper.

Well, signing off. Hope July is finishing well for you on your end. It's hard to believe that it's warm somewhere in the world right now. Oh, I am also going up to the Great Barrier Reef for a week next Friday. Bought the tickets a few months ago. Not great timing now, but it will give me the energy, I think, for that last burst of fieldwork and paper writing. But I will be around for another week if you want to reach me.

Allaine

To: Allaine Cerwonka allaine_cerwonka@politics.muwaye.unimelb.edu.au
From: Liisa Malkki lhmalkki@orion.oac.uci.edu

Date: Thursday, July 27, 1995
Subject: Re: musings on method

Hi there. I'm sorry. I think I didn't respond to your last e-mail before this one; things have
been too hectic. And this one has apparently sat in the system for a few days, too. I just
didn't tune in/boot up/log on at all for a while. There was too much to do and handle.
This latest letter of yours was fascinating, though I am sure it was mighty uncomfortable
for you. I think fieldwork is like that: things have a way of taking their own course and/or
becoming suddenly unmanageable. You go with the flow and try not to become a holier-
than-thou-disruption, and then you end up witnessing a strip search. It made me remember
something parallel I stumbled into in Tanzania. [Badly needing a break from fieldwork,] I
ended up going on a game-hunting trip with Swedish missionaries and Norwegian water
engineers. I didn't kill anything, but I saw plenty of killing and nearly got trampled by a
water buffalo herd because the idiot big white hunters did not know what they were doing.
And I (in my thin, white, Capezio sneakers) sank knee-deep into slimy mud as I tried to
carry the hindquarters of a bleeding warthog on my shoulders—to carry it to the car for
these people. The whole thing was horrible, and I am still haunted by the dead faces and
sweet eyes of the waterbuck and other animals they killed. I was thinking, I could've just
made noise and "saved" these animals.

Well, I think it's a little bit similar. Maybe the connection isn't apparent.

The paper for the conference sounds like an excellent idea. Altogether, I am impressed
by how well in hand everything seems to be there.

Did I tell you Anne McClintock's *Imperial Leather* [1995] has finally come out? Looks
interesting.

Are you getting addresses from the cops, too? So you can stay in touch with them. And
have any of them had you meet spouses or mates? I seem to remember you describing
how separate some of these social spheres or arenas are kept from each other.

I am going to go to a nice stationary store now to admire pens and fine papers. A
sensual pleasure one has to permit oneself often.

Let me know if you need any help at this end, as you prepare to come back.

Till soon,

Liisa

Afterthoughts

AC: Academia has a tradition of privileging the cognitive and ignoring, if not
disdaining, the corporeal. Ethnographic fieldwork is particularly challenging
because its practices blur some of the boundaries that typically operate

around our work, such as the separation of one's private life and working life, for instance. It also makes it more difficult to achieve the ideal of the disembodied intellect. Our bodies play into our intellectual work in vital ways, such as my having to cycle to all of my interviews, having to be able to keep up with police officers on patrol, or being expected to eat the food offered to me by my informants. Because of my mental, emotional, and physical immersion into fieldwork, I found it necessary to build in periods of detachment, which I could only achieve by physically leaving Melbourne.

Additionally, it is often at the level of the body that we register the contradictions of fieldwork and the awkwardness of being a person out of category. There was rarely a day I did not leave the police station without pains in my stomach from tension, exacerbated by eating the fast food that the police always ordered during the dinner shift. As Liisa's discussion here reveals, it is often when fieldwork gets too close or demanding physically that we are most disoriented by it. In Liisa's description it is the weight and the blood of the warthog on her shoulders, contrasted with her lightweight, white, Capezio sneakers, that embodies the moral ambiguity of the context for her (and perhaps even her naïveté going into the situation). As I wrote in my essay "Nervous Conditions," in my participation in what seemed to me an unnecessary strip search, it is at the level of the body that I initially registered my discomfort about the culture of the night shift at the police station. It was my sudden sense of claustrophobia in the interview room, with the naked body of a stranger before me, that forced my awareness of the invasiveness of my research behavior at that moment. And, as I wrote to Liisa, that physical experience allowed me to see how the atmosphere of the night shift encouraged me also to treat the shoplifter as someone to "process."

In this regard, the experience helped me to see the kind of thirst for greater access that I was bringing to fieldwork at that moment. These examples point to the way physical and emotional impressions can be very useful for analytical insights. However, that is not to say that in my mind the insights I gleaned (about myself, about police culture, or about fieldwork) were worth the ethical imposition I still feel I made in relation to the woman who was subjected to the strip search. But if we are going to make mistakes during fieldwork (and, alas, we all do), we might as well use them heuristically.

Both Liisa's and my own experiences during fieldwork highlight the way information about one's field site and about oneself is registered at the level of the body—stomach pains, tense or relaxed muscles, nervous laughter— all provide another layer of information about the ethnographer's sense of the context in which she is embedded. Like information we accumulate visually or by recording people's words, information that we register at the level of the body is not necessarily "true" or unfiltered by the researcher's positionality. It requires the same kind of cross-checking, critical scrutiny, etc. as we undertake in processing other forms of information gathered during fieldwork. Yet, in our rejection of the scientific model of detachment from our bodies, we should not necessarily take the body as a kind of easy or pure representation of truth in research. Diane Nelson cautions us that despite our critical awareness of the constructed meaning of bodies, we "tend to 'really' believe that the body tells the truth in ways that dissimulating words may not" (1999, 209).

While the fictional split between mind and body might be easier to maintain while writing conference papers that draw only on texts, for instance, fieldwork is an embodied form of knowledge production that engages with many aspects of one's being at once; the information we gather often involves our physical being, not simply our minds and imaginations. In this respect, fieldwork is less amenable to the reproduction of the binary split between mind and body. Moreover, it provides the *opportunity* to understand ideas and identities as they are configured materially in bodies and in our imaginings about the body.

To: Allaine Cerwonka allaine_cerwonka@politics.unimelb.edu.au
From: Liisa Malkki lhmalkki@orion.oac.uci.edu
Date: Tuesday, August 1, 1995
Subject: more musings on method

Dear Allaine,

I was just reading a review of a book called *Inside Culture* by David Halle [1993]; it's about the kinds of art, religious objects, etc. that people decorate their homes with, and it occurred to me that (though the book is about the United States) it might give you useable methodological ideas as to what to do with all your photographs and other materials. Do you have any insight or access to the cops' homes or home lives, in the way that you seem to have with the garden club people? (You should not worry about not getting access to some things; nothing is ever wide open.) I hope you continue in high spirits and the best of robust health. (This is the kind of greeting I am so often sent by friends and correspondents from Africa.) I don't like to think of myself as being in "the best of robust health," as I still have so much weight to lose after being pregnant.

   Well, anyway.

Liisa

To: Allaine Cerwonka allaine_cerwonka@politics.muwaye.unimelb.edu.au
From: Liisa Malkki lhmalkki@orion.oac.uci.edu
Date: Wednesday, August 9, 1995
Subject: travels

Dear Allaine,

Just letting you know that I'll be doing preliminary fieldwork in Montreal in August–September. My phone there will be (514)—. I am not sure I'll have e-mail access. Hope you are doing very well there. Looking forward to seeing you here again.

Liisa

To: Liisa Malkki lhmalkki@orion.oac.uci.edu
From: Allaine Cerwonka allaine_cerwonka@politics.muwaye.unimelb.edu.au
Date: Thursday, August 10, 1995
Subject: Re: travels

Hi Liisa,

I am back from ten days up North in the rain forest region. It is an amazing area. The rain forest is very, very dense and goes right down to the beach. So tourism and development are very much limited. And as if that weren't amazing enough, the Great Barrier Reef is only half an hour off shore and creates amazing colors in the water. I indulged in a bit of snorkeling and was delighted by the colors of the reef and the fish below. The beauty of the fish made me feel very plain and uninteresting in comparison. It's a really wonderful activity, snorkeling. It's so quiet under the water, and it's all about watching as opposed to acting on everything. I must admit that I don't understand the people who deliberately try to complicate their lives on vacation by bungie jumping and such things. We also did some kayaking and horseback riding in the region. It felt really, really good to be physical again after so many months of covering up my body against the Melbourne cold. I'm tired of winter.

I do not know if you will get a chance to check your e-mail before leaving for the field. If so, I hope you have a very productive and inspiring month. Montreal is a wonderful place. If you don't mind, I would like to keep sending you e-mail while you are away. It helps me to have someone to talk to about the things happening over here, even if you aren't able to respond. Plus, I have found that it is difficult to describe what a period in time was like once it is gone.

So, from here I will do about three more weeks of fieldwork and then start organizing my information and writing my conference paper. I have the green light for going out in the cop cars, as I think I have mentioned. It came through shortly before leaving for Cairns, so I went out once with my usual station but then once with another station. I can only go out when a car is scheduled, in addition to a van. Since there were none scheduled for Fitzroy, they called over to a neighboring station and got me in one of theirs. It was a good night out and gave me a chance to see whether there were certain things perhaps particular to my station, but not necessarily cop culture in general. A few things perhaps, but the cultures seemed very similar. This time a woman cop was senior person on the car. I find it very interesting talking to women cops about their sense of safety in the city. From their descriptions, they sound much more fearful than the garden club women. And perhaps more cynical than the men towards issues like rape (disbelieving the woman). That doesn't surprise me, however.

The images in your story about hunting in Tanzania were very powerful. I think it was the physicality of my encounter that was so surprising in that little interview room. Much like the horror of carrying the hindquarters of a bleeding warthog. It's the physicality and complicity that are emotionally powerful and morally confusing. But the confusing bits of this year have been the most intellectually engaging.

I am frustrated by the fact that my relationships with the cops are limited to the work sphere. I have gotten peeks at spouses when they show up to pick people up, but I have not had much interaction. It could be a number of things having to do with the character of this particular social world as well as the defenses that I have put up, despite my attempts to get in there with full gusto. I can be timid, despite myself. But time is not up yet, and I will keep an eye open for opportunity. These are guesses, but perhaps part of it has to do with the fact that most of the people are men and most are unmarried. Unmarried people are less prone to entertain in their homes. Then the married ones usually would do more entertaining, but in my experience it's usually women that are in charge of doing the social planning and inviting. And perhaps dinner parties are more of a middle-class thing, and many of the cops have a lot in common culturally with the working class. I have kept my ears open for something equivalent to the U.S. Super Bowl, but nothing so far.

There is one guy, who was the sergeant the night I went out on the "piss up" (Australian for drinking session), who had mentioned having me and Jim (whom he has never met) over for dinner. I think there could be advantages to talking with him one on one over dinner, but I'll have to do some thinking about whether I think he might interpret Jim's absence as a sexual invitation. I do find myself weighing safety as an issue with the cops, and that, along with differences in taste [habitus] might be something that they read and that keeps them more at a distance than I'd prefer. If I were a guy, I could just go off and play Australian rules football with them, and I would gain access to their hearts and lives immediately. Anyway, I will prod Rob some more about going over to his place for dinner, one way or another.

Well, happy travels. Very good to hear from you. I will keep in touch.

Allaine

To: Allaine Cerwonka allaine_cerwonka@politics.muwaye.unimelb.edu.au
From: Liisa Malkki lhmalkki@orion.oac.uci.edu
Date: Saturday, August 12, 1995
Subject: Re: travels

Hi,

Good to hear from you, as always. I hope I didn't worry you about access to women, home lives, etc. I was just asking and did not mean to suggest at all that you should have collected X or Y kind of material. I also think it's worth being self-conscious, as you are, about the kind of material and access your being a woman either blocks or enables. I suspect that it is more usual for men than women to do scholarly work on cops, and I suspect that they do get lots of good material through going to the Australian rules football something-or-other. But they do not necessarily get what you have found. Men, cops, people—they have to interact with lots of different kinds of people in the course of everyday life, and one should not assume *a priori* that the most natural or truest "habitat" of male cops is the company of other men, or other cops. That is, do what you do, and know that you are getting one slice of life and that you clearly have the power to reflect on many things that you can only observe from a distance. Participant observation means, I think, [moving in] a mixture of different social spheres—some you can participate in with ease; others you can only observe, or even hear about second-hand. Second-hand information is not to be sneezed at, either.

Yes, yes, please do keep writing to me, as I love to get these transmissions from you. I think I will, after all, be able to log on from time to time. I'm not sure, but I'll try. So, you may or may not hear from me.

A thought: when you start "writing up," it would be excellent in my view if you didn't try to "sociologize" your vocabulary and descriptive terms too much and allowed instead the "native terms" to do their work as naturally and as evocatively as they do in your letters to me. That is, something like a "piss up": why not keep the term, and other like terms, in your writing? It'll keep your dissertation ethnographically more accurate and livelier, and will make the manuscript more engaging.

Another thought: you felt nervous, I think, about not having done the correct thing, or done enough, when I asked you about the cops' home lives. This is a good preview case that gives you a hint of how a returning fieldworker feels—how fragile and inarticulate—when asked by colleagues at the home institution, "So, what did you find? What are your conclusions? What are you arguing? What's your evidence? What's your point in a nutshell?" People readily interrogate you in a manner that suggests they expect that you have accomplished a "total ethnography," that is, an in-the-round, full ethnography of the whole social universe that you studied in. Of course, this was always a fiction, even when ethnographers did manage to find isolated rural villages in the middle of nowhere. Upon reflection, no one would [explicitly, intentionally] ask such a thing [a total ethnography] of you; [but the post-fieldwork questions from colleagues sometimes add up to give you that impression].

If you are [initially] unable or unwilling to formulate answers to such questions, it is not because you don't know what you want to say, ultimately, but rather because you [probably] have too much material. Yours is not a narrow data set that is crunchable this way and that, and by any technicians who may set their hands to it. You have a year of honest-to-goodness, high-powered, ethnographic fieldwork under your belt, and that material can only be accessed right now by you. It is lodged in your head and in your private field notes. I am warning you not to get upset and not to feel that you "don't know anything" when you get back. It's natural to feel a little bit that way under the questioning of people who don't begin to know what you have been through and learned, which is most everyone. You may know too much, and will never be able to fit it all in the pages of a dissertation or book. Plenty of material and ideas will have to be filed for other writings. That's painful, too: what to omit. It is important, too, to show confidence in the methodologies [and strategies] that you have used, and not to allow ethnography to be frittered away in conversation into "no methods" at all.

When I returned from Tanzania, one question that upset me no end was, "How many people did you talk to? . . . What! You don't know? Well, how many informants?" I had to think about it a lot, and was worried that I had not counted them. Then I realized that I feared I had too few "primary informants." But I didn't. I had a handful of people I was very close to (key informants, as they are sometimes called), and then lots of other kinds of informants and chance meetings with strangers and one-time-only interviews and observations and reports of gossip and the like. I used all of the above in writing. Since I had lived in the setting for a year, I was enabled to make judgments about what was important or not, what was a one-time occurrence or a manifestation of a pattern, what evidentiary weight this or that bit of material could carry, and so on.

I guess I am trying to shield you from some of the pains involved in "coming home" from "the field." You'll go through these things in your own fashion, of course, but it might help somewhere along the way to have heard mention of similar issues from other ethnographers.

You might ask Jim (Ferguson, that is) for a look at the volume he is editing with Akhil Gupta on the concept of "the field" in anthropology. It's very good; I just edited the introductory essay for them. And I look forward to using the book in manuscript form for the methods course I'll be doing with Susan Greenhalgh in spring '96.

That snorkeling sounds like a joyride for the eyes. (Can one say that?) I mean, visually powerful. Sounds tropical, too. I hadn't realized you'd been laboring under wintry conditions! Poor thing! I had just thought it was summer, but of course you people are upside down! How long has it been winter there?

Read a nice short novel: *No New Land* by M.G. Vassanji [1994]. Rings very true. It's especially evocative when read after his other book, *Uhuru Street* [1991]. Both books are about Indians in/from Dar-es-Salaam.

Stay well, Allaine, and do keep writing. I'll check in once more, I expect, before leaving on the 15th.

Liisa

P.S. You might ask the garden club [people] for titles of their favorite gardening books and that kind of documentary back-up material. Also, if ever stuck for conversation topics, it is useful to ask people for recipes. What's your favorite Australian dish, etc.? When people talk about ingredients, they get surprisingly invested in the details. Just an idea, and not a very important one at that.

To: Liisa Malkki lhmalkki@orion.oac.uci.edu
From: Allaine Cerwonka allaine_cerwonka@politics.muwaye.unimelb.edu.au
Date: Wed, August 16, 1995
Subject:

Hello, hello wherever you are.

I am beginning this message with great frustration. I have just spent the last forty-five minutes corresponding with you, only to kick the plug out of the wall and lose the message! Ouch. The limits of technology. This may end up being very short as I am still mourning the loss of my last series of thoughts.

Well, I was in the middle of telling you that I came across Eve Darian-Smith's name on a History Department door. I have read and enjoyed some of her stuff. I believe you directed me toward her because she worked with Sally Falk Moore. I'll reread my articles by her and then swing by and talk with her. I am hoping to talk with a few of the local legends later this coming month.

Oh, I had written you about so many things already this evening. Damn. I am having the most amazing dreams at night. I can feel myself processing many things at once. I am working through saying good-bye to the people in the two field sites. It is sad to say good-bye to people I have come to like and to what is now a more comfortable world for me. I guess this is always the way. It's also difficult in terms of letting go of the collecting process. There is the anxiety that you picked up on of having left things unresearched. I worry that I have left the crucial question unasked, and at this point I can also see how many other things would be interesting to follow up, had I only the time. But then I think about you going off to Montreal, and I realize that there is time in the future to explore and develop what I did not get to this time. And my body tells me it's time to stop soon. I have maintained [a] level of awareness throughout this year that is very taxing on a long-term basis. I have been obsessed with my project, and everything I have done has been about it. So I look forward to having friends who don't necessarily have anything to teach me about Australian-ness.

I think it will be good to have September to think about my project in a more reflective manner: rehash what my questions have been, why I have researched in the manner I have, as well as what I have learned over the course of the year. It has been fortunate that many Australians I have met have felt comfortable questioning me about why I am researching Australian national identity in the way I have. I have gotten used to at least a certain series of questions. But yes, it is really easy to let alarm bells go off in my head and think, "Oh my god, yes, of course, I have done it all wrong and forgotten the most important thing!"

There have been many ways in which this has been a powerful year for me. An important one is that it has given me time away from my department at UCI. For me, that place has often presented an atmosphere of cross-examination about the value of critical theory/post-structuralism. I think I needed a year to really think through my research questions in their own terms and without having to justify them to a skeptical audience. I do not want the questions from members of my department to go away for good, because they are great preparation for the questions I will get on the job trail. But this year has allowed me to feel tougher and less apologetic about my approach. It disappoints me that a good chunk of academia is about posturing and being willing to push through your idea. I'm still not quite sure how to deal with Mark Petracca's [. . .] concern that I am totally unemployable. It will be satisfying to prove him wrong. I know he would actually like to be proved wrong for my sake, but his anxiety is yet another hurdle for me.

I am going out to the theatre with one of the garden club people. In the last month or so I have moved into another age group within the garden club (many aren't active members, but I have been referred to them by those who are). These have been women (some married, some not) who have children—teenagers. I have been delighted to find them so open in just a single interview. I have heard stories about people catching their husbands having affairs, concerns about children, etc. I am still giggling to myself about the story one woman told about her husband's lack of involvement in their daughter's life. I gently teased her about toeing the harder line [being the stricter disciplinarian] when it came to their daughter. She laughed and said that, yes, but her daughter knows that she cares about her and is aware of the details of her life. Her husband does not. In fact, her daughter's teacher had said that for an entire year she wasn't even aware that the girl had a father because she never mentioned him. One day her husband was the one to drop their daughter off at school, and he took her to the wrong school! He wasn't aware of where she went to school, even though it was a private school they sent their daughter to. This woman had a good sense of humor about the whole thing, but her husband did seem to be a bit of a concern to her.

Well, I better dash if I am to meet Judith at the theatre in time.

Allaine

⊹

To: Allaine Cerwonka allaine_cerwonka@politics.muwaye.unimelb.edu.au
From: Liisa Malkki lhmalkki@orion.oac.uci.edu
Date: Wednesday, August 23, 1995
Subject: Re: no subject

Hi,

EEEK! So this is fieldwork. I am finding myself very unprepared emotionally for this. I had thought that I'd arrive, develop some anxiety, and procrastinate for a few days before I contact people. You know, build up to it, but that didn't happen. We arrived in Montreal on the fifteenth, and on the following morning already a refugee friend was knocking at our door. We were all still in our pajamas, and I really didn't feel like talking to anyone before having a cup of coffee, but what can you do? It's been busy ever since. This is so different from the earlier research. Here, people have heard of me already, want to [have a look at] my book, can see why someone would want to research their lives, are open about many things—but very closed about others.

What a drag to lose that message. I do things like that too often. We can talk more when you come back, but I just wanted to say I thought you were thinking very useful thoughts about the return to the department at UCI. Let me know if I can help. Some people just dropped in. Got to go. I wish I could just sit and write for a bit longer, but next time. What's your departure date? It'll be a hard thing for you, I am sure, to leave. Talk to you soon.

Liisa

P.S. I think you should not worry about employability questions now. Just keep your peace of mind, write your chapters, and start applying for jobs much later. I think you'll be fine.

Tradition and Improvisation
in Ethnographic Field Research

LIISA H. MALKKI

> To name a sensibility, to draw its contours and to recount its history, requires
> deep sympathy modified by revulsion.
> —Susan Sontag, "Notes on Camp"

Introduction

Anthropology, as I have learned it, is traditionally the most eclectic and
interdisciplinary of disciplines. As Clyde Kluckhohn famously put it, anthropologists carry a kind of "intellectual poaching license" (cited in Geertz
1973). Over time, that license has been exercised in relation to many other
disciplines. In my graduate training, a memorable dictum came from Fred-
erick Maitland: "Anthropology will be history or it will be nothing" (Evans-
Pritchard 1961, 20). But there are remarkable differences of opinion as to
which disciplines are most closely allied to anthropology. Aside from history, contemporary sociocultural anthropology has made strong links to law,
structural linguistics, Marxist theory, philosophy, religious studies, feminist
theory, cultural studies, literary criticism, ethnic studies, social theory, and
sociology. But other time periods have seen these links elsewhere.

Yet, while judiciously exercising its poaching license, anthropology is
unquestionably a discipline with well-known intellectual traditions, or histories. There is also a specific anthropological sensibility. Anthropology is
not a social science *tout court*, but something else. What that something else
is has been notoriously difficult to name, precisely because it involves less a
subject matter—which, after all, overlaps with that of other disciplines in the

humanities and social sciences—than a sensibility. This sensibility is similar to Bourdieu's (2000) concept of professional "disposition."[1]

There are many things that still (remarkably perhaps, given our degrees of specialization) go without saying among sociocultural anthropologists—understandings that are widely shared. The first such understanding is that anthropology is what it is because it produces "situated knowledges" (Haraway 1991) through long-term, intensive, ethnographic fieldwork. How is this done? Anthropologists have had a challenging time of explaining this in general terms, even while many have produced brilliant ethnographic monographs based on long and innovative fieldwork. Since the manuals for ethnographic research that are widely used and respected by anthropologists are few and far between (to put it conservatively), and since ethnography is not usually taught as a set of standard or universally applicable methods, there is little that anthropologists can point to (other than the finished product) in explicit, ready defense of the methodological power of ethnographic work.[2]

When I began the e-mail correspondence with Allaine years ago, I became keenly aware that I was trying to say things to her that "go without saying" for anthropologists. So I assumed at any rate. But the "common sense" of anthropology is a complicated matter. As the weeks became months of correspondence, I realized two unsettling things. First, I was singularly uncertain at times as to what the things that go without saying were. Second, when I used our "working archive" (the e-mails) as a text in a course entitled "Practicum on Anthropological Fieldwork Techniques," my anthropology graduate students regularly expressed relief that the things that should go without saying were being said in our e-mails. For this reason alone, sustained conversations across disciplines are clarifying and, sometimes, enabling. Not only are anthropologists provoked into methodological and epistemological self-reflection, but non-anthropologists, too, improvising with methods taken from ethnography, can create something new and important. There are many improvisational dimensions to knowledge production and writing in general, but for ethnographic research, as I will suggest below, improvisation is indispensable. It requires a poaching license. Improvisation also entails a heightened sense of time and process.

In what follows, I begin with reflections on the specifically situated interdisciplinarities with which Allaine and I engaged. As will become evident, these tasks of negotiation and translation were not just a matter of a straightforward, one-to-one conversation between political science and anthropology. Much more complex and long-standing issues concerning empiricism, positivism, quantification, the nature of evidence, and the noisome ghost of "the scientific method" challenged us throughout. Here, I engage these issues only insofar as they are directly relevant to the intellectual project at hand, recognizing, of course, that a vast body of excellent work already exists in this area. It should be emphasized that my effort to think through questions of the ethics and politics of ethnographic field research are certainly not intended as a review of the literature on methods. I write in a practical spirit directly to the issues that were generated by our correspondence.

I will suggest ways of conceptualizing ethnographic field research as a complex process entailing (at least) three always co-present kinds of practice (see Moore 1978; Whitehead 1967, 90). Thus, ethnography, understood here as situated, long-term, empirical field research (as opposed to its other meaning as a genre of writing and a practice of representation), is simultaneously *a critical theoretical practice,* a *quotidian ethical practice,* and *an improvisational practice.* I conclude with reflections on process and temporality in ethnographic fieldwork.

Ethnography as a Critical Theoretical Practice

Much has been written in favor of inter- or cross-disciplinarity in anthropology and many other fields. Major funding agencies for social research are often particularly encouraging of projects demonstrating interdisciplinarity. In scholarly publishing, too, interdisciplinary work is valued. Programs and rosters of conferences organized around the world reveal a similar pattern. Graduate students in many doctoral programs are encouraged to do interdisciplinary course work, or they pursue such a route as a matter of course, as Allaine did. These contemporary trends fit ill and yet coexist with other institutional realities, and specifically this: the major and institutionally strongest departments in contemporary universities in the United States and elsewhere are still organized around long-standing disciplines. The system of awarding doctoral degrees still shapes scholarly knowledge production in disciplinary ways. When graduate students become job applicants in the academy, they are usually expected to hold a doctorate in the discipline to which they are applying. One of the most expedient mechanisms for reducing the pile of job applications facing a search committee is to weed out applicants with a doctorate in another discipline. The social and professional costs of doing interdisciplinary work are thus potentially very high for graduate students and untenured faculty. The tight market in academic jobs can become fearsome to negotiate, and there are also constant worries about the recognition and misrecognition of one's work in one's home discipline and outside it.

This raises formidable questions about advising or helping graduate students to pursue inter- or cross-disciplinary work, questions that continually preoccupied me as I worked with Allaine in her student days. This is what

I thought: is it ethical and responsible to encourage a student from outside my own department and discipline to conduct ethnographic fieldwork when her own discipline, political science, has traditionally valued and employed a very different set of research methods? What are the stakes for her, and do I have a realistic understanding of them? True, Allaine had herself pursued interdisciplinary linkages in the university long before she met me. But it is one thing to read widely and quite another to base one's entire dissertation research on an alien repertory of research techniques—techniques, more-over, that required more than a year of her time in a degree program that did not have such an extra year built into it. In deciding to pursue ethnographic research (or "real and serious fieldwork," as I think I put it to her at the time), Allaine would be out of step with her department in a number of ways.

It was evident that she had too strong a mind to be pushed into a project not of her own choosing, and that she had trained herself well—as a political scientist and a scholar—precisely through her own intellectual nomadism. It was also clear that she was highly regarded by her own faculty in political science at the University of California at Irvine; this undoubtedly afforded her more room for maneuvering than a different student might have had.

I was very interested in her project and aware of my desire and curiosity to see how it would materialize, but this was not sufficient to absolve me of worries: was she heading for treacherous or even un-navigable waters? In-deed, her advisors in political science worried about the same thing, and reasonably so. If, upon completion of the project, she produced a creature for which there was no appropriate cage, what would happen to her? Was I in some sense treating her as an "experimental doll" (Marks 1987)? The very form of this question suggests a passive role for Allaine, and I protest: It wasn't so! Even when we first met, we were more like colleagues than like teacher and student. While Allaine was an advanced graduate student at the time, I was still an untenured Assistant Professor, not many years beyond my own Ph.D. degree. Our different disciplinary "homes" and the fact that I was not her dissertation advisor probably contributed to the informality and ease of our relationship. I was also continually learning from our conver-sations together. She has never been a passive doll awaiting animation or instruction. Looking hard at the situation, however, the institutional and micropolitical hierarchies were there, and Allaine was structurally vulnera-ble. My relief and joy were great when Allaine's completed dissertation won the American Political Science Association (APSA) award for best dissertation in the category Race, Ethnicity, and Politics (1997); these feelings were com-pounded when her first academic position and the transformation of her dis-sertation into a book (Cerwonka 2004) seemed to come so painlessly. But the outcome might have been different, and that is why the old Enlightenment adage, "knowledge for the sake of knowledge," seems rather toothless at actually lived interdisciplinary crossroads.

Allaine's disciplinary nomadism (or transgressions, or poaching, or auto-didacticism, depending on the angle of view) involved intellectual negotiations, but also important political and social tasks of translation. In these negotiations and translations, many different sorts of issues surfaced, and chief among them were conventional understandings of "the scientific method" and of "social science." Her advisors put a hard but productive battery of questions to her (and to me, even if more discreetly): Why do ethnography? What can it accomplish that other strategies of knowledge production cannot? Is it empirical? And even if empirical, are its findings significant and *generalizable?* To answer the misgivings of the unconvinced was a challenging and serious task that Allaine and I have each tried to honor in our different ways. My brief reply follows.

I regard ethnographic field research as an invaluable and in certain respects superior mode of knowledge production among other powerful modes of knowledge production. Ethnography has never been a failed form of empiricism, "almost a science," the thing one does if one has no head for numbers or cares more about "feelings" than "facts." The conventionalized alignment of quantification with "science" and words with "not-science" is obviously spurious but still startlingly widespread. That is why I address it here. It is one of the many guises in which "the scientific method" can haunt social research as a "default mode of knowledge production," as Allaine once described it. ("The scientific method" can be characterized as an expectation that research should ideally follow a single, generalized logic of inquiry, often described in terms of the testing, or "falsifying," of hypotheses. The idea that even the natural sciences can be described in these terms is dubious. [See, e.g., Putnam 1978; Latour 1988; cf. Whitehead 1967].)

Malinowski, Boas, and other pioneers of anthropology pursued empirical research that they never hesitated to regard both as scientific and also as interpretive and experience-based. Only a later, narrower notion of science made ethnography "soft"—a "non-science" or a "not-quite-social-science." And only an even more recent misreading allows the ethnographer's principled, situated pursuit of social and cultural understanding to be styled as a "postmodern" or "relativistic" turn away from "science." Ethnographic field research, after the very early era of armchair ethnography (see Kuklick 1997), has always been both empirical research and a form of critical theoretical practice. This is not a recent development, postmodern or otherwise. It is knitted into the very backbone of anthropology. It is our tradition. It is perhaps useful to remind ourselves of this by reviewing some much older reflections on method in anthropology.

Edmund Leach's 1967 essay "An Anthropologist's Reflections on a Social Survey" is a close examination of a particular study, *The Disintegrating Village*, by Sarkar and Tambiah (1957). Based on a statistical survey of fifty-eight villages in Pata Dambara, Ceylon (now Sri Lanka), this study was regarded by Leach as a landmark work in Ceylon social studies. While he richly praised the work, the bulk of Leach's commentary consists of a lucid, carefully argued critique of the limitations of the social survey in "field sociology." His engagement was with far-reaching "principles of method" (Leach 1967, 76) rather than simply with the Pata Dambara survey. The histories of the scholars involved here are especially interesting to me because the sociological work of young Stanley Tambiah in the 1950s little resembles his brilliant, subsequent ethnographic and theoretical work in anthropology. He was (and is still) an invaluable teacher to me, among many others of his students. And Tambiah and Leach were to become, of course, close colleagues at Cambridge in the 1960s.

This is how Leach begins to map out the consequential differences between what he calls, too simply, "anthropological" and "sociological" methods:[3]

> In [the] area of field research, the differences between sociology and social anthropology do not lie in theory but in method. As a consequence of the fact that the principal research tool of the field sociologist is a command of statistics, it has become a necessary feature of sociological investigation that the "results" should be expressed in numbers. It follows that the units of sociological investigation must always be entities which can be expressed in numbers. [...] I would be the last to suggest that statistical investigations are necessarily mistaken in aim or application, but they are certainly limited in scope. It is my thesis that there is a wide range of sociological phenomena which are intrinsically inaccessible to statistical investigation of any kind. It is in this area of *non-statistical social fact* that the social anthropologist is professionally expert. (Leach 1967, 76–77; emphasis added)

Not all sociologists work with statistical surveys, of course—and there are anthropologists who rely on surveys—but in the present context it is analytically clarifying to foreground the premises, techniques, and products of statistical survey research. Leach's close attention to analytical premises in social anthropology and statistical sociology is also instructive: "The sociologist and the social anthropologist start with different premises about the nature of their subject matter. The sociologist with his statistical orientation presupposes that the field of observation consists of 'units of population,' 'individuals'; in contrast, the social anthropologist, with his non-statistical prejudices, thinks of his data as being made up of '*systems of relationship*'" (Leach 1967,

77; emphasis added). Again, this is too simple, because some statistical techniques are themselves concerned with "systems of relationship." But the contrast Leach draws between a qualitative anthropological focus on relationships and the typical survey's focus on the attributes of randomly selected
individuals is broadly accurate, and methodologically instructive.

> Differences in field research technique then logically follow. The sociologist
> assumes that the truths he is seeking to investigate are statistical truths, and, in
> the normal way, he endeavours to arrive at these truths by sampling procedures.
> Consequently the size of the "population" which can be investigated may be large
> in relation to the number of investigators; and the length of the enquiry may be
> correspondingly short. [. . .] In sharp contrast, an anthropologist will normally
> confine his attention to a single very small geographical area and endeavour to
> investigate the total network of interpersonal relationships which exists within
> that small area. The truths which he thus discovers are particular truths, and, if
> he is wise, he will be extremely cautious about attempts to generalise from these
> particulars. (Leach 1967, 78)

It is straightforward to see that the "particular truths" produced by anthropological fieldwork are "situated knowledges" (Haraway 1991). But it is also
necessary to recognize, naturally, that "statistical truths" are another form
of situated knowledge—differently situated, but situated nonetheless. One
of the common social characteristics of "statistical truths" is that they tend
to present themselves, and to be received, as results of unsituated knowledge production and as generally representative and authoritative for the social unit being researched. Yet, all researchers are in one manner or another
socially and politically situated, and the situation of the survey interview is
just one among many. This obviously does not mean that their work is un-
reliable—only that it requires, like all social research (indeed, like all research), to be interpreted.

> It is easy to see that the more obvious criticisms which anthropologists can make
> against sociologists are the simple converse of those which sociologists are likely
> to make against anthropologists. On the one hand, the sociologist with his sampling
> techniques and his questionnaire investigations appears to be presupposing uni-
> formities which perhaps do not really exist. In a sense, he is forced to assume that,
> already, before he ever starts his questionnaire enquiries, he knows, by intuition,
> just what are the significant variables concerning which it is worth while making
> enquiries. On the other hand, the microscopic investigations of the anthropologist
> may well be of such a particular nature as to have no general validity at all. Both ar-
> guments carry weight, and there is a commonsense implication that, if they hope

to achieve conclusions which have a general as opposed to a particular validity, the sociologist and the anthropologist ought to act as a team. With that view I am very largely in agreement. [Here], however, I am not so much concerned with the interdependence of anthropology and sociology as with their contradictions. (Leach 1967, 78–9)

Leach then goes on to analyze and reinterpret some of the findings of the Pata Dambara survey regarding land tenure, inheritance, and stratification. He demonstrates that a random selection of households following the statistical sociological model produces results that systematically misunderstand key social facts and institutions in the region. He proceeds to examine the apparent discrepancy in the survey results and shows that an anthropological, nonrandom analysis of "systems of relationship" among persons and households, land and wealth—as opposed to "units of population" randomly sampled—produces results that better explain the cultural and social processes at work. He notes that he arrives at his conclusion "by making the typically anthropological assumption that a social field does not consist of units of population but of persons in relation to one another" (Leach 1967, 80). Survey research tends to look for statistical relations among "individuals" and households with attributes, whereas anthropologists more commonly look for systems of social relations among people and institutions.

One of the merits of Leach's concise account is that he offers an analytical vocabulary for explaining to a non-anthropologist why the random sample (with all of its possibilities for generalization) should not be the ideal or goal in many research contexts.

Let me repeat, I am arguing by negation. My purpose is not to denounce all statistical types of sociological enquiry but rather to explain just why the social anthropologist claims to be able to reveal facts which escape the observation of the statistician. Precisely because he uses statistics, the sociologist must operate with a random sample of population. This means that *by definition* the units of population must be assumed to be unrelated to one another. It follows that no characteristics of the population which emerge from the enquiry can possibly be attributed to the interrelationships existing between different units. In contrast, the anthropologist explicitly concentrates on data which are *not* random. He purposely chooses a small field within which all the observable phenomena are closely interrelated and interdependent. (Leach 1967, 87; emphases in original)

What is more, standardized and apparently neutral survey questions in fact contain embedded cultural and ideological assumptions.

This is the crux. Dr. Tambiah makes the normal statistical sociologist's assumption that his questionnaire data can be treated as *independent evidence*. Individual questionnaires may be in error but, since the material has been collected on a "random" basis, the errors will cancel out. If then mathematical analysis of the questionnaires produces results which are in accordance with "legal expectation," this shows that practice and legal theory agree. But can we really say anything of the sort? Might it not be that all the questionnaires have, from the first, been drawn up to accord more closely with legal principles than with empirical facts? (Leach 1967, 83)

Here again we are back at the basic difference of attitude adopted by sociologists and anthropologists toward their raw material. The statistical sociologist takes it for granted that the truth which he is seeking is contained in his questionnaire answers and that mathematical technique is capable of revealing that truth; in contrast the anthropologist is suspicious of questionnaire data as such. I maintain that it is in the very nature of questionnaire investigation that the "results" tend to err in the direction of ideal stereotypes. Hence any attempt to investigate, by questionnaire research, the degree of fit between an ideal stereotype and actual practice is a waste of time. (Leach 1967, 85)

A parallel problem is likely to occur when a political scientist researching, say, nationalism interviews government officials or surveys citizens on their "political culture." (See also Bourdieu's critique of the opinion poll [2000, 67ff.] and Malinowski's critique of the questionnaire [1935, 319].) Here again, the knowledge produced tends to present itself as authoritative and to leave relatively invisible the situatedness and partialness of the results. If they are articulated, the situatedness of the researcher(s) and the partial (as opposed to God's-eye) views any project affords tend to be dealt with as unfortunate weaknesses, hardly ever as *analytical strengths*.

The tension between the two traditions of research contrasted by Leach was played out in Allaine's field research and in the course of our correspondence. I have dwelt on the tension at length because Leach's treatment of it goes a long way toward answering the questions about ethnography with which we began: Why do ethnography? What can it accomplish that other modes of research cannot? Is it empirical? Generalizable? Yes, it is deeply empirical. Yes, it can do things that statistical survey research cannot do. It is a powerful form of knowledge production that is (or can be) as deeply empirical as research gets. It is also theoretical from the start, because self-questioning about the form and the "object" of knowledge, about *the categories that structure the enquiry,* and about (as we would say today) one's will to knowledge are continually activated and reactivated by the socially situated, embodied practices of anthropological fieldwork. The generalizability of ethnographic modes of knowledge (the final element in the list of concerns given above), is, as Leach showed, a question that must be asked in the context of specific projects of research. And before this question becomes meaningful, it is necessary to ask: What is the unit of analysis at hand? And what the will to knowledge? In much classical anthropology, the unit of analysis was "a culture" or "a society" as a whole universe, and the will to knowledge was driven by holistic, totalizing research goals, that is, the desire and injunction to know "everything." Such anthropological holism was always an unattainable and wrong-headed ideal (see Gupta and Ferguson 1997; Geertz 1973, 40ff.).[4]

Long before Edmund Leach's time, Bronislaw Malinowski, in the Trobriand Islands in the 1930s, had already worked out some of the methodological ideas that came to be regarded as canonical ("traditional") in later anthropology. Malinowski never heard postmodernism spoken of, but he was very aware of the constructedness of facts and of the simultaneously theoretical and empirical nature of "fieldwork."

> The observer should not function as a mere automaton; a sort of combined camera and phonographic or shorthand recorder of native statements. *While making his observations, the fieldworker must constantly construct:* he must place isolated data in relation to one another and study the manner in which they integrate. To put it paradoxically, one could say that *"facts" do not exist in sociological any more than in physical reality;* that is, they do not dwell in the spatial and temporal continuum open to the untutored eye. The principles of social organisation, of legal constitution, of economics and religion have to constructed by the observer out of a multitude of manifestations of varying significance and relevance. It is these invisible realities, only to be discovered by inductive computation, by selection and construction, which are scientifically important in the study of culture. Land tenure is typical of such *"invisible facts."* (Malinowski 1935, 317; emphases added)

The "facts" or "data" are not, in other words, *objets trouvés* waiting to be discovered and recorded.[5] They are *made* (see Geertz 1973, 15–16; Malinowski 1935, 322n2). They are a social product, whether expressed in numbers, words, images, or other media. This clearly does not mean that they are not empirical. It is precisely their active construction by the researcher, Malinowski insists, that is "scientifically important in the study of culture."

Malinowski goes on to consider the nature of ethnographic practice; it is obvious to him that it is an inescapably theoretical practice:

The fieldworker in collecting his material has constantly to strive after a clear idea of what he really wants to know; in this case, a clear idea of what land tenure really is. And since this idea has gradually to emerge from the evidence before him, he must constantly switch over from observation and accumulated evidence to theoretical moulding, and then back to collecting data again. [. . .] Your ideas, therefore, will have to be extremely plastic and adjustable, for your concrete data, of course, cannot be "adjusted." [. . .] *Observations are impossible without theory; [. . .] theories must be formed before you start to observe, but readily dropped or at least remoulded in the course of observation and construction.* (Malinowski 1935, 321, emphasis added)

Clearly, the foregoing schematic discussion touches upon very old and much-rehearsed epistemological debates. The remarkable thing about them is that they are still so actively argued in some quarters, and often in terms of very simple either/or binarisms: objective : subjective :: quantitative : qualitative :: scientific : literary :: empirical : imaginative :: hard : soft, and even nowadays :: "scientific": "postmodernist."

Paul Willis, a central figure in British cultural studies, took up these binarisms more than twenty years ago.[6] In a particularly clear critical essay on method in ethnographic cultural studies, "Notes on Method" (1980), his aim is to identify the "really central principles of the 'qualitative' method" (Willis 1980, 88; and see also Willis 2000). He begins by remarking that mainstream, positivistic sociology has been obliged to accord participant observation and case study work "a legitimate place in the social sciences," but that this formulation of a *"methodological* variety" still leaves "the heartland of the positivist terrain untouched" (Willis 1980, 88). Thus, the notion of a methodological "variety" may be institutionally convenient, but it can also paper over differences that challenge each other too fundamentally to be a part of the same universe of knowledge production, while assimilating "qualitative" ways of knowing as a junior partner in an overarching positivist project.

In its recognition of a *technical* inability to record all that is relevant—and its yielding of this zone to another technique—positivism may actually preserve its deepest loyalty: to its object of inquiry truly as an "object." The duality and mutual exclusivity of the over-neatly opposed categories, "qualitative" methods and "quantitative" methods, suggest already that the "object" is viewed in the same unitary and distanced way even if the *mode* is changed—now you measure it, now you feel it. (Willis 1980, 88; emphases in original)

But, as anthropologists have long insisted, the very "object" of knowledge may change depending on whether a statistical relation or a social system of relations is privileged, and depending on what one's will to knowledge is. In this sense, the object of knowledge is never inert, lying somewhere out there in the landscape waiting to be "discovered"—or "felt."

Ethnography, Affect, and Quotidian Ethical Practice

This section begins with a discussion of the senses and affect, imagination and embodiment in anthropological fieldwork and then moves on to connect these with questions of ethics.

It is remarkable how often in everyday practices of knowledge production the term, *qualitative* comes to be aligned with matters of intuition and affect. "Now you measure it, now you feel it" (Willis 1980, 88; cf. Musil 1994, 134–49). What is this familiar binarism made of? The production of heteronormative gender binaries through practices of knowledge production is well known and well studied. Here, I want to pull out some other threads. First, this masculine : feminine :: hard : soft :: measurement : feeling :: objective : subjective :: quantitative : qualitative, binary apparatus assumes and even idealizes an absence of affect in the use of numbers. This is demonstrably a weak assumption. We are only too familiar with the emotive effects (and motivations) of interested numerical representations involving the exaggeration or minimization of things like civilian casualties in wars, death rates in genocides, or the measurable physiological effects of depleted uranium on people's bodies in the wake of the Gulf War. (Interestingly, in *The History of the Modern Fact* [1998], Mary Poovey has documented the early scholarly mistrust of statistics as being always too vulnerable to interested and emotive political manipulations. Statistics was considered a "soft" science on just these grounds.)

Despite the rather obvious co-presence of affective and ethical investments in even the most scientistic kinds of social research, there remains in "the scientific method" in default mode a "central insistence" on the "*passivity of the participant observer*" (Willis 1980, 89; emphasis added). The idealized erasure of the human, social presence of the researcher is evident in the ways in which "observation" is often defined. The normative expectation of the passivity of the researcher depends upon a "belief that the object of the research exists in [the] external world, with knowable external characteristics which must not be disturbed" (Willis 1980, 89; cf. Whitehead 1967, 88ff.). The idealized subject position for the researcher, then, is to strive to be "a fly on the wall," a quietly transparent observer. This is, at its worst, a voyeuristic and dishonest desire. It is true that "observation" is an element in the ethnographic conventions of "participant observation." But the participant observer is not a fly. On the one hand, one participates in good faith in the social contexts in which one is working. This presumably also entails conversations with people—conversations that make of the ethnographer, and of them, complexly social persons with social obligations. On the other hand, one observes—or tries to *see* and *hear* and use one's other senses well. To observe unobserved is usually an illusion. The actual fly on the wall shares this illusion at its own peril.

As Willis points out, human subjectivity and imagination are framed by social scientism as potential *contaminants* of research, blots:

> The concern is to minimize "distortion in the field," with the underlying fear that the *object* may be *contaminated* with the subjectivity of the researcher. Too easily it becomes an assumption of different orders of reality between the researched and the researcher. The insistent, almost neurotic, technical concern with the differentiation of PO [participant observation] from reportage and Art is also a reflection of the subterranean conviction that PO belongs with the "sciences" and must, in the end, respect objectivity. There is a clear sociological fear of naked subjectivity. The novel can wallow in subjectivity—this is how it creates "colour" and "atmosphere"—but how do we know that the author did not make it all up! So the research must be for a unified object which might be expected to present itself as *the same* to many minds. The first principle of PO, the postponement of theory, compounds the dangers of this covert positivism. It strengthens the notion that the object can present itself directly to the observer. (Willis 1980, 90; emphases in original)

Willis goes on to insist, like Malinowski and Leach (and many others) before him, that "in fact, there is no truly untheoretical way in which to 'see' an 'object.' The 'object' is only perceived and understood through an internal organization of data, mediated by conceptual constructs and ways of seeing the world" (Willis 1980, 90).

This statement provokes, as Willis noted earlier, a palpable positivistic fear that "theory can only, ultimately, demonstrate its own assumptions" (Willis 1980, 89). Thus, to simplify crudely, if every practice of research is always already theoretical, how can anything new be discovered? How can one see outside of theory? How can it be ensured that researchers are not just writing about themselves? The very form of these questions rests on the homology of binarisms discussed above. Willis's answer here is as follows: "However, we must recognize the ambition of the PO [participant-observation] principle in relation to theory. It has directed its followers towards a profoundly important methodological possibility—that of being "surprised," of reaching knowledge not prefigured in one's starting paradigm" (90).[7] We see this surprise emerging in Allaine's field experience. Her work in Melbourne was not a matter of the gradual accumulation of "data" into a stable structure, but of moments of puzzlement and sudden realization, of making and unmaking. This element of surprise often transformed her framing questions and led her to move continually back and forth between newfound understandings and older theoretical insights and questions, new methodological ideas and older, precomposed ones.

The capacity to be surprised requires imagination, which is one of the less directly "teachable" abilities that fieldwork demands (see Comaroff and Comaroff 1992; Mills 1959). The aspects of imagination at play in fieldwork are many. Theoretical imagination bleeds into social imagination and back again. Our senses provoke imagination in complex ways, as Stoler (2004); Reddy (2001); Herzfeld (2001, 2004); Seremetakis (1994); Stoller (1989), and others have shown. In the "thick processes" of fieldwork, affect and the senses (like thought) embody and gender the researcher in both predictable and unpredictable ways.

I can offer the sense of smell as a very simple example. In the refugee camp in which I worked in Tanzania, I remember noticing that I initially smelled different from many of the people there. I became aware of the smells of my own deodorant, soap, shampoo, and perfume from Southern California. On other people's bodies, I smelled sweat, smoky reminders of cooking fires, and a different kind of soap. Later, I became curious about where in the camp people got their soap, and I learned where and how it was made. In the process, I learned that it was very easy to ask people to talk about technical processes like soap-making; they knew that they were teaching me something definite and useful. This kind of conversation was much more effortless—and politically safer—than asking people outright about their lives and histories as refugees. Being taught about soap took a long time. In the process, I learned much more than I had expected about questions and themes that interested me more than soap. So, in a quite straightforward way, the sense of smell had yielded methodological and other insights, in addition to introducing me to several people I had not previously known. "Information" in a technical sense yielded "understanding" in theoretical and social senses. As Hannah Arendt (2005) wrote in another time, "Understanding, as distinguished from having correct information and scientific knowledge, is a complicated process which never produces unequivocal results. It is an unending activity by which, in constant change and variation, we come to terms with and reconcile ourselves to reality, that is, try to be at home in the world" (307).

At other times in the course of fieldwork in that refugee camp, fear forced me to think hard about my own imagination and to try to distinguish between paranoia and reasonable caution. Sitting alone at night with my affectionate tomcat, I sometimes felt my stomach tighten into knots as I imagined possible scenarios (mostly of getting kicked out of the camp before being able to complete my fieldwork, and of getting people into trouble with the authorities somehow simply by having sought their company). I had to work hard to sort out the possible scenarios from the likely scenarios, to trace the surfaces of my fear, and then to translate that into action and inaction. These night battles with my own imagination sharpened my senses, shaped my research strategies, taught me about the kinds of social performativity involved in being a "researcher" or a "student," and, most important, they raised continual ethical concerns about anonymity, confidentiality, informed consent, and the general safety of the people with whom I worked and lived. In this case, I would not know how neatly to separate affect from thought. More, insisting on that neat compartmentalization would have been analytically counterproductive.[8]

Yet, in the ethnographic monograph I wrote on the basis of the fieldwork in Tanzania (Malkki 1995), little remains of the centrality of affect and the senses in the process of my fieldwork. Whether it was fear or pleasure, boredom or comfort, pathos or humor, I tended to erase it from the final written product, perhaps appropriately.[9] Another thing I self-consciously avoided was writing long, narrative descriptions of the landscape, people's houses, their dress and mannerisms, and the moods or atmospheres of particular moments. I did not feel entitled to describe in that way, from the evidence of my own senses. Much later, in reading Mary Weismantel's excellent book *Cholas and Pishtacos* (2001), I realized that there might have been something quite conventionalized to my avoidance. She writes about a Puritanism of the senses in scholarly texts.[10] "Anxious to disavow exoticist writers of the past, ethnographers these days assiduously avoid expressing sensual enjoyment of the places where we work. Indeed, anthropology, once the relentless diarist of minutiae, now avoids the systematic recording of sense impressions, beset by an almost puritanical fear of admitting that they matter to us" (100). She notes that many ethnographers prefer—almost by default—to "move to a more distanced stance; and it is there, withdrawn from sensory knowledge, that they begin their analysis" (101; and see Herzfeld 2004, and 2001, 240–53; Fisher 2002; Seremetakis 1994; Passaro 1997; Foster 1996, 203ff.). Writing about visuality and visual anthropology, Anna Grimshaw has likewise identified "a puritan spirit running through anthropology as modern project," and she characterizes anthropology's relation to images and visuality (after Lucien Taylor) as one of "iconophobia" (Grimshaw 2001, 5; cf. Schneider and Wright 2006, 4; Belting 1994; Jay 1994).[11]

If we accept that fieldwork is an embodied, and embodying, form of knowledge production, why should we leave a considered awareness of the senses out of the project of creating ethnographic understanding? (In some quarters, participant observation is playfully known as "soak-and-poke" research.) And it just gets messier.

In 2000–2001, during a fellowship year at the Center for Advanced Study in the Behavioral Sciences in Stanford, California, I presented the e-mail correspondence between Allaine and myself to a multidisciplinary reading group of fellows. I received many productive comments (of which more further on). For the present purposes, the most productive feedback came as follows: "Do you *have* to have all these babies and washing machines in here?" This was a very interesting and surprising reaction, one that promptly announced itself: *"Datum!"* The correspondence included a few references to babies, to be sure, but I could not find any mention of washing machines. I later concluded from this that the commentator's referent was a generalized, vaguely feminine, mundane domesticity. The fine scholar who made the comment, in some frustration at having wasted his time reading such a long document, suggested that the correspondence was too long and that we should just pull out "the main points" and discuss them "more analytically," deleting all the rest. (The relevant homology might look like this: wet : dry :: domesticity : analysis :: life : work :: the senses : critical distance.)

The correspondence, in all its deliberate length, is meant to convey an inescapably temporal *process.* That process, the critical theoretical practice of ethnography, is typically long, often meandering, inescapably social, and temporally situated. More specifically, ethnography as process demands a critical awareness of the invisible social fact that multiple, different temporalities might be at play simultaneously. The process is inextricably embedded in relationally structured social lives,[12] quotidian routines,[13] events that become Events (see Malkki 1997), the panic time of deadlines,[14] the elongated time of boredom,[15] the cyclical time of the return of the expected,[16] the spiral time of returns to the recognizable or the remembered,[17] and so on. It engages the senses and the social and physical being of the ethnographer. It involves affect and makes demands on one's intuition. All of this is its analytical power and its messy challenge.

That you as an ethnographer work with what you are given—even as you make new things—means also that your gender, age, race, nationality, class, temperament, imagination, subjectivity, histories, and your whole social personhood are in some degree constitutive in the fieldwork process. In your field sites, you cannot be transparent, nor a fly. You take up social space as a person, and you've got to "play it as it lays" (Didion 1970). Gender matters in unexpected ways in all social research, and especially in the processes and relationships of ethnographic fieldwork (Butler 1993). In my own first year of research in Tanzania, I was socially "a student" and had no children. In a brief summer of research in Montreal, Canada, I was socially "a professor" and "a mother" of two young children. These differences of age and status produced significant differences in the kinds of questions I was able to ask, how and when I was able to hang around with people, how our social obligations as "a family" emerged, and so on. All this "goes without saying" in anthropology.

The babies and washing machines offended because of their messy, feminized concreteness in the specific context of scholarly writing. But that same "messiness" might have taken many different forms—this is not simply a comment about gender. The broad point here is that anthropological fieldwork is not usually a straightforward matter of working. It is also a matter of living. Ethnographic research practice is a way of being in the world. All this engages the senses and emotions, and it takes time. It is in this mundane, day-to-day way that the question of ethics emerges in ethnographic research, as the correspondence shows.

Questions of ethics appear again and again in Allaine's letters and in my efforts to reply to her. She questioned herself, for example, about where the lines between a friendship and a research relationship ought to lie, and more generally about the instrumentalities and forms of desire in social relationships during fieldwork. She worried about the intellectual curiosity and social circumstances that led her to witness a strip search at the police station that was one of her field sites. She confronted the ethics of sociality and gender politics in the company of police officers. She thought about the appropriateness of asking to photograph people's homes and gardens, and about securing permission to reproduce those images in her published work. I, for my part, reminded her to send thank-you notes to her informants, and realized then that in telling her things that "go without saying" for me, I was sounding very much like Miss Manners or Emily Post. I realized later the deeply class-specific nature of reminding her about the thank-you notes. A middle-class woman, I had been taught to write them somewhere along the way. It went without saying to me that it was "polite." This was part and parcel of a whole childhood world of injunctions that had become reflex. "Say thank you." "Don't mumble." "Don't speak or laugh too loudly." "Enunciate." "Look people in the eye." "Shake hands." "Let others go first." "Elbows off the table!" "Posture!" This was the common sense knitted into my spine by my northern European, culturally Lutheran, agnostic, middle-class family—hardly universal principles of good conduct, although some of it has proved serviceable in my work of ethnography.

The quotidian ethical practice that is fieldwork brings up questions that sometimes loudly announce themselves as "ethical dilemmas," while on other occasions they present themselves as "etiquette questions." "Manners" and ethics sit on a sliding scale that involves continuous cultural and other work of translation, in real time. Sometimes the translations go awry, and then one just has to try to go on from there.

All ethnographic field research is expected to have undergone an institutional review for the protection of "human subjects." The international, federal, and other guidelines used are meant to protect the rights and safety of those who might in any way be affected by the work. These screening processes are very important, but they do not begin to address the demands of ethnography as a quotidian ethical practice (Herzfeld 2001, 2004; Brenneis 1994; Patricia Marshall 2003; Farmer 2002; Meskell and Pels 2005).

The American Anthropological Association regularly publishes material on research ethics, and many fieldwork handbooks and textbooks also carry chapters on ethics. Thinking carefully about basic principles and textbook cases of ethical violations is important and often productive. Presumably for the sake of analytical clarity, textbook accounts and the training programs run by institutional review boards commonly present discrete ethics "cases"—sometimes very extreme cases like the Tuskegee Syphilis Experiment (Jones 1993).[18] While these offer useful thought experiments (as well as striking horror into any heart), they do not address the simpler, more ubiquitous ethical quandaries that crop up as one inhabits dynamic social processes and relationships that are often unpredictable, multiply entangled, difficult to interpret, and typically beyond the control of the researcher. These ethical challenges must be negotiated in real time, as they happen, and they are not neatly bounded. Sometimes they happen so quickly and imperceptibly that there is no time to react until later. At other times, it is what did not happen that generates the ethical soul-searching. This is hardly unique to ethnographic research; it comes with living in the world (Meskell and Pels 2005; Pels 1999; Garber, Hanssen, and Walkowitz 2000; Foucault 1997). Ethnography as ethical practice is necessarily social and therefore necessarily improvisational. There is, however, a strong anti-improvisational and positivist tendency in the wider institutional world of Human Subjects review boards and some funding agencies.[19]

Improvisation

The third working principle has been implicit in much of what has gone before, but it is perhaps the most important general lesson of my correspondence with Allaine. It is that ethnography is, and always has been, an improvisational practice. One of the reasons for my willful focus on earlier anthropologists—rather than more contemporary writers on the science question or writing culture (Clifford and Marcus 1986)— is that I want to say the key thing that has historically "gone without saying" in my discipline: in anthropology, as long as it has been a recognizable discipline, there has been a *tradition of improvisation*. It is not the case that there is an old, stable tradition with a fixed battery of methods, one "correct" way of doing fieldwork, and then a later movement toward postmodern fragmentation and "anything goes" improvisation. Rather, improvisation *is* the tradition. This comes through clearly in Clifford Geertz's classic 1973 essay, "Thick Description: Toward an Interpretive Theory of Culture," a key text in the field:

> In anthropology, or anyway social anthropology, what the practitioners do is ethnography. And it is in understanding what ethnography is, or more exactly *what doing ethnography is,* that a start can be made toward grasping what anthropological analysis amounts to as a form of knowledge. Thus, it must be immediately said, it is not a matter of methods. From one point of view, that of the textbook, doing ethnography is establishing rapport, selecting informants, transcribing texts, taking genealogies, mapping fields, keeping a diary, and so on. But it is not these things, techniques and received procedures, that define the enterprise. What defines it is the kind of intellectual effort it is: an elaborate venture in, to borrow a notion from Gilbert Ryle, "thick description." (5–6)

Geertz insists here that doing ethnography is not a matter of methods. This has too often been misunderstood to mean that anthropology has "no methods." True, it does not have a well-defined set of technical methods like analytic chemistry, for example. An anthropologist cannot be assured of her competence to carry out good field research simply through mastery of a known set of methods—be they (to extend Geertz's list a bit) interview techniques, household surveys, mapmaking, photography, media analysis, symbolic analyses of ritual, structural analyses of myths, questionnaires, the extended case method, tracking of the social drama, life histories, family histories, oral histories, genealogies, kinship analysis, analysis of court records, courtroom observation, archival research, linguistic analysis of speech acts, textual analysis, institutional ethnography, longitudinal studies, or other methods. These are all possible techniques in an open, flexible, highly context-dependent, and time-sensitive *repertory* of possibilities. The intelligent use of that repertory depends on critical, always already theoretical and contextual improvisational practices that, by definition, cannot and should not be a closed set. That they are not a closed set, hypostatizable as *"a methodology,"* is in part why doing ethnography is so difficult to teach in a standardized manner from a textbook. The ethnographer—specifically situated in a particular slice of space-time, and embedded in a social situation he does not control—must take on the risk and responsibility of improvisation, the creative use and perhaps remaking of the repertory. In this more methodological sense, too, the intellectual poaching license to which Kluckhohn referred is a practical necessity.

What, then, is the relationship between anthropology as empirical research and anthropology as an "art," a creative process? Anthropology has variously been called an "art," a "craft," a "science," "a human science," and a "social science." These working definitions, each perhaps ascendant at different moments, sit in an uneasy relationship to one another. And different anthropologists' intellectual temperaments lead them into different alignments in relation to these terms. I see ethnography as a form of situated empiricism (Malkki 1997) that is simultaneously, and without contradiction, an improvisational practice. As improvisation, ethnographic research demands forms of flexible intellectual openness and principled efforts to understand, knowledge and competence, and also forms of creativity and imagination. This, too, has long gone without saying. In 1936 Raymond Firth wrote that "social anthropology does have elements of an art [. . .], but it is not just an effort of the constructive imagination. Its generalizations must relate at some point to evidence of *what* who said and did where, when, and how. This leads to the heart of the problem of the status of empiricism in social anthropology. It is not a philosophical standpoint, it is a working principle" (Firth 1975, 18; emphasis in original).

More recently, the possibilities opened up by linking ethnographic research practices to artists' practices have been explored by Hal Foster (1996); Quetzil Castaneda (2006); Schneider and Wright (2006); Coles (2000); and others (see also Clifford 1986; and Wolcott 2005).[20] Taking Walter Benjamin's 1934 essay "The Author as Producer" as his starting point, Foster suggests that "a new paradigm structurally similar to the old 'Author as Producer' model has emerged in advanced art on the left: *the artist as ethnographer*" (1996, 172; emphasis in original). The ethnographic turn among artists was preceded, according to Foster, by "artist envy" in anthropology (180).[21] Castaneda develops a performative model of ethnographic research from theater and, specifically, from Augusto Boal's 1985 *Theatre of the Oppressed* (cf. Paulo Freire's *Pedagogy of the Oppressed* [1970]). The bridge I will make here is to music.

In the multidisciplinary reading group at the Center for Advanced Study in the Behavioral Sciences in Stanford, California, mentioned above, Mary-Louise Pratt made the observation that proved to be most enabling: "So, ethnography is really improvisational." It is thanks to her comment that we have since thought further about improvisation and fieldwork. In the same conversation, another colleague protested, "But where are the *rules?*! Are there no rules in anthropology??" In my thought-work, these two very different "clues" led me to read about improvisation in jazz. This vast literature still remains unfamiliar territory to me, but I will present here what use I have been able to make of it for present purposes. One of the key texts for me was Paul Berliner's *Thinking in Jazz: The Infinite Art of Improvisation* (1994); it is with this work that I principally engage here.[22]

First, I found in Berliner an answer to the foregoing question about "rules." Jazz musicians are often, mistakenly, thought to just stand up and make "something out of nothing," to play "out of their heads" (Berliner 1994, 2). A major dictionary states that "to improvise is to compose, or simultaneously compose and perform, on the spur of the moment and *without any preparation*" (Berliner 1994, 1; emphasis added; cf. Moten 2003, 63–64). "The popular conception of improvisation as 'performance without previous preparation' is fundamentally misleading. There is, in fact, a lifetime of preparation and knowledge behind every idea that an improviser performs" (Berliner 1994, 17). As Wynton Marsalis has said, "Jazz is not just, 'Well, man, this is what I feel like playing.' It's a very structured thing that comes down from a tradition and requires a lot of thought and study" (quoted in Berliner 1994, 63). Ethnography requires a similar commitment: to get to the point of improvising well, the ethnographer, like the jazz musician, must have devoted countless hours to practice and preparation of various kinds. (Learning field languages, reading relevant area literatures, writing theoretical essays, reading and critiquing famous ethnographies, and brief exploratory fieldwork trips are among the standard forms of preparation.) I also suggested earlier that competence for ethnographic fieldwork is not guaranteed by mastery of any one "set" of methods. In this respect, too, a comparison with learning jazz improvisation is pertinent: "Ultimately, *learning the tools and techniques of the art provides only the ground for the student's development.* To build the foundation, aspiring musicians must commit endless hours to practicing improvisation—mentally simulating the conditions of live performance events—if they are to acquire the cumulative experience upon which effective storytelling rests" (203; emphasis added). Storytelling is a key language metaphor in jazz (200–201).[23]

"One conventional way for young artists to share information is through informal study sessions, a mixture of socializing, shoptalk, and demonstrations known as hanging out" (Berliner 1994, 37). Here, the "young artists" could just as well read "young anthropologists." Much of the methodological learning of ethnography occurs outside the formal, preparatory "methods seminar." Occasionally, informal, apprentice-like relationships develop between faculty and students, or among students themselves, but much of the time the learning is autodidactic and actually occurs most directly during fieldwork (and during loosely structured "pre-fieldwork" visits of a few weeks or months to a field site).[24]

One learns context- and time-specific knowledge about particular research contexts as one lives and works in them. And then, in a very direct way, the people with whom one works teach one continually. Sometimes, this teaching happens unwittingly as ethnographers look and listen. At other times, the teaching is more explicit and purposive. Often, it is the people we call "key informants" who really teach us in this second sense. That pedagogical and social relationship involves great investments of time and commitment for both ethnographers and "key informants." It is often challenging to find ways of working with people that do not demand too much of their time or thoroughly inconvenience them. The autodidactic dimension of fieldwork appears to be familiar in the jazz world too: "The jazz community's traditional educational system places its emphasis on learning rather than on teaching, shifting to students the responsibility for determining what they need to learn, how they will go about learning, and from whom" (Berliner 1994, 51).

I also came to think about orality in the teaching of anthropology through Berliner: "In fact, much of the jazz repertory remains part of the community's oral tradition and is not published as single music sheet items or in fake books" (Berliner 1994, 93). The professional practices of anthropology include significant oral dimensions, in which the ambiguities and mistakes of fieldwork live on, whether as rumors about colleagues, as shared reminiscences, or as instructive anecdotes to students (see Klemp et al. 2006; see also Monson 1996; Sawyer 2000).

While the discipline of anthropology, like jazz, values innovation and creative originality, a significant part of the learning and doing of fieldwork (and of jazz improvisation) consists of imitating and quoting, riffs and licks (Berliner 1994, 95, 192). "The great players always give homage to their predecessors by recalling certain things they did. They give it in appreciation and in understanding of the validity of their predecessors. Being able to quote from songs and solos is always part of a mature artist because he's aware of the contribution of others and its impact, how valid it is. Something that is really valid is timeless" (Arthur Rhames, quoted in Berliner 1994, 103–4).

It is perhaps in terms of temporality that the most useful analogies between ethnographic improvisation and jazz improvisation can be made. Neither form of making things in the world involves simple linear time alone. There is a continual "tacking back and forth" between the familiar and the unfamiliar, the plan and its execution, theoretical insights and surprising empirical discoveries. This might be conceptualized as a cyclical (or spiral) temporality that exists among other kinds of temporal processes and rhythms in the field (cf. Kubler 1962). Likewise, there is in jazz "a perpetual cycle between improvised and precomposed components of the artists' knowledge as it pertains to the entire body of construction materials on any and every level of solo invention. [. . .] The proportion of precomposition to improvising is likewise subject to continual change throughout a performance" (Berliner 1994, 222, 242).

The cyclical nature of the critical theoretical process of ethnography is also manifest in the taking of risks and the making of mistakes, rethinking and reordering one's questions and priorities.

> As the multiple associations of their ideas wash over improvisers, they put into operation their well-practiced skills at negotiating the many possibilities. They select some for development and tightly manage their interrelationships. Besides those unexpected transformations that periodically arise from the discrepancy between conception and execution, improvisers constantly strive to put their thoughts together in different ways, going over old ground in search of new. The activity is much like creative thinking in language, in which the routine process is largely devoted to rethinking. [. . .] It is in dramatic movements from formerly mastered phrases to unrehearsed patterns, from commonly transacted physical maneuvers to those outside the body's reach or hold, and from familiar frames of reference within compositional forms to uncalculated structural positions, that improvisers typically push the limits of their artistry. (Berliner 1994, 216–17)

This account of improvising rings very true in relation to my own experience of fieldwork, although I was hardly in possession of "well-practiced skills," especially at the beginning. When things were going unexpectedly well during fieldwork in Tanzania, I thought of it at the time as a heady, nervous, even blissful state of "channeling." I was "playing above my head." Something other, better, than me was generating the insights that took form and "worked." A part of it was undoubtedly that I was being *taught* by the people around me in Tanzania. They expected more of me than I did of myself. On these occasions, I felt intensely alive. Berliner cites a jazz artist as follows: "Thinking in motion and creating art on the edge of certainty and surprise, is to be 'very alive, absolutely caught up in the moment'" (220).

> Descartes, in naming wonder the first of the passions, described wonder as an impassioned state that makes learning possible. [. . .] Wonder occurs at the horizon line of what is potentially knowable, but not known. We learn about this horizon line when we find ourselves in a state of wonder. Surprise has guided us to something where we can invest energy and time in a profitable way. (Fisher 2002, 1–2)

Another key parallel is that the jazz improviser plays in real time, often in front of a live audience or together with other musicians. The ethnographer, too, has to negotiate fieldwork in real time, in "live" social contexts. The processes and practices of fieldwork rarely follow the compositional script envisioned in the initial research proposal, and, in the course of the typical period of one year of fieldwork, it is impossible (and undesirable) for all of one's actions to be instrumental, that is, purposively directed solely toward professional goals. Life happens in the course of the work, as it should. There are false starts, adjustments of research questions, mistakes, and surprises along the way. Encounters with informants can be like live performances. You cannot go back to un-say or un-do things; you just make the best of it. As Art Farmer has said, "If an idea comes to you and you don't make it, you have to experience making something else out of it. That happens all the time when you're improvising" (Farmer, quoted in Berliner 1994, 211).

The key contribution of our e-mail correspondence in published form is, then, that it expresses something of the improvisational process of ethnographic fieldwork *as it happens in real time*. This record or working archive is therefore long and filled with quotidian or idiosyncratic details that seem unnecessary. It covers the whole period of a year of Allaine's fieldwork. Some readers of the manuscript have expressed frustration with this:

> This text is so long and meandering. Couldn't you boil it down to the main points? Write a real methods book and use a couple of the e-mails to illustrate your points.

> We live in an era of sound bites. Nobody has the time to read something like this anymore.

The logic of sound bites performs an authoritative mastery over the complexities of life and politics. An expert is there to pat down doubt and to plug up the little holes through which questions might seep in. Ethnography is, by its very nature, antithetical to forms of "expertise" that close down possibilities and choke off questioning. It is processual. It is as Art Farmer once remarked: "Nothing is ever fully realized, and you never say, 'Well, this is it.' You're always on your way somewhere"—or as Don Pate put it, 'otherwhere'" (quoted in Berliner 1994, 285, 251; cf. Moore 1978; Arendt 2005).

I began with the question of why it is so hard to say the things that "go without saying" in anthropological fieldwork. It is hard, not because there are "no methods" in fieldwork, but because it is like trying to tell a musician how to improvise. And I return to the fact that this is not a "methodology textbook." We hope that this record of one specific process may be useful to others (whether in anthropology or other disciplines), not by telling how to do it, but by showing how it happened, in real time. An accomplished, white saxophonist once worried to Dizzy Gillespie that "in playing jazz he was 'stealing' black people's music." Gillespie said, "You can't steal a gift." He added: "If you can hear it you can have it."[25]

Endnotes

1. We would like to thank Michael Herzfeld (2001, 2004, and personal communication) for his insights on Bourdieu's (2000) concept of "disposition." See also Durkheim on professional ethics (2001 [1957],14–27 ff.).

2. Many sociologists have, of course, written on ethnographic method, but generally with a different sensibility.

3. This is a serious oversimplification on Leach's part—there is a strong sociological tradition in ethnography and critical theory, while some anthropologists also use surveys.

4. Malinowski was hardly alone in this; the social construction idea is of course very old; see Kant, Weber, Berger, Luckmann, and others.

5. The idea of simply "stumbling upon" or finding facts lying around, waiting to be collected, is reminiscent of how Disney's Donald Duck cartoons portrayed Uncle Scrooge innocently "finding" pots of gold lying around in the tropics. As Dorfman and Mattelart (1991) put it, Scrooge's pots of gold are a result of systems of relationship. At issue were systems of the disempowerment of specific categories of people, and of the imperialist extraction of resources and labor, to which Disney unfailingly applied the eraser.

6. Willis's classic 1981 ethnography, *Learning to Labour,* has been very influential in anthropology; see, for example, Lave 1988.

7. "This is not to allow back an unbridled, intuitive 'naturalism' on impoverished terms. [. . .] We must recognize the necessarily theoretical form of what we 'discover'" (Willis 1980, 91).

8. Charles Hirschkind's work on ethics, affect, aurality, and the Islamic revival in Cairo open up new possibilities for thinking about the interrelationships between ethics and affect in ethnographic fieldwork (2006a, b).

9. I would like to thank Michael Herzfeld for his enabling insights on the challenges of representing affect in ethnographic writing (personal communication, 2005).

10. Cf. Hans Belting: "The Reformation taught the dominion of the word, which suppressed all the other religious signs. Christianity had always been a revelation through the word but now the word took an unprecedented monopoly and aura"; Belting goes on to cite Luther: "The kingdom of God is a kingdom of hearing, not of seeing" (1994, 465).

11. Arnd Schneider and Christopher Wright argue that "anthropology's iconophobia and self-imposed restriction of visual expression to text-based models needs to be overcome by a critical engagement with a range of material and sensual practices in the contemporary arts" (2006, 4). See also Coles 2000.

12. The researcher's desire to dwell in the slowed time of rest and thought may be disrupted by an informant's sense of urgency, or vice versa.

13. See, for example, Bourdieu on *habitus* (2000); and de Certeau on such matters in *The Practice of Everyday Life* (1984).

14. The researcher might be feeling the panic of the impending end of fieldwork, the "return from the field," while the people with whom she has worked may feel the yawning of time into the future. They may feel that the researcher has become a part of life as it is, while the latter may feel guilt over her all too prompt and definite departure. The different temporalities inhabited provoke ethical dilemmas and quandaries.

15. Time may seem endless during uninformative interviews, long engagements with bureaucracy, or (as happened to me) when car trouble occurs and one is stranded in the thick of a forest infested by tsetse flies with no apparent prospect of being rescued.

16. The cyclical time of the expected might take the form of the weekly laundry day, monthly rent checks, or annual taxes.

17. The ethnographer might remember or recognize suddenly, in the course of an interview, that what the person across the table is saying has been said by others in other guises in the course of other interviews. Recognition of a pattern spurs her to return to previous field notes, enabling her to understand them in a new way. In the course of this process, the ethnographer realizes that she has returned to an earlier point, but in a different key. She has in the meantime been transformed by new forms of understanding. This seems to me to be a matter of spiral time.

18. See Marshall 2003 on the histories of ethical codes of conduct in scientific research, including the Nuremberg Code of 1947, the Helsinki Declaration of the World Medical Association 2001 (originally formulated in 1964), and the Belmont Report in the United States. See also Macklin 2001.

19. Donald Brenneis, personal communication, 2002. Herzfeld (2004); and Shore and Wright (2000) have written extensively about the bureaucratization of ethics.

20. Here, Thet Shein Win has generously guided me to key contemporary texts on linkages between anthropology and art.

21. On this point, see Coles 2000; and Schneider and Wright 2006, 3.

22. I would like to thank Ray McDermott and Kevin O'Neill for their thoughtful conversations about jazz with me and for pointing me to sources. See, for example, Sharon Welch's essay on Foucault and the jazz aesthetic (2005, 79–103); Smith 1994; Klemp et al. 2006; Moten 2003.

23. See also Lave 1988; and Lave and Wenger 1991 on situated learning.

24. See Herzfeld 2004 on apprenticeship and Durkheim 2001 [1957], 22–27, on the guild, the family, and professional membership.

25. This quotation is from Gillespie's obituary in the *Economist* (February 7, 2002).

REFERENCES

Alcoff, Linda Martin. 2003. "Gadamer's Feminist Epistemology." In *Feminist Interpretations of Hans-Georg Gadamer*, ed. L. Code. University Park: Pennsylvania State University Press.

Alloula, Malek. 1986. *The Colonial Harem*. Minneapolis: University of Minnesota Press.

Almond, Gabriel. 1990. *A Discipline Divided: Schools and Sects in Political Science*. Newbury Park, CA: Sage.

Almond, Gabriel, and Sidney Verba. 1963. *The Civic Culture: Political Attitudes and Democracy in Five Nations*. Princeton, NJ: Princeton University Press.

Anderson, Benedict. 1991. *Imagined Communities: Reflections on the Origin and Spread of Nationalism*. New York: Verso.

Appadurai, Arjun. 1986. "Introduction: Commodities and the Politics of Value." In *The Social Life of Things*, ed. A. Appadurai. New York: Cambridge University Press.

———. 1991. "Global Ethnoscapes: Notes and Queries for a Transnational Anthropology." In Fox 1991.

Arendt, Hannah. 2005. *Essays in Understanding, 1930–1954: Formation, Exile, Totalitarianism*. New York: Schocken Books.

Balibar, Etienne, and Immanuel Wallerstein. 1991. *Race, Nation, Class: Ambiguous Identities*. Trans. C. Turner. New York: Verso.

Behar, Ruth. 1996. *The Vulnerable Observer: Anthropology That Breaks Your Heart*. Boston: Beacon Press.

Belting, Hans. 1994. *Likeness and Presence: A History of the Image Before the Era of Art*. Trans. E. Jephcott. Chicago: University of Chicago Press.

Berger, John. 1973. *Ways of Seeing*. New York: Viking Press.

Berliner, Paul. 1994. *Thinking in Jazz: The Infinite Art of Improvisation*. Chicago: University of Chicago Press.

Bhabha, Homi K., ed. 1990. *Nation and Narration*. London: Routledge.

Blainey, Geoffrey. 1975. *The Tyranny of Distance: How Distance Shaped Australia's History*. Melbourne: Macmillan.

Blunt, Alison, and Gillian Rose, eds. 1994. *Writing Women and Space: Colonial and Postcolonial Geographies*. New York: Guilford Press.

Boal, Augusto. 1985. *Theatre of the Oppressed*. New York: Theatre Communications Group.

Bornstein, Erica. 2003. *The Spirit of Development: Protestant NGOs, Morality, and Economics in Zimbabwe*. New York: Routledge.

Bourdieu, Pierre. 2000. *Pascalian Meditations*. Trans. R. Nice. Stanford, CA: Stanford University Press.

Boyer, Dominic. 2005. *Spirit and System: Media, Intellectuals, and the Dialectic in Modern German Culture*. Chicago: University of Chicago Press.

Brenneis, Donald. 1994. "Discourse and Discipline at the National Research Council: A Bureaucratic *Bildungsroman*." *Cultural Anthropology* 9, no. 1: 23–26.

Briggs, Jean. 1970. *Never in Anger: Portrait of an Eskimo Family*. Cambridge, MA: Harvard University Press.

Butler, Judith. 1993. *Bodies That Matter: On the Discursive Limits of Sex*. New York: Routledge.

Caldeira, Teresa Pires do Rio. 2000. *City of Walls: Crime, Segregation, and Citizenship in São Paulo*. Berkeley and Los Angeles: University of California Press.

Castaneda, Quetzil. 2006. "The Invisible Theatre of Ethnography: Performative Principles of Fieldwork." *Anthropological Quarterly* 79, no. 1: 47–76.

Cerwonka, Allaine. 1997. "Space and Nation in a Global Era: In Search of Australia." PhD diss., Department of Politics and Society, University of California–Irvine.

———. 2004. *Native to the Nation: Disciplining Landscapes and Bodies in Australia*. Minneapolis: University of Minnesota Press.

Chambers, Iain. 1985. "The Obscured Metropolis." *Australian Journal of Cultural Studies* 3, no. 2: 1–23.

Clifford, James. 1997. *Routes: Travel and Translation in the Late Twentieth Century*. Cambridge, MA: Harvard University Press.

———. 1986. "Introduction: Partial Truths." In Clifford and Marcus 1986.

Clifford, James, and George Marcus. 1986. *Writing Culture: The Politics and Poetics of Ethnography*. Berkeley and Los Angeles: University of California Press.

Code, Lorraine. 2003. "Introduction: Why Feminists Do Not Read Gadamer." In *Feminist Interpretations of Hans-Georg Gadamer*, ed. L. Code, University Park: Pennsylvania State University Press.

Cohen, Lawrence. 1998. *No Aging in India: Alzheimer's, the Bad Family, and Other Modern Things*. Berkeley and Los Angeles: University of California Press.

Cohen, William David. 1994. *The Combing of History*. Chicago: University of Chicago Press.

Coles, Alex, ed. 2000. *De-, Dis-, Ex-: Site-Specificity: The Ethnographic Turn*. London: Blackdog.

Comaroff, Jean. 1985. *Body of Power, Spirit of Resistance: The Culture and History of a South African People*. Chicago: University of Chicago Press.

Comaroff, Jean, and John Comaroff. 1992. *Ethnography and the Historical Imagination*. Boulder, CO: Westview Press.

Cosgrove, Denis, and Stephen Daniels. 1988. *The Iconography of Landscape: Essays on the Symbolic Representation, Design, and Use of Past Environments*. New York: Cambridge University Press.

Dangarembga, Tsitsi. 1988. *Nervous Conditions*. Seattle, WA: Seal Press.

Danielsen, Dan, and Karen Engle, eds. 1995. *After Identity: A Reader in Law and Culture*. New York: Routledge.

de Certeau, Michel. 1984. *The Practice of Everyday Life*. Trans. S. F. Rendall. Berkeley and Los Angeles: University of California Press.

Dewey, James. 1980[1934]. *Art as Experience*. New York: Perigree.

di Leonardo, Micaela, ed. 1991. *Gender at the Crossroads of Knowledge: Feminist Anthropology in the Postmodern Era*. Berkeley and Los Angeles: University of California Press.

Didion, Joan. 1970. *Play It As It Lays*. New York: Farrar, Straus, and Giroux.

Dilthey, Wilhelm. 1972. "The Rise of Hermeneutics." Trans. F. Jameson, *New Literary History: A Journal of Theory and Interpretation*. 3, no. 2 (Winter): 229–44.

Donzelot, Jacques. 1979. *The Policing of Families*. New York: Pantheon.

Dorfman and Mattelart. 1991. *How to Read Donald Duck: Imperialist Ideology in the Disney Comic*. New York: International General. (Orig. pub. 1971.)

Douglas, Mary. 1995. *Purity and Danger: An Analysis of the Concepts of Pollution and Taboo*. London: Routledge and Kegan Paul. (Orig. pub. 1966.)

DuBois, Cora. 1980. "Some Anthropological Hindsights." *Annual Review of Anthropology* 9, no. 1: 1–13.

Durkheim, Emile. 2001 [1957]. *Professional Ethics and Civic Morals*. 3rd ed. New York: Routledge.

Emerson, Robert, Rachel Fretz, and Linda Shaw. 1995. *Writing Ethnographic Fieldnotes*. Chicago: University of Chicago Press.

Epstein, A. L., ed. 1967. *The Craft of Social Anthropology*. London: Tavistock.

Evans-Pritchard, E. E. 1960. *The Nuer: A Description of the Modes of Livelihood and Political Institutions of a Nilotic People*. Oxford: Clarendon Press.

———. 1961. *Anthropology and History*. Manchester, UK: Manchester University Press.

Fabian, Johannes. 1995. "Ethnographic Misunderstanding and the Perils of Context." *American Anthropologist* 97, no. 1: 41–50.

———. 1983. *Time and the Other: How Anthropology Makes Its Object*. New York: Columbia University Press.

Farmer, Paul. 2002. "Can Transnational Research be Ethical in the Developing World?" *Lancet* 360, no. 9342:1266.

Fenno, Richard F. 1978. *Home Style: House Members in Their Districts*. Boston: Little, Brown.

Ferguson, James. 1994. *The Anti-Politics Machine: Development, Depoliticization, and Bureaucratic Power in Lesotho*. Minneapolis: University of Minnesota Press.

Firth, Raymond. 1975. *We, the Tikopia: A Sociological Study of Kinship in Primitive Polynesia*. London: Allen and Unwin. (Orig. pub. 1936.)

Fisher, Philip. 2002. *The Vehement Passions*. Princeton, NJ: Princeton University Press.

Foster, Hal. 1996. *The Return of the Real*. Cambridge, MA: MIT Press.

Foucault, Michel. 1972. *The Archeology of Knowledge and the Discourse on Language*. New York: Pantheon.

———. 1978. *Discipline and Punish*. New York: Pantheon.

———. 1997. "Ethics: Subjectivity and Truth." In *Essential Works of Foucault, 1954–1984*, vol. 1., ed. P. Rabinow. New York: New Press.

Fox, Richard, ed. 1991. *Recapturing Anthropology: Working in the Present*. Santa Fe, NM: School of American Research Press.

Freeman, Carla. 2001. "Is Local: Global as Feminine: Masculine: Rethinking the Gender of Globalization." *Signs* 26, no. 4: 1007–38.

Freire, Paulo. 1970. *Pedagogy of the Oppressed*. New York: Seabury.

Garber, Marjorie, Beatrice Hanssen, and Rebecca L. Walkowitz, eds. 2000. *The Turn to Ethics*. New York: Routledge.

Gadamer, Hans-Georg. 1999. *Truth and Method*. 2nd ed. Trans. J. Weinsheimer and D. G. Marshall. New York: Continuum.

Geertz, Clifford. 1973. *The Interpretation of Cultures: Selected Essays*. New York: Basic Books.

————. 1985. *Local Knowledge: Further Essays in Interpretive Anthropology*. New York: Basic Books.

Gibson, Ross. 1992. *South of the West: Postcolonialism and the Narrative Construction of Australia*. Bloomington: University of Indiana Press.

Gilroy, Paul. 1991. *'There Ain't No Black in the Union Jack: The Cultural Politics of Race and Nation*. Chicago: University of Chicago Press.

Ginzburg, Carlo. 1989. *Clues, Myths, and the Historical Method*. Trans. John and Anne C. Tedeschi. Baltimore, MD: Johns Hopkins University Press.

Goody, Jack. 1993. *The Culture of Flowers*. New York: Cambridge University Press.

Grayling, A. C., ed. 1995. *Philosophy: A Guide Through the Subject*. Oxford: University of Oxford Press.

Gramsci, Antonio. 1991. *Selections from the Prison Notebooks*. Ed. Quentin Hoare and Geoffrey Novell Smith. London: Lawrence & Wishart. (Orig. pub. 1971.)

1991, C1971

Grimshaw, Anna. 2001. *Ethnographer's Eye: Ways of Seeing in Modern Anthropology*. Cambridge: Cambridge University Press.

Grosz, Elizabeth. 1993. "Bodies and Knowledges: Feminism and the Crisis of Reason." In *Feminist Epistemologies*, ed. L. Alcoff and E. Potter. New York: Routledge.

————. 1994. *Volatile Bodies: Toward a Corporeal Feminism*. Bloomington: Indiana University Press.

Gunnell, John. 1993. *The Descent of Political Theory*. Chicago: University of Chicago Press.

Gupta, Akhil, and James Ferguson, eds. 1992. "Beyond Culture: Space, Identity, and the Politics of Difference." *Cultural Anthropology* 7, no. 1: 6–23.

————. 1997a. *Anthropological Locations: Boundaries and Grounds of a Field Science*. Berkeley and Los Angeles: University of California Press.

————. 1997b. *Culture, Power, Place: Explorations in Critical Anthropology*. Durham, NC: Duke University Press.

Halle, David. 1993. *Inside Culture: Art and Class in the American Home*. Chicago: University of Chicago Press.

Hannerz, Ulf, and Orvar Lofgren. 1994. "The Nation in the Global Village." *Cultural Studies* 8, no. 2: 198–207.

Haraway, Donna J. 1991. "Situated Knowledges: The Science Question in Feminism and the Privilege of Partial Perspective." In *Simians, Cyborgs, and Women: The Reinvention of Nature*. New York: Routledge.

Harding, Sandra, ed. 1987. *Feminism and Methodology*. Bloomington: Indiana University Press.

————. 1991. *Whose Science? Whose Knowledge? Thinking from Women's Lives*. Ithaca, NY: Cornell University Press.

Harvey, David. 1989. *The Condition of Postmodernity: An Enquiry into the Origins of Cultural Change*. Cambridge, MA: Blackwell.

Hayes, E. Nelson, and T. Hayes. 1974. "The Anthropologist as Hero." In *Claude Lévi-Strauss: The Anthropologist as Hero*, ed. E. N. Hayes and T. Hayes. Cambridge, MA: MIT Press.

Hebdige, Dick. 1993. *Going Global: Culture in the Nineties*. Multimedia presentation to the Department of Anthropology Colloquium Series, University of California at Irvine, March 16.

Heidegger, Martin. 1962. *Being and Time*. New York: Harper and Row.

Herzfeld, Michael. 2001. *Anthropology: Theoretical Practice in Culture and Society*. Oxford: Blackwell.

————. 2004. *The Body Impolitic: Artisans and Artifice in the Global Hierarchy of Value.* Chicago: University of Chicago Press.

Hirschkind, Charles. 2006a. *The Ethical Soundscape: Cassette Sermons and Islamic Counterpublics.* New York: Columbia University Press.

————. 2006b. *The Ethics of Death and the Islamic Revival.* Colloquium presentation, Department of Cultural and Social Anthropology, Stanford University, May 8, 2006.

Howes, David. 1996. "Introduction: Commodities and Cultural Borders." In *Cross-Cultural Consumption: Global Markets, Local Realities,* ed. D. Howes. London: Routledge.

————. 2003. *Sensual Relations: Engaging the Senses in Culture and Social Theory.* Ann Arbor: University of Michigan Press.

Jay, Martin. 1994. *Downcast Eyes: The Denigration of Vision in Twentieth-Century French Thought.* Berkeley and Los Angeles: University of California Press.

Johnson, Louise. 1994. "Occupying the Suburban Frontier: Accommodating Difference on Melbourne's Urban Fringe." In Blunt and Rose 1994.

Jones, James H. 1993. *Bad Blood: The Tuskegee Syphilis Experiment.* New York: Free Press.

Kapferer, Bruce. 1988. *Legends of People, Myths of State: Violence, Intolerance, and Political Culture in Sri Lanka and Australia.* Washington: Smithsonian Institution Press.

King, Gary. 1989. *Unifying Political Methodology: The Likelihood Theory of Statistical Inference.* Cambridge: Cambridge University Press.

King, Gary, Robert Keohane, and Sidney Verba. 1994. *Designing Social Inquiry.* Princeton, NJ: Princeton University Press.

Klemp, Nathaniel, and Ray McDermott, Jason Raley, Matthew Thibeault, Kimberly Powell, and Daniel J. Levitin. 2006. *Plans, Takes, and Mis-takes: Sequence and Learning in Jazz.* Unpublished ms.

Kubler, George. 1962. The Shape of Time: Remarks on the History of Things. New Haven, CT: Yale University Press.

Kuklick, Henrika. 1997. "After Ishmael: The Fieldwork Tradition and Its Future." In Gupta and Ferguson 1997a.

Langford, Ruby. 1988. *Don't Take Your Love to Town.* Sydney: Penguin Books.

Latour, Bruno. 1988. *Science in Action: How to Follow Scientists and Engineers Through Society.* Cambridge, MA: Harvard University Press.

Lave, Jean. 1988. *Cognition in Practice.* London: Cambridge University Press.

Lave, Jean, and Etienne Wenger. 1991. *Situated Learning: Legitimate Peripheral Participation.* New York: Cambridge University Press.

Leach, Edmund. 1967. "An Anthropologist's Reflections on a Social Survey." In *Anthropologists in the Field,* ed. G. Jongmans and P. C. W. Gutkind. Assen, The Netherlands: Van Gorcum.

Lessing, Doris May. 1994. *Under My Skin: My Autobiography to 1949.* New York: Harper-Collins.

Lévi-Strauss, Claude. 1962. *The Savage Mind.* Chicago: University of Chicago Press.

Lewis, Martin, and Karen Wigen. 1997. *The Myth of Continents: A Critique of Metageography.* Berkeley and Los Angeles: University of California Press.

Lutz, Catherine. 1995. "The Gender of Theory." In *Women Writing Culture,* ed. R. Behar and D. Gordon. Berkeley and Los Angeles: University of California Press.

Macklin, R. 2001. "After Helsinki: Unresolved Issues in International Research." *Kennedy Institute of Ethics Journal* 11, no. 1: 17–36.

Malinowski, Bronislaw. 1978. *Coral Gardens and Their Magic: A Study of the Methods of Tilling the Soil and of Agricultural Rites of the Trobriand Islands.* 2 vols. New York: American Book Company. (Orig. pub. 1935.)

———. 1967. *A Diary in the Strict Sense of the Term.* London: Routledge and Kegan Paul.

Malkki, Liisa H. 1992. "National Geographic: Rooting of Peoples and the Territorialization of National Identity among Scholars and Refugees." *Cultural Anthropology* 7, no. 1: 24–44.

———. 1995. *Purity and Exile: Violence, Memory, and National Cosmology among Hutu Refugees in Tanzania.* Chicago: University of Chicago Press.

———. 1996. "Speechless Emissaries: Refugees, Humanitarianism, and Dehistoricization." *Cultural Anthropology* 11, no. 3: 377–404.

———. 1997. "News and Culture: Transitory Phenomena and the Fieldwork Tradition." In Gupta and Ferguson 1997a.

Marcus, George. 1998. *Ethnography through Thick and Thin.* Princeton, NJ: Princeton University Press.

Marks, Shula, ed. 1987. *Not Either an Experimental Doll: The Separate Worlds of Three South African Women.* Bloomington: Indiana University Press.

Marshall, Patricia. 2003. "Human Subjects Protections, Institutional Review Boards, and Cultural Anthropological Research." *Anthropological Quarterly* 76, no. 2: 269–85.

Massey, Doreen. 1994. *Space, Place and Gender.* Minneapolis: University of Minnesota Press.

Mauss, Marcel. 1967. *The Gift: The Form and Reason for Exchange in Archaic Societies.* Trans. I. Cunnison. New York: W. W. Norton. (Orig. pub. 1954.)

———. 1973. "Techniques of the Body." *Economy and Society* 2, no. 1: 70–88. (Orig. pub. 1934.)

McClintock, Anne. 1995. *Imperial Leather: Race, Gender, and Sexuality in the Colonial Context.* New York: Routledge.

Meskell, Lynn, and Peter Pels, eds. 2005. *Embedding Ethics: Shifting Boundaries of the Anthropological Profession.* London: Berg.

Michaels, Eric. 1994. *Bad Aboriginal Art: Tradition, Media and Technological Horizons.* Minneapolis: University of Minnesota Press.

Mills, C. Wright. 1959. *The Sociological Imagination.* New York: Oxford University Press.

Mills, David, and Robert Gibb. 2001. "Centre and Periphery: An Interview with Paul Willis." *Cultural Anthropology* 16, no. 3: 388–414.

Minh-ha, Trinh T. 1989. *Women, Native, Other: Writing Postcolonialism and Feminism.* Bloomington: Indiana University Press.

Monroe, Kristen Renwick, ed. 1997. *Contemporary Empirical Political Theory.* Berkeley and Los Angeles: University of California Press.

Monson, Ingrid. 1996. *Saying Something: Jazz Improvisation and Interaction.* Chicago: University of Chicago Press.

Montuschi, Eleonora. 2003. *The Objects of Social Science Research.* London: Continuum.

Moore, Sally Falk. 1975. "Epilogue: Uncertainties in Situations: Indeterminacies in Culture." In *Symbol and Politics in Communal Ideology,* ed. S. F. Moore and B. Myerhoff. Ithaca, NY: Cornell University Press.

———. 1978. *Law as Process: An Anthropological Approach.* New York: Routledge & Kegan Paul.

———. 1987. "Explaining the Present: Theoretical Dilemmas in Processual Anthropology." *American Ethnologist* 14, no. 4: 727–51.

————. 1993. "The Ethnography of the Present and the Analysis of Process." In *Assessing Cultural Anthropology*, ed. R. Borofsky. New York: McGraw-Hill.

————. 2005. *Law and Anthropology: A Reader*. Malden, MA: Blackwell.

Moreno, Eva. 1995. "My Chastity Belt: Avoiding Seduction in Tonga." In *Taboo: Sex, Identity and Erotic Subjectivity in Anthropological Fieldwork*, eds. D. Kulick and M. Wilson. New York: Routledge.

Moten, Fred. 2003. *In the Break: The Aesthetics of the Black Radical Tradition*. Minnesota: University of Minnesota Press.

Musil, Robert. 1994. *Precision and Soul: Essays and Addresses*. Ed. and Trans. B. Pike and D. S. Luft. Chicago: University of Chicago Press.

Nader, Laura. 1972. "Up the Anthropologist: Perspectives Gained from Studying Up." In *Reinventing Anthropology*, ed. D. H. Hymes. New York: Pantheon Books.

Naples, Nancy. 2003. *Feminism and Method: Ethnography, Discourse Analysis, and Activist Research*. New York: Routledge.

Nelson, Diane M. 1999. *A Finger in the Wound: Body Politics in Quincentennial Guatemala*. Berkeley and Los Angeles: University of California Press.

Passaro, Joanne. 1997. "You Can't Take the Subway to the Field! Village Epistemologies in the Global Village." In Gupta and Ferguson 1997a.

Patai, Daphne. 1991. "U.S. Academics and Third World Women: Is Ethical Research Possible?" In *Women's Words: The Feminist Practice of Oral History*, ed. S. Berger Gluck and D. Patai. New York: Routledge Press.

Pels, Peter. 1999. "Professions of Duplexity: A Prehistory of Ethical Codes in Anthropology." *Current Anthropology* 40, no. 3: 101–36.

Piven, Frances Fox, and Richard A. Cloward. 1971. *Regulating the Poor: The Functions of Public Welfare*. New York: Pantheon Books.

Poovey, Mary. 1998. *A History of the Modern Fact: Problems of Knowledge in the Sciences of Wealth and Society*. Chicago: University of Chicago Press.

Pratt, Mary Louise. 1986. "Fieldwork in Common Places." In Clifford and Marcus 1986.

Putnam, Hilary. 1978. *Meaning and the Moral Sciences*. London: Routledge.

Rabinow, Paul. 1977. *Reflections on Fieldwork in Morocco*. Berkeley and Los Angeles: University of California Press.

Rabinow, Paul, and William M. Sullivan. 1979. *Interpretive Social Science: A Reader*. Berkeley and Los Angeles: University of California Press.

Reddy, William. 2001. *The Navigation of Feeling: A Framework for the History of Emotions*. Cambridge: Cambridge University Press.

Reinharz, Shulamit. 1992. *Feminist Methods in Social Research*. New York: Oxford University Press.

Riley, Denise. 1988. *Am I That Name? Feminism and the Category of Women in History*. Basingstoke, UK: Macmillan.

Rosaldo, Renato. 1989. *Culture and Truth: The Remaking of Social Analysis*. Boston: Beacon Press.

Sarkar, N. K., and S. J. Tambiah. 1957. *The Disintegrating Village: Report of a Socio-economic Survey Conducted by the University of Ceylon*. Colombo, Ceylon [Sri Lanka]: Ceylon University Press Board.

Sartre, Jean Paul. 1963. *Search for a Method*. Trans. H. E. Barnes. New York: Alfred A. Knopf.

Sawyer, R. K. 2000. "Improvisation and the Creative Process." *The Journal of Aesthetics and Art Criticism* 58:149–61.

Schaffer, Kay. 1994. "Colonizing Gender in Colonial Australia: The Eliza Fraser Story." In Blunt and Rose 1994.

Scheer, Robert. 1988. "Eating Tuna Fish, Talking Death." In *Eating Tuna Fish, Talking Death: Essays on the Pornography of Power*. New York: Hill and Wang.

Schleiermacher, Friedrich D. E. 1994. "Foundations: General Theory and the Art of Interpretation." In *The Hermeneutics Reader*, ed. K. Mueller-Vollmer. New York: Continuum.

Schlesinger, Arthur Meier. 1992. *The Disuniting of America*. New York: W. W. Norton.

Schneider, Arnd, and Christopher Wright. 2006. *Contemporary Art and Anthropology*. New York: Berg.

Seremetakis, C. Nadia. 1994. *The Senses Still: Perception and Memory as Material Culture in Modernity*. Boulder, CO: Westview Press.

Shore, Cris, and Susan Wright. 2000. "Coercive Accountability: The Rise of Audit Culture in Higher Education." In *Audit Cultures: Anthropological Studies in Accountability, Ethics, and the Academy*, ed. M. Strathern. London: Routledge.

Soja, Edward. 1989. *Postmodern Geographies: The Reassertion of Space in Critical Social Theory*. London: Verso.

Sontag, Susan. 1990. "Notes on Camp." In *Against Interpretation and Other Essays*. New York: Anchor.

———. 2001. *On Photography*. New York: Picador. (Orig. pub. 1977.)

Squiers, Carol, ed. 1990. *The Critical Image: Essays on Contemporary Photography*. Seattle: Bay Press.

Steedman, Carolyn. 1986. *Landscape for a Good Woman: A Story of Two Lives*. London: Virago.

Stewart, Susan. 1993. *On Longing: Narratives of the Miniature, the Gigantic, the Souvenir, the Collection*. Baltimore, MD: Johns Hopkins University Press.

Stoler, Ann Laura. 2004. "Affective States." In *A Companion to the Anthropology of Politics*, ed. D. Nugent and J. Vincent. New York: Blackwell.

Stoller, Paul. 1989. *The Taste of Ethnographic Things: The Senses in Anthropology*. Philadelphia: University of Pennsylvania Press.

Tambiah, Stanley Jeyaraja. 1985. *Culture, Thought, and Social Action: An Anthropological Perspective*. Cambridge, MA: Harvard University Press.

Tsing, Anna Lowenhaupt. 1993. *In the Realm of the Diamond Queen: Marginality in Out of the Way Places*. Princeton, NJ: Princeton University Press.

———. 2005. *Friction: An Ethnography of Global Connection*. Princeton, NJ: Princeton University Press.

van Binsbergen, Wim. 1981. "The Unit of Study and the Interpretation of Ethnicity." *Journal of Southern African Studies* 8, no. 1: 51–81.

Vassanji, M. G. 1991. *Uhuru Street: Short Stories*. Portsmouth, NH: Heinemann.

———. 1994. *No New Land*. Toronto: McClelland & Stewart.

Verba, Sidney. 1965. "Conclusion: Comparative Political Culture." In *Political Culture and Political Development*, ed. L. W. Pye and S. Verba. Princeton, NJ: Princeton University Press.

Visweswaran, Kamala. 1994. *Fictions of Feminist Ethnography*. Minneapolis: University of Minnesota Press.

Ware, Vron. 1992. *Beyond the Pale: White Women, Racism, and History*. New York: Verso.

Warren, Kay. 2001. *The Symbolism of Subordination: Indian Identity in a Guatemalan Town*. Austin: University of Texas Press. (Orig. pub. 1978.)

Watts, Michael J. 1992. "Space for Everything (A Commentary)." *Cultural Anthropology* 7, no. 1: 115–29.

Weberman, David. 2000. "A New Defense of Gadamer's Hermeneutics." *Philosophy and Phenomenological Research* 60, no. 1 (January): 45–65.

———. 2003. "Is Hermeneutics Really Universal Despite the Heterogeneity of Its Objects?" In *Understanding Gadamer*, ed. M. Wischke and M. Hofer. Darmstadt., Germany: Wissenschaftliche Buchgesellschaft.

Wedeen, Lisa. 1999. *Ambiguities of Domination: Politics, Rhetoric and Symbols in Contemporary Syria*. Chicago: University of Chicago Press.

———. 2002. "Conceptualizing Culture: Possibilities for Political Science." *American Political Science Review* 96, no. 4: 713–28.

Weismantel, Mary. 2001. *Cholas and Pishtacos: Stories of Race and Sex in the Andes*. Chicago: University of Chicago Press.

Welch, Sharon. 2005. "'Lush Life': Foucault's Analytics of Power and Jazz." In *The Blackwell Companion to Postmodern Theology*, ed. G. Ward. New York: Blackwell.

White, Richard. 1981. *Inventing Australia: Images and Identities: 1688–1980*. Sydney: Allen & Unwin.

Whitehead, Alfred North. 1967. *Science and the Modern World*. New York: Free Press. (Orig. pub. 1925.)

Williams, Raymond. 1977. *Marxism and Literature*. Oxford: Oxford University Press.

Willis, Paul. 1980. "Notes on Method" In *Culture, Media, Language*, ed. S. Hall, D. Hobson, A. Lowe, and P. Willis. London: Hutchinson.

———. 1981. *Learning to Labor*. New York: Columbia University Press.

———. 1997. "TIES: Theoretically Informed Ethnographic Study." In *Anthropology and Cultural Studies*, ed. S. Nugent and C. Shore. New York: Pluto.

———. 2000. *Ethnographic Imagination*. Cambridge: Polity Press

Wilson, Alexander. 1992. *The Culture of Nature: North American Landscape from Disney to the Exxon Valdez*. Cambridge, MA: Blackwell.

Winterson, Jeanette. 1987. *The Passion*. New York: Atlantic Monthly Press.

Wolcott, Harry F. 2005. *The Art of Fieldwork*. Walnut Creek, CA: Alta Mira Press.

Wolf, Diane, ed. 1996. *Feminist Dilemmas in Fieldwork*. Boulder, CO: Westview Press.

INDEX

aboriginality: as Australianness, 42, 47, 62–
63, 66; commodification and marketing
of, 62, 106, 123; politics of, 49, 106, 108–
9; spatiality of, policing, 16, 72, 101, 133;
spirituality of, 49, 66
affect, 4–5, 21, 33–37, 91–93, 99, 173–79,
186n8; and the body, 33–36, 175–76;
fear, and research, 175–76; mind/body
opposition, 33; reflexivity, 33
Africa, 36, 77–78, 88–89, 113–14, 140–41,
142–44, 154
Anderson, Benedict, 41, 42, 107
anthropology: apprentice-like pedagogical
relationships, 182; as an art and as empirical research, 181; assumptions about
ethics, epistemology, strategies, 4; expectations of a totalizing vision, 29, 171;
"fusion of horizons," 23, 30, 32; and what
"goes without saying," 3, 13, 29, 163,
178, 180, 185; immersion, 7; as philosophical humanism, 131; positivism, 30,
172; research as process, 4; and romantic
stereotypes, 6, 56, 124; as sensibility, 13,
23, 162–63
Appadurai, Arjun, 68, 127
Arendt, Hannah, 175, 185
Asia, conception of, 18, 42, 67, 72, 78, 101,
110–11, 114
Australia, 106–7, 113; and aboriginality, 66,
69; as Asia, 18, 67, 101; Australianness
as multiculturalism, 55, 62–63, 72, 108,
111; as Commonwealth, 18; immigration
politics, 72; nationalism, 41ff., 52; spatial
practices, 26

babies, 48, 50, 68–69, 84, 120, 177
Balibar, Etienne, 78

Behar, Ruth, 33
behavioral revolution in political science,
11–13
Belting, Hans, 176, 186n10
Berliner, Paul, 182–86
Binsbergen, Wim van, 75
Bornstein, Erica, 79
Bourdieu, Pierre, 2, 13, 118, 163, 170,
187n13; critique by, of the opinion poll,
170; on habitus and sensibility, 13, 162–
63
Boyer, Dominick, 35; on intellectual labor as
artisanal, 35
Brenneis, Donald, 187n19
bricolage, 39nn9–10; ethnography as, 23; and
improvisation, 24
Britain and empire, 18, 42, 53, 111
Burundi, 102–3
Butler, Judith, 177

Caldeira, Teresa, 67, 84, 101
Cash, John, 58, 61, 115, 116–18, 120
categories: cultural, 9; disciplinary, 8–10; and
interpretation of empirical details, 4; and
maintenance of social order, 10; national
identity, 41–42; in post-structuralism, 17;
social groupings, 75, 79–80, 88–89
Certeau, Michel de, 16, 88, 133, 149, 187n13;
"tactical raids of the weak," 16, 133
childhood memories: productivity of narratives, 46, 127
Clifford, James, 30, 31, 39–40, 40n14, 127,
135, 141, 179, 181; and George Marcus,
2, 179
Code, Lorraine, 23
Cohen, David William, 48
Cohen, Lawrence, 80

Comaroff, Jean, 78, 113
Commonwealth: and gardening, 53, 54, 111;
    social imagination of, 42, 72
culture: concept of, in political science, 11–
    12; influence of materialist and rational
    choice theorists, 11–12; modernization
    theory, 11; uses of the Geertzian concept
    of, 12

Dangarembga, Tsitsi, 56. *See also* "nervous
    conditions"
"data," 57
Didion, Joan, 177
di Leonardo, Micaela, 40n13
Dilthey, Wilhelm, 15
Donzelot, Jacques, 88
Douglas, Mary, 9, 10

empiricism: expectations in political science,
    117; the gap between theory and empiri-
    cal research, 4; practice of, in fieldwork,
    4; research as scientific and interpretive,
    165
environmentalism, 19, 51, 54; and aborigi-
    nality, 49, 54; and nationalism, 19; and
    nativism, 116
ethical issues in fieldwork, 178–79; "bias"
    or prejudice, 30–32; confidentiality,
    147; friendship, 96–99; power relations,
    15–16, 31–32, 34, 88, 95, 129, 150–51;
    self-presentation, 94, 98, 140; trust and
    the potential for harm, 92, 95, 131–32;
    uses of photographs, 67–68, 180
ethics, 131–32, 143–44, 152–54; affect, 2–4,
    31–33, 34–36, 175–76, 186n8; "do no
    harm," 131; and friendship, 93, 97–98;
    as "manners," 178; and personhood, 31,
    94ff.; politics of contact and "fusion,"
    23, 32; in the positivist model, 23, 31–33;
    research as "mercenary," 93, 95, 97–98
ethnicity, as expected object of anthropolog-
    ical research, 46, 54, 56, 73, 128, 130
ethnographer as chameleon, 95
ethnography: and artistic practice, 181; as an
    attempt to understand, 57, 131–32; and
    auto-didacticism, 183; as critical theo-
    retical practice, 164–73; as hermeneutic
    process, 4–5, 16, 19; and false expecta-
    tions of "total" ethnography, 29; forms
    of, in fieldwork, 6–7; generalizability,

170–71; improvisation and methodol-
    ogy, 24–25, 179–81; mythic view, 5–6;
    as "no methods" embodiment, 35–36;
    152–54; non-totalizing theoretical in-
    sights, 14–15, 19; not hypostatizable as "a
    methodology," 180; as process, 2, 19–20,
    36, 177; reading theory, 124–25; simi-
    larities of, with jazz improvisation, 23,
    183–84; tacking between ethnographic
    evidence and theoretical concepts, 15–
    16, 54

Fabian, Johannes, 57; "ethnographic mis-
    understanding," 6; temporal otherness,
    68
Farmer, Art, 185
field notes, 80–84; flexibility of, 24–25, 79; in-
    formants, 47–48; participant observation,
    308–9; representativeness of, 65, 74–75,
    78, 167–70; safekeeping of, 79; as writing
    genre, 80
fieldwork: and affect, 5, 37, 91–93; conven-
    tionalized separation of, from "reading
    theory," 124–25; ethical dimensions, 2,
    31–33; immersion, 7; interview strate-
    gies, 21, 24, 45–46, 64–65, 67, 76–77,
    85, 127, 130, 141; versus "life," 6–7, 53,
    139–40; mind/body split, 154; nervous
    conditions, 38, 56, 114–15, 118, 140;
    objectivity, 25–26, 30–32, 96; partic-
    ipant observation, 24, 30–33, 70, 76;
    participant observation, as "soaking and
    poking," 121; positionality, 25–26, 31,
    174; post-fieldwork adjustment, 126, 158;
    presentation of self, 87–88, 94–95, 97,
    140; situated knowledges, 36, 78, 87, 163,
    168; socio-spatial travel, 103–4; status of
    participation in the scientific method,
    157, 173–74; temporality, 6, 183–84;
    "that which goes without saying" in an-
    thropology, 3, 13, 29, 163, 178, 180, 185;
    uncertainties and structural indetermina-
    cies, 56–57. *See also* field notes; fieldwork
    process; fieldwork sites; friendship and
    fieldwork; improvisation; mistakes in
    fieldwork
fieldwork process: Bourdieuan system of,
    118; challenges and choices, 3; character
    of, 4–6; concerns in initial phases of
    research, 73–74; dialectic of guessing

and validation, 19; differences in types of anthropological/social research, 167–69; in interdisciplinary research, 4; process of theory building, 37; realist model, 5; real time, 5–6, 37; relationships among experience, self, and the alterity of the research object, 30–31; research practices, 6–7; in shifting circumstances, 21

fieldwork sites, 21, 26–28; as a form of motivated and stylized dislocation, 104; institutions as, 47–48, 50, 52; selection of, 26, 27–28, 46–47, 54, 55–56, 59, 60, 61, 64–66, 69–71, 72–74, 121, 126

Firth, Raymond, 181

Foster, Hal, 181

Foucault, Michel, 88, 179, 187n22

friendship and fieldwork, 93–94, 96; ethics of, 97–98

Gadamer, Hans-Georg, 4, 5, 15, 22–23, 24, 25–26, 30, 31–32, 37, 39nn11–12; "fusion of horizons," 23, 30, 32; and "tact," 22

gardening: African cultivators, 77; cottage gardens, 72; East Melbourne Gardening Club, 61; English roses, 64; "gardening essentialism," 53; imported English trees, 53; indigeneity, 62, 107; native species as symbols of Australianness, 53, 62, 69, 106; theft of plants, 52; Trobriand gardeners, 77; weather as vocabulary, 77

gardeners: and class, 65, 113; not "grassroots" or "cultural" enough to be informants, 54, 128, 130; sociality of, 21, 134

Geertz, Clifford, 2, 4, 12, 15, 20, 21–23, 39, 80, 171, 180

generalizability, 59, 61–62, 72, 74–75, 113, 117, 121, 130, 158, 170–71

Gillespie, Dizzy, 186, 187n25

Gilroy, Paul, 132

Goody, Jack, 134, 135, 136

Gramsci, Antonio, 42

Grayling, A.C., 4

Grimshaw, Anna, 68, 176

Grosz, Elizabeth, 33; and Descartes, 33

Gunnell, John, 13

Gupta, Akhil, and James Ferguson, 6, 7, 40n15, 70, 75, 103–4, 109, 141, 158, 171

Haraway, Donna, 25, 27, 36, 78, 87, 163, 168

Harding, Sandra, 40n13

Harvey, David, 66

Heidegger, Martin, 25–26

hermeneutics: affect and body as resources in, 33–36; process of, in interdisciplinary ethnographic research, 2–4, 5, 16, 39n4; as process of understanding, 22

Herzfeld, Michael, 7, 14, 176, 179, 187n24; "schooling the body," 35

human subjects, 179

immersion: and globalization, 7; ideal of total immersion, 121, 171

improvisation, 20–22, 179–86; and bricolage, 23–25; "be flexible," 79; in ethnographic research, 23–24, 25, 181; in fieldwork, 20–23, 37, 162–64, 179–80; in interdisciplinary projects, 3; parallels with jazz, 2, 183–85

"informants": as term, 57, 59, 87; as "ordinary people," 87–88, 95–96

interdisciplinarity: borrowing between political science and anthropology, 12; disciplinary obstacles and other roadblocks, 8–11, 13, 165; liminality, 8ff.; and professional marketability, 9; as a sensibility or disposition, 13–14

interpretive social science, 2, 10

Jay, Martin, 176

joking, 81, 90, 121–22; police humor, 134, 150–51

Kluckhohn, Clyde, 162; the anthropological "poaching license," 162

knowledge production: emotional landscape of, 37; ethical link to power, 95, 96; ethnographic field research, 166; ethnography in an interpretive mode, 2–3, 8, 14; interdisciplinarity as process of, 14; masculine/feminine dichotomy, 7–8; methodological orthodoxies, 8, 118; range of emotions as model, 5; researcher's responsibilities, 130–32; scientific paradigm in the social sciences, 130; situated knowledges, 25, 28, 168; statistical truths, 167–70

landscape, 18, 55–56; and national identity, 65, 69, 106, 126
Lave, Jean, 187n23
Leach, Edmund, 167–71, 174, 186n3
Levi-Strauss, Claude, 23–24, 39nn9–10

Malinowski, Bronislaw, 6–7, 15, 37, 68, 91, 166, 170–71, 174, 186n4; critique of the questionnaire, 170
Marcus, George, 6, 179
Marsalis, Wynton, 182
Meskell, Lynn, and Peter Pels, 179
Minh-Ha, Trinh T., 5, 39n1
mistakes in fieldwork: the strip search, 33–34, 35–36, 150–51, 152; the warthog story, 152, 156
Monroe, Kristen Renwick, 12, 39n4
Montreal, Canada, 2, 6–7, 161, 177–78
Moore, Sally Falk, 2, 17, 19, 39n7, 56, 159, 185; "fieldwork in a post-structural period," 19

Nader, Laura, 88
Naples, Nancy, 40n13
nationalism, 41ff.; and memory, 52; and the transnational, 70; as "war of position," 42
Nelson, Diane, 35, 40n19, 154
"nervous conditions," 38, 56, 96, 114, 118, 140
Not Either an Experimental Doll (Marks), 115, 165

objectivity/subjectivity, 22–23, 25, 30–33, 40n14, 173–74; and disembodiment, 35
observation, 24, 76, 173–74

participant observation, as "soaking and poking," 119, 121–22, 177
Passaro, Joanne, 32–33, 96, 176
Pata Dambara, 167, 169–70
Petracca, Mark, 9, 73, 115, 116–17; advising, 105–12, 112–14; and the Kroger supermarket analogy, 9; worries about employability, 160–61
photography: as research technique, 67–68, 142, 180; copyright and permissions, 67, 142, 144
police: concept of "crooks," 81, 120, 133, 136, 145; concerns about misconduct, 21,

91–92, 129–30, 145–46, 148; interviews and interrogations, 85, 86–87, 90–91; policing practices, 82–84; policing and space, 134, 136; politics of gender, 35, 85, 148; the power of the uniform, 146; sociality, 21, 36, 89
political science: "political culture" and Geertz's concept of culture, 11–12; expectations of generalizability, 27, 73, 117; research methods, 10–12, 22, 73, 172
Poovey, Mary, 173
positionality, 25–33, 80; and gender, 29, 157; "ordinary people" as fiction, 87–89; and personhood, 25, 28, 31, 36; and "situated knowledges," 25–26; "studying up" (Laura Nader), 88
positivism: concept of "bias," 28, 31; expectation of social/laboratory sameness, 97; ideal of objectivity, 34; ideal of objectivity and objectification of subject, 172; influence of researcher, 31; pervasiveness in political science, 12, 73; positivist sociology, 172, 174; as research model, 29–30; and review boards, 179
post-structuralism, 17, 19
Pratt, Mary Louise, 30, 40n14, 80, 181

Rabinow, Paul, and William Sullivan, 2, 16, 17, 19
rational choice theory, 10–11
representativeness: expectations of, 27, 46–48, 56, 61–62, 72, 73, 74–75, 117, 130; sampling, 75
research: anthropological and interdisciplinary, 4; empirical, 2, 13; epistemology and hermeneutic process, 3, 8; ethics, 2, 4; ethnographic, 1–3, 4–5, 6, 8–9, 11, 37, 117–19; expectations, 29–30; interdisciplinary, 8, 9, 10, 13; methods of, 4–5; practice of, 3, 4–5, 6–7; dangers of predation, 142, 143–44; process of, 2; sensibility, 13–14, 22–23
Rhames, Arthur, 183
Ricoeur, Paul, 4, 19
Rosaldo, Renato, 5, 21, 39n1

Sartre, Jean-Paul, 137–38
scientific method, as "default mode of knowledge production," 166

Schleiermacher, Friedrich, 15, 39n5

senses, 18–19, 99, 111, 121–22, 123, 127, 149, 175; Puritanism of the, 176; "soaking and poking," 119, 121–22, 177

sensibility: anthropology as, 20, 23, 162; and habitus, 13, 162ff

Seremetakis, Nadia, 46, 176

social geography, 18, 109–11

social structures, 11, 14–15, 19–20, 54, 127, 183–84

Soja, Edward, 18, 66

Sontag, Susan, 68, 162

space and place, 19, 26; politics of class and neighborhoods, 92–93

spatial practices, 19; mapping, 15–16; and national identity, 18, 74; resistance to control, 16; theory and hermeneutics, 16; state control of Aboriginal geographies, 16

statistical research, 167–72

structuralism, 16–17; and totalizing ethnography, 17

subjectivity, 36

tacking: analogous to jazz improvisation, 183–85; between part and whole, 15, 16, 19, 125; in building theory, 19; dialectic of guessing and validation, 4, 19; knowledge production, 54; process of, 15–16

Tambiah, Stanley, 78, 167, 170

Tanzania, 6–7, 88, 102–3, 124–25, 139, 140–41, 143–44, 152, 158

temporality, 4–5, 17, 100–102, 127, 177, 187nn14–17; anthropological representations of, 6, 17, 177; circular and spiral time, 183–84; generational time, 77, 127; and jazz improvisation, 183–84; linear time, 37; and process, 36, 177; "sound bites" versus process, 185; time and the body, 36–37, 44

totalization, 17, 19, 29, 158, 171

"tradition," 166, 180; of field-note writing, 80

Tsing, Anna, 7, 14

units of analysis, 75, 167–72

Visweswaran, Kamala, 40n13

vivisection, ethnography as, 132

"walking tours" as a research technique, 149

Ware, Vron, 132

Warren, Kay, 80

Watts, Michael, 66–67

Weberman, David, 31, 39n11

Wedeen, Lisa, 11–12

Weismantel, Mary, 176

Williams, Raymond, 70–71, 106

Willis, Paul, 17, 35, 39n6, 118, 171, 172–74, 186n6; "flat discursivism," 35